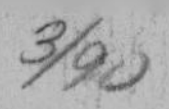

D1604330

Remem-
bering
Josephine

* * *

Remembering Josephine

* * *

by Stephen Papich

The Bobbs-Merrill Company, Inc.
Indianapolis/New York

Published by the Bobbs-Merrill Company, Inc.
Indianapolis New York

Designed by Winston Potter
Manufactured in the United States of America

First printing

Library of Congress Cataloging in Publication Data
Papich, Stephen.
Remembering Josephine Baker.
1. Baker, Josephine, 1906–1975. 2. Dancing.
I. Title.
GV1785.B3P36 793.3'2'0924 [B] 76-11628
ISBN 0-672-52257-8

To
KATHERINE DUNHAM

Without her, I could not have had
my own "time" in the theatre.

Without that "time," I would not
have met Josephine Baker,

and this book would not have been
written.

Contents

Foreword ix
A Tribute xi
Preface xv
Chapter 1 *The Legend of Josephine Baker* 3
Chapter 2 *East St. Louis—The Roots* 11
Chapter 3 *"No drinkin', no smokin', no . . ." With Bessie Smith* 20
Chapter 4 *The Early Years in Show Business* 34
Chapter 5 *The Folies Bergère* 50
Chapter 6 *Black Queen of the Music Hall* 58
Chapter 7 *La belle vie à Paris* 65
Chapter 8 *The Crown Prince of Sweden* 71
Chapter 9 *Years of Greatness* 93
Chapter 10 *Back to New York* 100
Chapter 11 *The Rumble of War* 108
Chapter 12 *In the Resistance* 118
Chapter 13 *The Children of Brotherhood* 131
Chapter 14 *Château des Milandes* 139
Chapter 15 *The Costs of Love* 148
Chapter 16 *Old Man Trouble Comes Again* 164
Chapter 17 *The Feud with Walter Winchell* 173
Chapter 18 *"Take It or Leave It"—A Study in Disaster* 180
Chapter 19 *Bill Taub* 186
Chapter 20 *Josephine Baker Arrested!* 197
Chapter 21 *Facing the Music* 201
Chapter 22 *Telling It Like It Is* 209
Chapter 23 *Zsa Zsa Gabor Lends a Hand* 214
Chapter 24 *"The Cat's Food Dish Brought Five Francs"* 223
Chapter 25 *Tears for France* 226
Chapter 26 *The Final Curtain* 228
Index 233

Foreword

Sometime in the middle of August, in 1961, my phone started ringing about three in the morning. When it rang at that hour, I knew who would be on the other end.

It was Josephine Baker, calling from her château in the south of France. I had never heard her speak so excitedly. She had just received a letter from Bosley Crowther, then the eminent motion picture critic of *The New York Times*.

Mr. Crowther and I had been having certain discussions about the possibility of his doing the Josephine Baker biography. Regrettably, the deal was never consummated.

But what had thrilled her so much was the glowing manner in which he had written to her.

"Well, Stephen," she said, "you can imagine how happy I am right now, when I received this letter from Mr. Crowther. I have received a million letters in my lifetime, but I have never received one that made me so happy. I can hardly wait to meet him."

In everything that he wrote, Mr. Crowther wrote beautifully, and his letter to Josephine was no exception.

I had wanted someone who had not known her to do a foreword for this book—to give his impressions as an "outsider," so to speak.

Then it occurred to me to use Mr. Crowther's letter instead.

He had never met her, but his feelings about Josephine are very evident, and of course so beautifully put. Following are some of Mr. Crowther's comments.

August 7, 1961

Dear Miss Baker:

I am so excited by the prospect Steve Papich has proposed of meeting you with the intention of writing your biography that I want you to know my feelings and anticipations of what may be achieved—which accounts for this rather personal letter from someone you do not know.

In the first place, I have to tell you I have been an admirer of yours for years, ever since I first saw you perform in Paris in 1928 when I was a visiting college student and you were the brilliant star of (as I recall) the Folies Bergère. But, then, who is there that saw you in those dazzling, delightful days that did not become an enduring admirer of the incomparable Josephine?

Through the years, I have followed with interest the course of your intriguing career, because it always seemed to me there was a very special dramatic cachet to your personality. Then I saw you perform here at the Strand Theatre in 1951 and suddenly it struck me, as I sat there watching you again after many years, what an intense and interesting drama could be written around your life.

I was thinking then in terms of a novel or a play, and the thought of it stuck in my mind as something I might some day like to do. Thus, when I got Steve Papich's inquiry as to whether I might be interested in doing your biography, the suggestion fell upon a mind that was already alert to the possibilities.

You wonder what it is that I find so fascinating and significant about your life? Is it merely the dazzle and sensation of your theatrical and romantic experiences? No. Many stars have had dazzling and spectacular theatrical careers. And many women in the theatre (and out of it) have had sensational romantic affairs. These, of course, are a part—an important part—of the warp and weft of your life. But they are interesting and special only because they flow into it naturally and give vivid and exciting color to the full fabric of your career.

And that career, as I now see it, from the comparatively little I yet know, represents the fulfillment of a person of courage, determination and strength. You started life with little except a burning ambition and fortitude. You made yourself successful by striving and exercising your strengths. But by success I mean something more than becoming a famous star. I mean becoming a fine, strong human being, compassionate and generous. And that, I believe, you are.

This growth of an individual is what interests me and makes me feel that your biography, fully and honestly presented, would be rich and meaningful.

Sincerely,

Bosley Crowther

Miss Josephine Baker
Château des Milandes
Castelnaud-Fayrac
Dordogne
France

for JOSEPHINE

They fired a volley of twenty-one guns, and the sound ricocheted in the Place de la Madeleine. It was an honor they reserved for kings and presidents. And she rested once more on the steps of the Madeleine, as she had done fifty years before.

And the soldiers of the Army of France fought for the privilege of bearing her coffin, and they bore it high, as if it were some great shield, and it was.

Now she, triumphant in victory, could no longer bear it herself, so they bore it for her, with her body on it. And over her body they placed the Tricolor of France, and on that they placed her Legion of Honor, their country's highest award.

And the people of Paris stood silent in the streets, and with their silence they honored her, and the wind carried to them her soft laugh, as it had done for fifty years.

Au revoir, *Josephine, good-bye. For night has come.*

from Stephen . . .

Preface

I have decided to call what I have written about Josephine Baker *Remembering*, principally because she herself was remembering as we would talk. I have tried to be as accurate as possible, but many times Josephine confused dates and incidents. It had been an incredibly long career for her, and so much had happened that her confusion was understandable.

Sometimes in the retelling, and there was much of this, she attributed one incident or event to a different party at a different time. It is unimportant, really. What is important is the event itself. Actually, many times the same incident did occur with several different people. To really tell the story of Josephine Baker would require volumes. She always really thought of it as three careers in one: her life in the theatre, her life during World War II, and her life as a humanitarian.

I have attempted also to quote her as accurately as possible. If the dialogue sometimes sounds strange to the reader, that is how she spoke and wrote. She spoke with great long pauses, then her thoughts would rush out, and one had a hard time comprehending.

At times she would bring up a subject that had not been discussed for days, expecting the listener to immediately grasp what it was that she was trying to say.

She could recall some insignificant little detail of a piece of her wardrobe that was worn perhaps in the early 1930s, but she would have a difficult time remembering what she had for lunch.

She required little sleep. Frequently my telephone would ring at 5:30 in the morning, and she would come on the line, wide awake after having gone to bed at 1:00 A.M.

Her secret was little catnaps. Many times while we were traveling together on planes, she would be talking to me and suddenly drop off to sleep in the middle of the conversation. Then, a half hour later, she would awaken abruptly, as if she had never napped, and continue on the same subject.

I never once in the entire length of our friendship questioned one of her stories, or interrupted her to tell her that she had told me a story before. Usually they were exactly as I had heard them the first time, but were just as exciting on the second hearing.

Many times we would be sitting quietly, and she would start a story about someone or something, forgetting that I had been there, too. I always let her continue.

"You know, Stephen, one time I was at Betty Grable's house in Hollywood. She had the most beautiful mouth. When they did those close-ups of her, that mouth was something."

I had been at Betty Grable's house with her when she and Betty had talked about her mouth. Tommy Wonder had introduced Josephine to Betty at the Huntington Hartford Theatre in Hollywood, and after the performance we all went over to Betty's house for a late supper.

Betty told Josephine that before any close-up was done of her for those great pictures that were produced at Twentieth Century–Fox, she always chewed a mouthful of redhots!

"My God, you don't say." Josephine just stared at her.

That night, when I came backstage and rapped on her dressing-room door, she said, "Come in," with a strange accent. There she was, with a mouthful of redhots, examining her mouth and lips in the mirror. Ever after, she always chewed some kind of red candy before she went on, and it always produced the same result—that red mouth, with its great slash of fire-engine-red lipstick.

I had been a choreographer at Fox and had worked on a couple of the old Grable pictures. I never saw her chewing on any redhots at any time. But I happen to know that that is what she told Josephine, because I was there when she said it. *Whether she did it or not, she said she did,* and that, I guess, is what was important to Josephine.

Much will be said about this book, I am sure. Even now, while it is still in the typewritten version, my phone will ring and someone will question the authenticity of a certain story.

I sometimes wonder what "authenticity" really means. Every Josephine Baker story, like a Judy Garland story, must have been told a thousand times. If you liked Josephine Baker you embellished the story just a little in the telling, and if you did not like her you played it down just a little, so that by the time the story made the rounds, it could hardly be compared to the original. And then a person would telephone me about an "authentic" story *he* had heard, assuming it to be the *real* one.

And on and on it goes.

Josephine Baker told me stories at all hours of the night and the day. There was never any set time. These stories usually came in her hotel suite, while she was lying in bed, cuddling some little puppy or kitten, a Turkish towel wrapped about her head. I heard them on planes and on trains and on boats. I heard them even in prison with her. Once, while we were traveling with Bill Chandler, Tommy Wonder, and Don Dellair, we were stranded for four days in Gander, Newfoundland, by an Air France strike; it turned out to be one marvelous storytelling session.

Sometimes I would go into her bedroom at the Château des Milandes, and she would be in bed, drinking chocolate. These were the terrible times in the 1960s, and she would do anything to avoid the issue that concerned her most at that time—money, or I should say the lack of it. To forget her present troubles, she would reach back into those times long past and dredge up something that had given her great happiness at the time. She would try to extract from it just an ounce more of that same happiness, and it was good to see the lines around her face ease up as she relived those times.

"Sit down, Stephen, have some chocolate. I was just lying here thinking about the Dolly Sisters. God, did we have fun. One time Miss [Mistinguett] hid in their apartment for a week, hiding from Maurice [Chevalier]. We all acted as though we did not know where she was, and told wild stories of how we had looked for her all day long. You know, I think they're buried out there in Hollywood somewhere. Next time we're out there, take me to the cemetery. I'd like to talk to them for a while."

Then back would come the lines in her face as "Old Man Trouble" returned.

"Well, I can fight it only one day at a time, no more. So, for today, I've fought enough."

I knew when the subject of money had to be dropped. On those days I tried to lead her into another story, and she always obliged, happy to be away from her money problems even momentarily.

The following, then, is the story of Josephine Baker. It is as she told it to me, and I have tried to record it as faithfully as possible. Of course, Josephine told her story, or parts of it, to others too. It may be that she told it the same way or that she told it differently. If their versions disagree with mine, that is really no problem. Let them record their own versions, as I have done mine.

Almost always, wherever she appeared in the world, Josephine would find someone in the audience staring at her through binoculars. Then, when she finished a number, she would throw up her hands as if to hide behind them, and, looking out at those people, she would invariably say, "Oh, sir, oh, madame . . . please fold those funny things up and put them away . . . don't look through them anymore . . . please hold on to your illusions!"

Her audiences adored the little gimmick. Following this, of course, every other pair of binoculars in the house would go up to someone's eyes.

But I believe that Josephine *did* want them to hold on to their illusions. For she invariably held on to her own. She once said to me, "My whole life, in the theatre and out, has been an illusion! You know, sometimes I think I'd do that song, but then Dietrich has done it, and I don't want them to make any comparisons."

When speaking or writing about a famous personality of the theatre, it is difficult to separate fact from illusion. If you pursue "facts" as diligently as I suppose one should, then you invariably lose something of the aura that surrounds the great stars. For it is just this illusion, this aura, that makes them great.

* * *

I have not stripped Josephine of her illusions about herself. I, too, wish everyone to hang on to his own illusions about himself—and about Josephine.

"My God, Stephen, sometimes life is terrible, isn't it? Let's forget about it and think of happy times—then I'll feel good. Let's be happy today. I think I'll write a fairy tale."

And then she would sit down and proceed to do so.

I do not want to intimate that my book is a "fairy tale," even though at times it reads like one. There are parts of her life that I would *not* reveal under *any* circumstances.

David Picker, the very prominent motion picture producer, flew to Detroit to discuss with Josephine and me the possibility of producing her life story on film. The deal was never concluded. Josephine demanded what even I considered an outrageous amount of money. He was a real gentleman and politely told her that that was not within his capabilities, and perhaps she should seek another producer.

I remember his taking us to dinner that evening. Mr. Picker seemed to me to be a producer of the old order. He engaged a limousine for her and made special arrangements in a very fine Chinese restaurant. He had somehow discovered that Josephine loved Chinese food.

I remember very well the last thing she said to him that evening as she was getting out of the car in front of our hotel:

"If we do it, Mr. Picker, let it be a happy film. . . . Let's not dwell on the sad parts or the unpleasant parts of my life. Forget the details. . . . Who cares on what day I was born, or on what date I was in a certain city or in a certain show? Make it so that when I come to the theatre to see it, I can be happy all over again!"

That is what I want this book to be also.

Remem-bering Josephine

"When they do your life story in the movies, Miss Baker, who do you think could play your role?"

"I would like to meet the woman who has the courage even to play my life story in a film. . . .

. . . I do not believe the woman exists who would have the courage to have *lived* it as I have done."

(In a press interview at the Music Center
in Los Angeles, California, September 20, 1973)

Chapter 1

"You must accept me for what I am, Stephen, and when you do that with me, or anyone, you will have a friend for life."

* * *

I first met Josephine Baker sometime in the late 1940s—perhaps 1948 or 1949. (I too am bad with dates. Like Josephine, "Time is my worst enemy. I am not friendly with it.") I was working at the time with Katherine Dunham, who was appearing in Paris at the Théâtre de Champs Elysées.

Everyone has his certain time, and Katherine Dunham was certainly having hers. She was the rage of Paris, as were her singers, dancers, and musicians. She was a brilliant director and choreographer who was far ahead of her time, and still is.

I believe that Josephine was jealous of her. She should have been. For a time, the French talked about Katherine Dunham and not Josephine Baker. Josephine considered her something of an intruder. She called Katherine "that colored woman from America."

Years later I toyed with the idea of having Miss Dunham choreograph and direct a revue with Josephine. I think it could have worked, too. Now, regrettably, it is too late.

At any rate, I was shopping in the Fauchon with one of the dancers, and the first thing I spotted was a little puppy running around among a display of chickens. Then I saw those elegantly manicured hands plumping chicken breasts to see how fat they were.

There wasn't much doubt. It was Josephine Baker. My friend Tommy Gomez introduced us. That was the beginning.

The last time I saw her was in 1973, in Los Angeles. A few months prior to this she had been the rage of Los Angeles in her final performance in that city. Her engagement at the Music Center was sold out, and on the final night thousands were turned away.

She had left behind her a stunned city. Following her final performance, the people in the audience had screamed wildly and refused to leave. To get her out of the theatre, it was necessary for my assistant, Robert Wood, to drive the car onto the stage dock through the loading doors. But then, as we drove out, a mob of people gradually surrounded the car, and it could not move.

An old black woman pressing in on the passenger side held a little girl of about eight or nine years up to the window so that the child could see Josephine. Great tears were streaming down the black woman's cheeks. She wanted this child to remember Josephine Baker.

Josephine was so touched that she rolled down the window and took the child's hand. Then she handed her her handkerchief and a red rose she was carrying. The child did not understand, but the woman and the rest of her fans did. They applauded her.

Then the crowd slowly fell back, and we proceeded to drive away from the theatre. Perhaps they knew what I did not—that that would be the last time they would see Josephine.

"My God, they really love me, don't they? I always thought they did, but I never *really* realized it until now."

As we drove out Sunset Boulevard toward the Beverly Hills Hotel, she was silent for a long time.

"If you had told me all this, I wouldn't have believed it. But now I have to, don't I, 'cause I'm the one, I guess, who has made it all happen."

Then, a few months later, Josephine, being Josephine, did something absolutely outrageous. Against my advice and that of everyone else, she accepted an engagement to appear for an independent promoter in the Beverly Hilton Hotel.

I begged her not to do it. I knew the history of what was happening there. I tried to reason with her. To return so quickly would only defeat everything she had accomplished in her engagement at the Music Center.

"But what can I do?" she asked. "I've already signed the contract."

I advised her to break it. That would be nothing new to her.

She would not. I warned her that she would not get paid, and that she would have the usual problems with hotel bills, air fares, and so on.

I should have saved my breath.

"Perhaps I am wrong," she told me, "but you must accept me for what I am, Stephen, and when you do that with me, or anyone, you will have a friend for life."

It was good advice.

Of course, the engagement at the Hilton was a true disaster. It was poorly publicized. Musicians were not paid. There were unpaid hotel bills. And worst of all, there was no audience. She was in and out of town before anyone knew it.

During the first two days of the Hilton engagement, I was working at the Music Center in the midst of another concert and hadn't had the time to see her. Then Haroldine Browning and her father, Ivan Browning, old friends of Josephine, called me and begged me to come immediately to the Beverly Hilton, as Josephine needed me at once. Of course I went.

"My God, Stephen, you were right. *It has been a shambles!*" she said, enunciating each word. We could only laugh.

"Now, Robert, you take little Moustique in the living room and play with him and Fifi, while Stephen and I get this all straightened out."

I could have done it over the telephone. It was the same old story. Of course there were unpaid bills, unpaid salaries, plane tickets to take care of, baggage to handle, and so on.

Mr. Browning, his daughter and son-in-law, and Robert Wood and I took her to the airport.

When we got there, she insisted on talking to Sammy Davis, Jr. I placed the call for her, and his wife answered. Josephine asked whether Sammy could do anything for her in Las Vegas. Of course I had been through that before, but I let her talk; maybe he could do something.

I got her onto the plane. She was exhausted. She took a seat in the nearly empty plane and immediately pulled out the arm rests, and we made a bed for her. I tucked the two puppies in beside her and arranged the pillows. I knew she would sleep all the way to Paris.

"You were so right, Stephen. What a disaster. Thank God you came over."

Then she forgot the incident completely. It was always that way.

"Now, look here, I want you to come to Monte Carlo and see this new revue, and then you will meet with Mr. Nederlander at the Palace, and we will come here next season. You know, I'm tired, but I need the money *so* badly. You know that. I have so much catching up to do."

I had to leave the plane, and, as I had done hundreds of times before, I automatically checked all the baggage that was to be shipped as freight. As usual it included forty or fifty pieces and weighed about half a ton.

I stood for a long time and watched the Air France plane rumble off into the night. . . .

A few months later I wrote Josephine what I thought was a devastating and sobering letter. I had conveyed to her an offer for the rights to her life story from Bob Banner, a very well established American television producer. I had thought the offer extremely generous, much better than any other she had received. But she had refused point-blank. I was furious, as she had constantly been prodding me to secure such an offer for her.

A few days later she telephoned me. I sat down, expecting the worst to hit me over the telephone. "Now look here, Stephen," she began, "you must not be upset about this offer we have. We'll get better ones; you'll see. For a lot more money." She was not the least disturbed by the content of my letter. She was accepting me for what I was—a friend.

I tried to explain that someone would one day "beat us to the punch." She sang me her answer: "Maybe you're right, and maybe you're wrong . . ."

We talked briefly about her upcoming U.S. tour, and then she started telling me about the new revue she was rehearsing. It seems that she had done nothing so lavish since the old days with Henri Varna at the Casino de Paris. I was delighted.

The old excitement, the old Josephine, were all there. I will always regret that I too could not have been there.

* * *

On April 12, 1975, as I was busily preparing a huge American tour for her for the 1975–76 season, Josephine Baker, while rehearsing a new number at the Bobino Music Hall in Paris, suddenly dropped to the stage. She died two days later in the Salpêtrière Hospital.

"I never took the easy path, always the rough one. Even in the theatre. I don't know *why* I'm rehearsing myself to death. But, you know, when I took the rough path, I decided it made it a little easier for those who followed me." It was a statement she made continually.

She had another favorite saying. Josephine loved the Italian language, and was fluent in it. Whenever she emerged from one of her many battles or skirmishes—and there were many—she would say, "*Addio senza rancore*" ("Farewell without bitterness").

When she fell on the Bobino stage, if her life flashed in front of her, as it is supposed to do for all of us, she probably said, very quietly, "*Addio senza rancore.*"

I took many of the paths with Josephine. Some of them were smooth, some of them very rough. I tried to be a true friend. I hope I succeeded.

* * *

"If I live to be a thousand, I'll never get everything done."

What she did get done was something. She was a woman who changed the course of history. She never set out to do that; it just happened that way.

But she did not accomplish what she wanted most to do. By her own admission, Josephine could not make the "brotherhood" theme of her life work. Her formula failed; in its failure, it helped to bankrupt her—and, ultimately, to destroy her.

It is a legacy she now leaves to another, somewhere in the world, to accomplish for her. But she went a long way in laying the foundations.

It might sound now like a small accomplishment. It was not. She helped to move many people some distance along the rocky path with her.

Above all, she wanted to be "someone" in the United States. Regrettably she was not. All the more regrettably, she never took the time to try to explain herself. Perhaps she did not know how.

There is no doubt that she was a real star—whatever that is supposed to mean. But she was also a humanitarian, a patriot, and a mother.

She was also a friend. I know.

When she died in France, they carried her to the Place de la Madeleine. And because she was a soldier of France, she received a military funeral.

As her funeral cortège moved down the great avenue of the Champs Elysées, it passed the Théâtre de Champs Elysées, where Henri Varna, while auditioning her, had laughed at the "little pieces of iron" on her shoes. It passed the Arc de Triomphe, where she had stood at the Liberation with General De Gaulle.

It passed the Théâtre de Folies Bergère, and it passed the Casino de Paris. The people in those neighborhoods waited for her in front of those theatres.

Then it moved to the Bobino Music Hall on the Left Bank, and they placed a huge cross of orchids on the back of her hearse.

As the cortège slowly wound its way out of the gates of Paris, the men stopped and removed their hats, and the women waved their little white handkerchiefs. It was a gesture they reserved for ones they loved.

In the countryside, on its journey to the south of France, the people stopped as well, doffing their hats and waving their white handkerchiefs.

Josephine was laid to rest near her villa in Roquebrune-Cap-Martin, outside Monte Carlo. From her tomb can be seen the blue of the ocean.

But Josephine is not there. She is on the stage of the Folies Bergère. She is in the Palladium in London. She is in the Teatro l'Opera in Rio de Janeiro. She is on the stage of Carnegie Hall in New York.

And if you do not believe me, you must go to one of those places. And when it is quiet, and the stage and the house are dark, you will hear her. The breeze will carry her soft laugh to you. Then, if you believe, as I do, you will see her. You will see those egrets, and those feathers, and those sequins. You will see her smile and bow to you.

And if she knows you, you might hear her thousand violins playing those haunting melodies. And maybe even while you are watching, a prince will come and take her in his arms, and they will wrap themselves in sable and dance. . . .

Sunrise

Chapter 2

"Mama, can we go watch the cakewalk tonight? . . .
I love to watch them hookers from St. Louis dance!"

* * *

Josephine Baker was born sometime during the early years of the century, either 1903 or 1906—it is a little difficult to determine. I recall that once, while we were flying from Montreal to Paris, I noticed that her passport said 1903. Then, on her last visit to Los Angeles, I noticed that her new passport now said 1906. Perhaps, as did many people in those days, she needed to be older than she really was for some reason or other.

But, as Josephine said, "Who cares? If they remember those minor things, the day and year I was born, then that means they're more interested in that than what I've done with my life."

Josephine's mother, Carie Baker, was a washerwoman. It is difficult to determine who Josephine's father was. When I pressed it ever so slightly, she would change the subject. It was something she assiduously avoided. It probably will never really be fully explained.

Josephine had two sisters and a brother. I knew her sister Margaret; she had devoted her life to Josephine. Maybe someday Margaret will write her own story, and perhaps she should. Between the two sisters there were battles, arguments, and recriminations; there were insinuations and denials. There was also a great deal of love. For it is not likely that Margaret would have stayed around as long as she did, seeing Josephine through the thick and the thin, if love had not been there.

I once asked Josephine when her brother and other sister died. She said she did not want to talk about it.

There was also a nephew, Richard Martin, who was the son of Josephine's brother. She knew very little of him. In 1974 she wrote me about Richard because she was very concerned about his welfare. For some reason the

F.B.I. and INTERPOL were searching for him, and they had come to her villa at Roquebrune-Cap-Martin.

"I have never been around Richard since he was born," she wrote me. "I must admit that I know practically nothing about him apart from what my sister Margaret has told me, but we must think he is undoubtedly active, from what I read in the papers."

She felt that Richard had betrayed her, that he had collaborated with others to write stories about her and had attempted to produce an unauthorized biography of her. I do not know if this is true. I met him only once, very briefly. At that time he seemed to care very much for his Aunt Tumpy, as he called her.

Josephine was a real loner. Early in life she separated herself from her family. She remained a loner her entire life.

She recalled that in her young years her family was constantly moving from one place to another—sometimes just ahead of the rent collector, and sometimes for other reasons. The "other reasons" are the ones that seemed to stick in her mind. It was a fire that burned on her forehead, both literally and figuratively, until the day she died.

Then the Baker family moved to Boxcar Town, in East St. Louis, Illinois. Boxcar Town was a jungle of boxcars that had been made into "homes" by the railroad to house the black laborers brought up from the South. The cars could not have been in worse condition, having been abandoned by the railroad only after they had deteriorated badly. On the sides of some could still be discerned "LACKAWANNA," "ILLINOIS CENTRAL," "L&N," and so on. Doors and windows were cut into them haphazardly, their positions determined, it seemed, by wherever the carpenter happened to be standing.

It was as if some giant had taken the cars and tossed them next to the switching center. Night and day the blacks heard the groaning of the steam giants, pulling and shoving their loads. The hissing steam, the constant warning whistles, and the banging of car against car were heard incessantly.

The blacks living in Boxcar Town did their best to turn the dilapidated structures into homes. It was a pathetic effort. Josephine recalled making "a little garden in front, and I made a little fence out of rocks. I planted some geraniums, but they never had a chance to come up."

It was in Boxcar Town, about 1917, that Josephine experienced something that radically changed her life. She would have been about ten or eleven, if we use the 1906 birthdate.

Josephine remembered that it was a big night, a Saturday night. There was a full moon, and "we didn't need all those lanterns hanging around that we normally had. You could see real good.

"You know, in those days nobody had any money. But everyone looked forward to Saturday night because that was Rag Night. I remember there was one man who sort of ran the dances. He would go around on Saturday night putting up little white rags on sticks and tacking rags to the sides of the boxcars, so that the visitors from East St. Louis and St. Louis could find their way through Boxcar Town. They just "followed the rag." You know, that all started in Chicago with the rent parties. And that's how ragtime got its name.

"But, boy, how I loved those Saturday nights! I remember all the ladies used to say, 'Thank the Lord for Saturday night.' "

Josephine remembered that it had been a long day for her. She had gone to St. Louis, where her mother had sent her to collect for some laundry they had done sometime before. She had not been successful. She had only enough money to get home on the streetcar.

Her mother was hanging a few more clothes on a line she had strung between shacks. Her mother prided herself on her fine laundering. She had taught Josephine how to wash, starch and iron, and years later it was not unusual to walk into her dressing room and see her pressing out some personal garment.

Josephine recalled sitting on a little bench outside their boxcar when Jimmy, the man who ran the dances, came by.

"Hey, Josephine, you gonna get that cake tonight?"

He was, of course, referring to the big event of the evening. After the struts and drags and slow drags and all, the last event of the night would be the cakewalk, and the dancers would kick high for a cake as it was being held up by some little girl or boy. "Whoever kicked it into the air got fifty cents," Josephine recalled later. "Boy, that was a lot of money."

Her mother answered for her. "How's Josephine gonna get the cake if she ain't got a dime to get in, Jimmy?"

"Yeah, that's right, sister, you gotta have the dime."

Her mother just tilted her head and, smiling, said, "But if you paid your wash bill, Jimmy, like as not she'd have one."

"Well, you know, I reckon if anyone as little as Josephine snuck under the rope nobody'd ever see her. And about my bill, Mrs. Baker, I sure appreciate your doin' my clothes, and soon's this strike is over, I'm taking care of it, sure."

Josephine recalled that most of the time when her mother washed for the blacks she did not get paid. Not because they did not want to: They simply had no money. Then the ladies would repay her by carrying water for her, and cleaning her "house," and sending over pots of greens and rice and beans and all.

But it was a Saturday night again. Time to forget. Time to have some fun.

"Mama, can we go watch the cakewalk tonight? I love to watch them hookers from St. Louis dance."

It was the first time she had ever used the word "hooker." Her mother was shocked.

"Josephine! Where you learnin' that?"

She came over to the bench and sat next to Josephine.

"I don't ever want to hear you use that word again. You don't know nothing about nobody unless you see it firsthand yourself. Now don't you ever forget that."

Then Josephine let loose the bombshell.

"Yes, Mama, but they *are* hookers, 'cause one of them told me so. And she said in a couple of years I could go over to St. Louis and be a hooker too, and wear all those hot clothes."

* * *

Years later Josephine's mother told me this story. We were in the Château des Milandes, the fabulous country home of Josephine, who by that time was a great star of the Paris music halls. Mrs. Baker seemed ill at ease, surrounded as she was by luxury—by the Aubusson carpets, the Louis XIV furniture. The servants made her uncomfortable, and she could not speak the language. She hesitated even to go into the kitchen. But when the servants would leave, she would go in and begin fixing something for herself to eat—"my kinda cookin'," she called it.

She is buried now in the little cemetery behind the church, across the road from that great mansion. I was glad she was not there to see the destruction of Josephine.

* * *

But that was years later, and much had happened to Josephine Baker. Now her mother tried to be stern with Josephine. Maybe some of it stuck, and maybe it did not.

"Josephine Baker, if I ever see you talkin' to one of them women you ain't never gonna see no cakewalk again, let alone dance one. You hear me?"

"Mama was tired even then," said Josephine later. "She told me that she was not always going to be able to look after me. She asked me to do what she said. She told me that it was a long life ahead, and that every time I turned around there would be trouble for me. 'Old Man Trouble' she called it. She told me she wouldn't always be around to help me out. How true that was. But I was glad Mama was gone then. I could never have faced her when those terrible things were happening to me.

"Mama said for me to stay away from them St. Louis women. I never did. You know, some of my best and oldest friends were hookers."

But on that night long ago, Josephine could hear the little band striking up those struts and drags and one-steps and two-steps. She could recall even in her last years the marvelous names of those songs.

"You know, that was some good music. There was 'Silver Heels' and 'Razzazza Mazzazza' and the 'Georgia Camp Meetin'.' "

Then she would laugh as those names rolled out.

"We laugh now, but then those songs were hot stuff. When I heard that music, I just sort of stood up straight and walked around like I could do it all, too. And you know, it didn't take me long to learn, either."

Josephine and her mother walked to a little square surrounded by boxcars. A dance floor had been built out of smooth railroad ties, and it was lit with hissing gas-pressure lamps. Their mantles threw a stark white light over the entire scene.

The little band was playing the first rag of the night. Josephine remembered the drummer. "He tied his drum around his waist so he could move, then he would move around the floor, strutting and beating that drum, and turning somersaults. Boy, he was something."

A large crowd surrounded the dance platform, and many were moving forward to give Jimmy the dime admission that permitted them to come onto the platform. They took seats on the benches surrounding the floor.

There was great activity and tremendous excitement. Her mother held Josephine in front of her as if to protect her. They both watched as the couples who had paid their dime began the first "big strut" around the floor.

"They didn't have any clothes, but how those girls managed to dig around through their little boxes and find something to put on, I'll never know. But then they didn't need anything, really, 'cause they could really dance.

"But the *big stuff* always arrived later in the night. They were the girls from St. Louis. Boy, they were the *real* St. Louis women. I remember the madam was named Billie, and she had a Packard, mind you. A *Packard*. Do you remember that car?"

I assured her that I did. She told me that years later when she had money she had wanted to buy a Packard, but somebody had persuaded her to get a Daimler instead. She said she always regretted it.

"Those hookers had it together. It was silk and satin and colors everywhere. You know, they would take one shade, and every piece of clothing would be that shade. There would be shades of lavender, or red, or blue. Even those funny bloomers. And those hats—you cannot believe those hats.

"Years later, when I got my first really *great* hat in the Casino, I thought to myself, I wonder what poor old Billie would think if she saw this.

"But that Billie, she was smart. She was always in white and cream. I never saw her in anything else, and I'll never forget that night, 'cause she came with white foxes too, and it was her birthday."

Madam Billie must have been something indeed when she strutted up, leading her girls. The St. Louis hookers knew where to come for a real hot night of dancing.

When they arrived, Josephine said the place used to go wild.

"How much, Jimmy?" shouted Billie. "How much for me and the girls?"

He counted ten people. "A dollar even, Billie."

She reached into her bosom, and out came a twenty-dollar bill, which she waved around. Everyone gasped. "Well, here's twenty dollars, brother—'cause everyone's gonna dance on Billie tonight."

She planted her feet on the dance floor, threw the foxes over her shoulder, and continued.

"And say happy birthday, folks, 'cause I'm forty today, and I'm the top of the St. Louis women. Ain't no more like Billie, and ain't gonna be no more either. I've been around for forty years, and I intend to be around for another forty."

The horns sang out, and the drums hit, and the banjos seemed to scream, and when the band hit the chorus of "Silver Heels," Billie passed by where Josephine and her mother were standing. For a moment she stood still, chin held high. She adjusted her hat, then that fabulous black leg with its white laced boots slowly came out of her white silk gown. She pointed her right hand straight out in front of her, and with her left she dropped those white foxes and dragged them behind her.

"You know, I was breathless. I had never seen anything like that. I couldn't believe it. My eyes just bugged out of my head."

The crowd screamed. Billie was hot stuff, and she knew it. The other dancers followed her, and the crowd applauded and shouted.

"Boy, were they happy. They had forgotten their troubles for just a short while, and they were having some real fun."

Very likely, "Silver Heels" had never sounded better. Perhaps that sound, that wonderful music and laughter, only served to excite all the more the group of men assembling on the outside of Boxcar Town.

* * *

"Remember now, boys, I want a nigger's head for every club I'm handing out tonight."

Inside the tiny railroad switching office on the outside edge of Boxcar Town about thirty-five or forty men were crowded. They were railroad thugs and detectives. They were strikebreakers. They were rednecks. They were "nigger-haters."

The report of the subsequent congressional investigation stated:

> . . . in the ensuing hours, 312 buildings and 44 railroad boxcars were burned. Property damage was put at $393,600. It is impossible to say how many perished.
>
> Negroes fled to the shacks and boxcars in which they lived. The matchwood dwellings were fired and occupants cut down with rifles and shotgun fire when they ran out to escape the flames.
>
> One man was beaten to death, a boy shot and killed and a woman's scalp torn off . . .

Until I had read the excerpts from the congressional investigation into the East St. Louis riots, it was difficult to believe what Josephine had told me.

Again, as she had her entire life, she had minimized it. Obviously it was more dreadful than even she had remembered.

The "strikebreakers," each of whom was paid twenty dollars, were armed with clubs and kerosene-filled coffee cans. They were told that for every nigger they "got" it would mean a job for a decent white man. They were to watch the sky, and when one of the detectives threw his lighted torch high into the air, they were to move in. They were told also, "In the morning, I don't wanna see nothin' but ashes."

As they surrounded Boxcar Town, the thugs and detectives and strikebreakers looked high into the night sky, waiting for their signal.

* * *

Now the big time of the night had come. Jimmy came out with the "cake."

"It was a poor old painted chocolate cake made out of wood. It had several layers. It was painted brown, and it had some holes in the top where you could stick some candles," Josephine remembered.

He finished fitting the candles, and one of the dancers lit them. This little scene took place next to the spot where Josephine and her mother were standing. Finally Jimmy fitted a pole into the bottom of the cake, and he held it high.

Then he spotted Josephine. "Come on, Josephine—your turn tonight to carry the cake."

Josephine was thrilled. Her mother held her back, but it was only for a second. In an instant, Josephine was up on the floor, holding the swaying stick with the cake on top.

The little band broke into "Georgia Camp Meetin'," and Josephine held the cake in front of her a little above eye level as she led the dancers off into the strut, preliminary to the high kicking. She loved every moment of it.

She kept her eye on Madam Billie, who had put one hand on her hip, thrown her head back, and stepped forward with the aristocratic air of a lady born to nobility. Her beautiful legs kicked forward through the slit in her white gown.

"I'll never forget that night. It was the first time I had ever carried the cake. I decided that no one was going to outdo me. I watched Madam Billie, and I put my hand on my hip, and I held that cake real high. I threw back my head, just like she did, and I let go with one real good kick. You know, I was good, too!"

"I led them off like they had never been led before. Boy, that crowd roared, and Billie laughed. I looked over at Mama, and even she was smiling. I was some real hot stuff, and I knew it."

Unknown to anyone, the thugs were moving quietly through the dark streets, clubs, guns, torches, and coal oil in hand.

In the little square on the platform, the dance was reaching its peak. Josephine moved to the center of the floor with the cake. She held it just right for the first low kicks, then with each chorus of music it went a little higher. She shouted at them to kick higher.

The crowd also shouted for their favorites. But it was Madam Billie's birthday, and she cried, "Let me at the cake, folks. I want that fifty cents prize. I might need it in my old age."

Then, in a great turn and a lift, Billie's dance partner lifted her high onto his chest, and in a wonderful high kick, showing those marvelous white laced boots and her lace-edged underwear, Billie sent the cake with its lighted candles high into the night sky. . . .

The crowd roared as the cake, candles still ablaze, went up and up, and their eyes and their laughing and smiling faces followed it upward.

Then in an instant, those expressions changed to ones of horror. What they saw now, instead of the cake, which had already fallen, was a flaming torch. It seemed to hang in the sky for a moment. Then it dropped quickly into the center of the dance floor.

It landed near Josephine, and it showered kerosene over her and everyone. She gave a terrified scream, and immediately her mother rushed up onto the platform and pulled her back.

Pandemonium broke loose. A volley of shots was fired, and the thugs and strikebreakers raced through the streets throwing coal oil and torches through the windows of the boxcars.

As the blacks ran down the streets toward their homes they were met with clubs and guns, and the massacre began.

There was terror and disbelief as the torches and clubs and guns did their work on men, women, and children alike.

Those who could, fled for their lives. Josephine and her mother made it to their boxcar. They watched through the window, paralyzed with fright, as Jimmy and a black woman were clubbed to death before their eyes.

Josephine remembers her mother's wash line, its clothes blazing and waving in the wind. Then a torch came through the window, and Josephine and her mother ran for the back door and into the dirt street.

They ran on and on. Finally they came to the clearing in front of Boxcar Town and hid behind a tree and some bushes. Her mother pulled her down and threw her apron over Josephine's eyes so that she could not see. Josephine pulled the apron from her face in time to see Madam Billie running for her Packard. Her beautiful white outfit was covered with blood, which was streaming from a huge gash in the side of her face.

Josephine saw her make it into the front seat. But as she tried to raise the window and start the car, the thugs ran up. Billie threw her hands in front of her to protect herself; one of the thugs pushed his lighted torch into her face and shouted, "Happy birthday, nigger!"

Josephine remembered that she screamed, and that the scream kept coming out of her mouth even after her mother had clamped her hand so tightly over her mouth that she could no longer breathe.

She watched the huge Packard go up in a mass of flames.

Then, as quickly as it had begun, it was over, and there was silence. Josephine and her mother stayed in the bushes for what seemed hours. Soon the sun began to rise. They looked over Boxcar Town. Not one boxcar was standing. There was only smoke and ashes.

When the sun came up, and they could see other people moving around, they came very slowly out of their hiding place. Mama found an old potato sack and gave it to Josephine to carry. They tried to find their old house to see what they might recover of their meager possessions.

There was nothing—nothing but the dead. Hundreds of them.

Josephine and her mother hurried out of Boxcar Town. Josephine did not look back—just as she would not look back when the Germans took her Paris townhouse and destroyed it, or when she lost her great château in the south of France. Throughout her life, she looked only forward.

"In my wildest dreams then," she said later, "I could not have believed what would happen to me."

As she and her mother walked out of what was left of Boxcar Town, Josephine continued to look ahead. On the horizon, much was waiting for Josephine Baker from East St. Louis, Illinois—much that she could not possibly foresee.

But now she was only a child in the wings. Slowly she walked toward that great stage on which she was to play out her life.

Chapter 3

"I ain't offerin' you no singin' and dancin' job. I'm offerin' you a maid's job. If you want it, you leave tonight. Ten dollars a week and train fare. No drinkin', no smokin' dope, and no fuckin' the musicians."

* * *

There was a nip in the air. It was the first cold nip of the year, an announcement that summer was over and fall and winter were coming. The leaves were dropping from the trees, blowing and swirling down the street, mixed with the dust.

The old Booker T. Washington Theatre sat in the middle of the block. A few blacks moved up and down the street attending to their business, oblivious to what was going on inside.

There was a little box office, and on both sides of the lobby there were posters of the current attractions.

On the front of the marquee they had placed the starring attraction for that week. It read:

BES IE SMITH

Either one of the "S's" had fallen down or there was not another one available to put in Bessie Smith's name. Very likely it did not matter much to her.

On one side of the lobby stood a beautiful photograph of Bessie Smith in a white gown, her hair pulled straight back. She was standing between the parted theatre curtains and displaying a broad smile. At the top it said, BESSIE SMITH—this time with both "S's"—and at the bottom, EMPRESS OF THE BLUES.

On the other side of the lobby hung a poster of two black vaudevillians.

It was a photo enlargement, and one could tell that it had traveled extensively. Hand lettering across the bottom announced that it was BERT AND BENNY.

It was still early in the day, but all the performers were in the theatre. The little Sterno cans were sputtering under pots and pans in the dressing room, and Bessie Smith, her maid, the musicians, and Bert and Benny were having a little lunch just prior to this matinee performance.

Bessie did not feel well in St. Louis; it was "too far north" for her. She was having problems, both with her career and in her personal life. On this particular day she was hitting a "gang of gin," and, for that matter, maybe a "pigfoot" too. The pigfoot didn't matter much. It was the gin.

The market where Josephine usually went to shop was on the far side of the Booker T. Washington Theatre. It was fortunate for Josephine Baker—and for the rest of the world—that that market was located where it was, and fortunate too that Bessie Smith was having a bad day.

* * *

Mrs. Baker and her little family, including Josephine, were now living in an apartment in the city. It had been one dreary tenement after another since the tragic riot and the burning of Boxcar Town.

They ironed and washed for both whites and blacks in the neighborhood, and Josephine remembered going by trolley car to deliver the laundry.

It must have been an even more depressing situation, particularly for Josephine. If they were not put out, they were robbed out. One day she came home to find that all the furniture—what little there was—had been stolen. There was not even a towel left, and even the washing that had been "taken in" was gone.

"My God, they even took the Sears Roebuck catalog, and you know what that meant."

Josephine remembered the day well. It was cool; the leaves were falling, and it looked like rain. The window of the flat was steamed up from the piles of wash. She stopped her ironing and walked over to the window. As she leaned against it, she started to draw a picture in the steam, then erased it with her hand.

She stood there a long time, just staring out into the little backyard behind the tenement. She watched the fire slowly sputter out under the great black washtub where her mother had the clothes boiling. She saw the rain falling on the already wet clothes. When she looked to the right, she saw the tenement next to hers, and after that only another tenement, and another tenement, and on and on. She looked up at the sky; it was almost black with rain clouds.

Behind her she could hear the scrub, scrub, scrub of the clothes being rubbed over the washboard. When the rain began to beat against the window, she turned away. She walked to the table where she was ironing pleated blouses. She blew into the charcoal in the iron to make it hotter.

For a long time she ironed away, thinking of nothing but the prison she was in. It seemed utterly hopeless. She resigned herself to a life of drudgery.

"What do you want for supper, baby?" Her mother probably sensed Josephine's despair. She sensed also that there was little that could be done about it.

Josephine knew there was little or no money in the house. She had just returned from a long trip on the trolley to collect for the washing. It should have been about twenty dollars. She returned with two.

"I don't care," replied Josephine, ironing and blowing up the charcoal alternately.

"I said, Josephine, what—do—you—want—for—supper?" Her mother spoke each word very slowly, as if she had reached the end of her road.

Josephine did not speak for a long time. She only continued ironing.

"Josephine, you turn around this minute and speak to me!"

Then it all came out at once. She whipped around, and the words came tumbling out of her. She never forgot them. She regretted them all her life. In a thousand ways in later years she tried to erase them, to make up for them.

"I don't want nothin' for supper. I don't want nothin' for breakfast. I don't want nothin' from you ever. I don't want this cheap apartment, or that thin little secondhand summer coat you're makin' me wear in the winter. You hear me? I don't want nothin'!"

Now she screamed, and, taking the pleated blouse, she threw it on the floor and kicked it across the room. The charcoal-burning iron went next.

". . . No, no, no, I don't want nothin', and I sure as damn hell don't want nobody else's dirty washing and ironin'."

She started to speak again, to continue, but she was stopped in mid-sentence by a flat wet hand to the side of her face.

She stood as if paralyzed for a moment. She had never been struck by her mother before; neither had Margaret or the other children.

But it brought her to some semblance of sense. She threw her arms around the woman she loved.

"Oh, Mama, Mama. I'm so sorry. I don't mean them things, Mama, but how long are we gonna stay here and take care of other people's wash? When is somebody gonna take care of *our* wash? Can't you see, Mama, I'm sick of it, and I know you are too. We ain't got nothin' and we ain't ever gonna have anything. Half the time we don't even get paid. You know too, don't you? Most of the time we don't even have food in the house, and we work here all day."

Now tears were streaming down her face. Her mother took her damp apron and wiped them slowly from her own face and from Josephine's.

"Mama, I don't want it anymore, and I don't want it for you either. I want us to get out of here. I want us to run away. Oh, Mama, please, please, let's just walk out right now. Let's just leave all this dirty washin' and ironin'. We'll manage somehow. Let's just leave it. Oh, please, please, Mama. I'm so unhappy. Let's just walk out that door now."

They stared at each other a long time. Her mother sat heavily in the rocking chair. Now the rain was beating hard against the window. Josephine felt as if it were trying to get in at her. Soon, she knew, the rain would turn into snow, and the snow would beat against the window and try to get in at her too.

Years later she was reminded of this pathetic scene she had played. This time she was in the private railroad car of a prince who was soon to become a king. They had made love, and when she raised the shade, the same snowflakes were beating against the window trying to get in at her. They glistened on the window like the diamond bracelets she wore.

"You know, Stephen, I guess that's why I don't like the snow and rain. It reminds me of that awful time back home in America. You know, I can't figure it out. I love America, but it seems when I'm in America all I have is bad luck. I guess I have to face facts. America just doesn't like me."

But that day, with the same rain beating against the window, her mother spoke, slowly, and Josephine listened.

"I know, Josephine. You know, you're right, too. I never wanted to do somebody else's dirty washin', and I don't want it for you either. But right now there ain't nothin' else we can do. Right now we're stuck, baby, and Old Man Trouble is right out that door waitin' for us to come through it.

"Josephine, if only you would stay in school like the other children. When you learn somethin', you'll get us both out of here. There just ain't no other way. You gotta be smarter than them other people. If you ain't, you're gonna be here all your life, just like me, with a lot of little babies to feed, and nothin' to feed them with. You gotta be one step ahead of the rest of the people. You gotta learn to lead them, and make them follow you, baby. You can't follow them. And I'm tellin' you, the place to start is in school, where you can learn how to do it."

She looked at Josephine a long time.

"Someday, girl, when you're grown up, you're gonna be real beautiful."

She paused, as if reliving what was probably her one great moment of happiness. "You know, baby, one time I was in Chicago, where I met your daddy, and he took me to a show, and I saw all those beautiful light-skinned colored girls dancin' and singin', and later I thought my Josephine could do that if she had someone to show her. I was happy, then, baby; then your daddy left, and here we are. But I think of that show up in Chicago a lot.

"You know, I ain't sayin' you could do that too, but maybe when I save a little up I could send you to Chicago. Maybe even to New York. Then you know what? You could go up to Harlem and find a rich man and get married and have some beautiful babies of your own. Then you could send for Mama, and boy, would we strut around Harlem. All of us, Josephine. We'd show them Harlem people what they're made of in St. Louis. You know, Josephine, I'm feelin' lucky, and tomorrow when I go out I'm gonna play a number, and if I win, I'm gonna give you half of it. What do you think of that?"

Josephine looked at her mother for a long time. There is little doubt that she loved her immensely. It is regrettable that she did not know how to show that love. In later years she gave tremendous love across the footlights to her audiences, and they returned it. But she could never give that same love to an individual, or to her family.

She never gave it to her mother, or to Margaret, or very likely to her other sister or her brother. For years she told me about how she loved Richard, her nephew in St. Louis. She did not. She could not give of herself to an individual. She did not know how; she gave all of herself to her audiences. At a time when she could have helped Richard, she decided that she did not know him, and even accused him of trying to capitalize on her career.

Josephine probably wanted to take her mother in her arms and love her. But she did not. Perhaps her mother did not know how to take Josephine and give her her own love.

"Listen, Josephine, I mean it. If I hit that number, I will give you half of it. But you gotta promise me one thing. You'll go back to school tomorrow morning. You gotta promise me also you won't use them cuss words no more. Every time I hear them words it kills me a little bit. And you know I've gotta stay alive long enough to see you get out of this place. You know there ain't nothin' I wouldn't do for you and the others, Josephine. But, you know . . ."

Mama paused for a very long time, looking at the rain beating against the window.

". . . I just don't know how to do it."

* * *

"Mama, you got any money at all?"

Now Josephine wanted a change of scene. One wonders if she had made up her mind at that moment or a little later in the day. She never said.

"Tomorrow I'll go to school. And when I come home, I'll help you iron at night. I think I'll be a teacher, and when I get some money I'll get a great big house over in St. Louis, and I promise you, Mama, every day we'll send the laundry out. We ain't even gonna have an iron in the house!

"Mama, you got any money at all? 'Cause I'm going out and get some greens and fatback, and I'm gonna make you a pile of cornbread, and we're gonna celebrate, and put the plates on this table, and eat like real people do. I'm tired of the table being an ironing board."

"Josephine, I got that two dollars you brought home this morning. Why don't you take whatever you need? Get Mama a piece of cake, too, will you, baby? Just get anything you want, and when you get back, I'll have this washin' and ironin' out of the way, and we'll have a real little party just for ourselves. You know, Josephine, right now I feel so good, I just feel like I'm gonna hit that number."

Mama did not hit her number; Josephine hit it instead. She did not know it when she walked out that door on that rainy day long ago, but when it hit, it paid off in a thousand ways that she could not possibly have imagined.

* * *

"Mama, just give me a quarter now, that's all I need for shopping. What kind of cake would you like? A piece of angel food?"

Her mother took a cup and fished out a quarter. She handed it to Josephine, who was putting on her thin little coat.

"And you know, baby, I'm gonna get you a new coat too, and one for Margaret and myself, and when we go up to Harlem we all goin' to be somethin' else. Now you hurry back, hear?"

Josephine Baker walked out that door sometime in the early 1920s. She never recalled the exact date. She did not want to. She had hated it all. She did not turn back. As she closed the door behind her, she leaned against it for a moment and took a great deep breath. Then she gave a vicious kick high into the empty air.

"Old Man Trouble, get outta my way, 'cause I'm comin' through!"

* * *

The rain had stopped, and the leaves were again blowing up and down the street. Josephine looked up at the marquee of the Booker T. Washington Theatre. It said:

BES IE SMITH

Even then Josephine had heard a great deal about Bessie Smith. She used to love to go to a neighbor's house and listen to records. She loved the ragtime ones particularly, and the blues. She said that whenever Bessie sang, it almost made her cry.

At first she did not pay much attention to the theatre as she passed by. Then, out of the corner of her eye, she spotted a sign that read "Matinee Today." From inside the theatre she could hear the band playing. The performance was just starting.

Then Josephine noticed the large poster of Bessie Smith and began to study it closely. Her lips moved as she read, "Empress of the Blues." Empress of the Blues—she liked that. She had heard about queens and empresses and all that. They taught her in school that somebody in Russia had killed some empress not too long ago, but she couldn't remember much about it. She knew that couldn't happen to Bessie Smith, because, after all, she wasn't a real empress.

She walked over to the other side and examined the tattered enlarged photograph of the second-billed act. It was Bert and Benny. Underneath their names they were billed as "The Two Hot Jigs." She smiled a little. They were dressed in outrageous outfits—Bert in a very tired set of tails, wired up and sticking out, probably in imitation of Bert Williams's famous chicken outfit. The other one, Benny, was in ridiculous drag. He wore a skirt, his pants having been rolled up to the knees. His feet were clad in heavy workman's boots. He had on a woman's blouse and a great string of beads around his neck which he was fingering. But the thing Josephine never forgot was the great big sunbonnet on his head, tied with a huge ribbon under the chin. His eyes were crossed.

Josephine looked at the photograph for a long time. Then she laughed. She crossed her eyes, in imitation of Benny in the photograph.

But then she moved away. She was thinking of what she would cook Mama for dinner. She started walking up the street toward the market. She was going to get some chitlins, she thought, but she didn't know how to fix them or cook them, and she knew Mama would have to do that, and she didn't want her to have to do anything tonight. She wanted to do it all for her. She settled on the greens, with a piece of fatback. And also some rice and beans, and the cake. She moved along.

"Then, I don't know what happened to me. I just had to stand still for a moment. Something stopped me dead in my tracks, as if they had put a great big glass wall in front of me. I just could not move. I was paralyzed. I could not imagine what it was. I just could not move! I was glad there were no other people on the street. They would have thought I was crazy. Like I was frozen to death. Then I came out of it a little. And I began to hear that music coming out of the theatre. It just seemed to be pulling me back and drawing me into that theatre.

"You know, I had never been in a theatre before. I didn't know anything about it. I had been to a movie once, and I loved it, but I had never been in a real theatre. You know, I think it was God telling me to go back there 'cause He wanted to do something with me, and He wanted me to do something for Him.

"If He had showed me what He had in store for me, maybe I would not have gone in. But maybe I would have, anyway. When I think about my life, I guess the real problem was only in the 1960s. And that was my fault. Not His. So if I had it to do all over again, and God gave me that chance, I guess I'd do it again."

Josephine turned slowly and headed back toward the theatre. When she got to the box office she saw a card that said "25¢." That was exactly what she had in the pocket of her thin little coat.

Slowly she took the quarter out and shoved it through the little hole in the glass. She remembered that she kept her finger on it for a while. Then she just let go. The woman in the box office handed her a ticket. "Better hurry, honey, the show's just startin'."

"You know, I'll never forget that woman, whoever she was, or wherever she is, when she said, 'Better hurry, honey.' 'Cause then I just ran, and I guess I've been runnin' ever since."

She pulled open the theatre door, and the music blasted out at her. She didn't know the song then, but she got to learn it, and all her life she never forgot it.

It was "Bake That Chicken Pie." She flew down the aisle and sat in the front row just as the vaudeville team of Bert and Benny were making their entrance.

There were fewer than thirty people in the house, but Bert and Benny were giving it their all. Time was very likely running out on them and on their material. It was the beginning of the end of the era of race songs and coon songs, but they obviously had not yet found that out.

Josephine was fascinated. She watched Benny in his drag outfit. She could not take her eyes off him. He was playing the female end, and cracking the jokes in a high-pitched voice.

". . . Now if you wanna make a nigger feel good, here's all you have to do . . ." And on and on the song went, about stealing a chicken from your neighbor's yard and baking a homemade chicken pie.

* * *

One day, years later, while Josephine and I were standing in the garden of the Milandes, her great château, a little black man walked up. He took a handkerchief and wiped his brow. It had been a long walk, and obviously a long journey.

"Josephine, you don't remember me, do you?"

Josephine squinted her eyes and studied him for a long time. A thousand things flashed through her mind. Finally she focused on the right item, and very slowly, her eyes filling with tears, she said, "Benny, I'll never forget you as long as I live." She threw her arms around him.

"Josephine, I just wanted to see you again before I died."

"Oh, my God, you've come to see me now, when times are so bad for me. Benny, why didn't you come when times were good and you could have seen me at the top?"

"Josephine, you'll always be at the top for me—and everyone else too!"

That night in the music room of the château, Josephine talked and Benny talked and Mama talked. It was the only time I ever saw Mama when she looked happy. I will never forget how young she looked that night.

Then it was a thousand stories, and a thousand reminiscences again. It was tears and laughter and talk and "good soul food," as Josephine said.

And I was happy for her, for she was momentarily forgetting her problems, and forgetting that Old Man Trouble was just outside the door.

Then they talked of how Benny had taught Josephine all he knew. When they got to the part of how, as a joke on Bert, while she was Bessie's maid, Josephine went on for Benny, sunbonnet and all, they suddenly stopped.

"Why don't we just do it once, for old time's sake, Josephine?" Benny said.

And they did it again as they had done it years before in some dingy theatre in Memphis, Tennessee. They did "Bake That Chicken Pie." Only now it was in the elegant music room of her château. But those two people, Benny and Josephine, were still on that little stage somewhere in Memphis.

Every movement, every gesture, every word was perfect, with Benny doing Bert's part, and Josephine doing Benny's.

It is one of those moments that, when it is all over, everyone says that he wishes they would have had a camera to capture it. One never does have that camera. One is not meant to capture it. It is hidden somewhere in the universe. Someday, possibly, that moment will come again. Maybe someone will push the right button, and we will again hear, ". . . oh, how I wish to heaven . . . that I get the biggest slice!"

I never heard Josephine use any type of racial slur. She never used the terms "nigger," "wop," "kike," or anything remotely like them. However, it did not bother her to sing "Chicken Pie," with all its racial slurs and words.

"You know, it's only a song, and it is funny, and sometimes I do hum it a little and think about those times."

* * *

But that day in the Booker T. Washington Theatre, as a much younger Benny finished the last bar of "Chicken Pie," he crossed his eyes and looked right at Josephine.

Josephine shrieked with delight. Then she slid down in her seat and crossed her eyes too.

That, then, was the beginning.

"I never knew where I was. I forgot all about the people in the theatre, and about the world, and about St. Louis. I even forgot about Mama and the dinner I was supposed to fix, and I even forgot who I was."

She remembered Bessie Smith, and more of Bert and Benny, and the little band. Then, before she realized what had happened, it was all over, and the house lights came up, and everyone left but Josephine. She sat there for a long time.

She had no intention of leaving the theatre. She wanted to go backstage, but didn't know how. She walked up some steps and crossed over the apron of the stage. She found the center part of the curtain and walked through.

It was the first time she had ever stood on a theatre stage.

It was dark, and she remembered looking at the bandstand. The musicians had left their instruments leaning against their stands or chairs. She looked right, then left, and started walking into the wings.

Then suddenly she stopped. Sitting on a box of prop stairs was Benny. His arms were resting on his knees. Sweat was pouring down his face. He was still wearing the bonnet, only the ribbon was now untied. The skirt was thrown back, and he was smoking a cigarette. He had been watching Josephine.

"Hey, girl, come here . . . what you want?"

"I wanna see Miss Smith."

"Well, Miss Smith ain't seein' nobody this afternoon, or tonight, or tomorrow either. What you want to see Miss Smith for?"

Josephine looked him over for a moment. She figured it was now or never.

"I wanna job . . . a job as a singer and a dancer. I'm good too."

The words kept pouring out of her. Her mother would have been shocked.

"I danced over in St. Louis in Proctor's all last summer. I was dancin' in Chicago too, in a show before it went to New York. They wouldn't take me 'cause I wasn't old enough then. But I am now. I'm twenty-one."

She stood up straight and dropped off her thin little coat to show her figure.

Benny had been studying her through the cigarette smoke. He had heard this story in different versions in every city he had played for the last forty years.

"You know, Steve," he told me years later in the Milandes, "I was just about to chase Josephine out and tell her to git on home to her mama, when Bessie came shoutin' out that dressin'-room door.

" 'Where is that lyin' nigger?' she screamed. 'Where is that little son of a bitch? Leavin' me cold food in my room, and she's out over in St. Louis cattin' around. And I'm payin' that lowdown nigger bitch my good money, and look what's happenin' to me.' "

Bessie Smith had emerged from her dressing door. Her beautiful white satin gown was covered with spilled food.

Neither Josephine nor Benny could believe what they were seeing. She was covered with catsup and grease and sauce and gin from her lips to her shoes. She could not have been more drunk.

Benny went up and tried to pick the bits of food off her gown. Josephine followed.

"I'm gonna kill that lyin' son of a bitch the minute she walks in this theatre. This wouldn't have happened if she hadn't left me here alone. What am I gonna do now?"

She had backed into the dressing room, and Benny had followed. Josephine stood in the doorway.

Perhaps she sensed an opportunity. Perhaps she really wanted to help. Bessie Smith seemed oblivious to the fact that she was even there.

"I can fix that, Miss Smith. I know how. It's easy for me. My mama taught me how to wash and iron. I do good laundry for the white folks in St. Louis. I can wash your dress and have it dried and ironed in a couple of hours. I'll do it right here in this sink for you."

Bessie looked at her through gin-blurred eyes.

"Who in the hell are you, nigger?"

Josephine hesitated, but only for a moment. "I'm a friend of Benny's here." She looked pleadingly at Benny. He only stared back at her.

"Then git me outta this goddamn dress."

Once she was out of it, she dropped back onto the couch and in nothing flat had passed out, snoring.

"God, I remember, could Bessie Smith ever snore. It would shake the whole theatre. And when she opened her mouth, the whole room went blue with cuss words."

Josephine was as good as her word. In less than two hours she had carefully washed the dress, dried it between towels, and was just putting the finishing touches on it when Bessie awoke. Josephine started to leave the room.

"Where you goin', girl?" This time she did not call her "nigger." Bessie looked at the beautifully cleaned and pressed dress that Josephine had hung on a rack.

"I was just leavin', Miss Smith. I got your dress all fixed up and it's hangin' up there."

"Come here." She pointed to her purse on the dressing table. "In that pocketbook there you'll find a dollar for yourself."

Josephine walked over to the dressing table and opened the purse. Inside she saw not one dollar but hundreds in several great rolls. She fished out just one dollar. Bessie watched carefully all the while.

"Least, you're an honest nigger. Where you goin' now?"

"I gotta go home now, Miss Smith."

"Stop that Miss Smith shit and call me Bessie."

"Yes, Bessie."

"You wanna job?"

Josephine thought for a moment. Benny had walked up and was standing in the door. He eyed Josephine carefully.

"Bessie, I can't sing, and I can't dance, and I ain't no friend of Benny's. It was all a lie. And I never was in no dancing show over in Chicago either." She was about to continue when Bessie interrupted.

"Bitch, I ain't offerin' you no singin' and dancin' job. I'm offerin' you a maid's job. If you want it you leave tonight. Ten dollars a week and train fare. No drinkin', no smokin' dope, and no fuckin' the musicians."

Josephine's mind was working fast. She didn't know how to answer. It seemed like this was her opportunity to escape. To run away. That was all she could think of. She must escape, run away. But she was also thinking about what would happen to her mother. She did not get an opportunity to make up her own mind; it was made up for her.

"And you can start right now . . . get me some gin." Bessie fell back on the couch, and Josephine moved toward the gin bottle.

* * *

That night two things were happening simultaneously.

Josephine was sitting backstage on a little stool. On stage Bessie Smith was singing. Josephine took a small piece of paper and a pencil and began writing.

> Dear Mama: I'm sorry it has to be this way. But it's the only way for me to get away. I'm going with Bessie Smith. Here's a dollar for you Mama. I'll send for you one day when I get that great big house I told you about. I love you Mama.
>
> Joe

She took the dollar bill Bessie had given her. She flattened it out and, folding it in the letter, inserted it in the envelope. She sealed the envelope and addressed it.

She quickly slipped the letter into her pocket as she saw Bessie coming off the stage, sweating heavily. Bessie reached for the gin glass that Josephine handed her.

On the other side of town, Josephine's mother was terrified. Josephine had not returned. All afternoon she had been wearing a path between the window and the door, peering outside and down the hall.

She imagined the worst. Then, when night came, she ran down the hall. As she threw a shawl over her shoulders and pulled her hat down on her head, she pounded on her neighbor's door.

"My God, somethin's happened to Josephine. She's been gone since afternoon. She ain't ever done this before. She went out to buy me some supper, and she ain't come back yet."

She was hysterical. Her neighbor grabbed her coat and hat also, and they ran down the corridor and down the stairs into the street below.

"I gotta find her. Oh, my poor baby. Somethin's happened to my poor Josephine. You gotta come with me to find my baby. Oh, my God, what am I gonna do if somethin's happened to my little baby?"

When she reached the street she began calling for Josephine. She ran first to the store, which was now closed, and on her way she passed the theatre. The performance was going on.

She ran back to her home with her friend, asking everyone she met if they had seen her daughter. She described her in detail.

Then, exhausted, she returned to her apartment, hoping that Josephine would be there. It was empty.

She fell into her chair and could not be consoled by the neighbors. Tears streaked down her face as one of the neighbors went to the police station to report Josephine Baker missing.

* * *

Early in the morning in the St. Louis railroad station, a train was waiting to depart for the South. There were a few white passengers entering the Pullman cars. Down the platform came the members of the Bessie Smith troupe. There were the musicians and Bert and Benny, and then Bessie Smith and, beside her, Josephine Baker, carrying two large valises.

The conductor was calling, "All aboaaard!" He assisted the white women passengers up the steps and into the Pullman cars. The black porters were waving at Bessie Smith, for they had recognized her immediately.

The conductor continued announcing the last call and announcing the cities on the route.

"Panama Limited . . . Paducah, Memphis, Jackson . . . Natchez, Baton Rouge . . . and New Orleans." He spotted the members of the Bessie Smith troupe struggling along the side of the train, and without missing a beat he continued: "Niggers in the last car, all niggers in the last car. All aboaaaard . . ."

Wordlessly they made their way to the last car. Compared to the Pullman it was decidedly a third-rate day coach. Inside, half a dozen blacks occupied the seats. Most were already asleep. Bessie dropped into a seat, opened her purse, took a great slug out of a pint of gin, leaned over, and looked out the window.

"You want something, Bessie, some water or something?" Josephine asked.

Bessie shook her head no. Outside, the conductor was making his final call.

Josephine walked out onto the platform that separated their car from the first-class Pullman cars in front. The steps had been covered, but the top door between the cars had been left open. She pulled the collar of her thin little coat about her shoulders as she looked out.

She stared blankly for a long time. She was dazed, thinking of nothing. Then, as the sound of the air brakes being released jolted her, she leaned forward a little and spoke ever so softly.

"Good-bye, Mama . . ." A tear formed in her eye.

The train gave a jerk forward. Then Josephine sucked in her breath, squared her shoulders, and spoke again.

"Good-bye, St. Louis . . . good-bye, East St. Louis, too," she almost shouted.

The train began moving rapidly out of the station. The wheels were clicking against the tracks.

Now she leaned over and looked through the window at the dreary scenery passing by. It had started to rain. She planted her feet firmly on the steel floor, balancing herself against the swaying of the train. She clutched the collar of the cheap coat to her throat as if it were some marvelous fur piece, and with defiance in her eyes and in her voice, difficult to understand in one so young, she shouted, "Yeah . . . good-bye, St. Louis. I'm leavin' here a nobody . . ."

The train was now streaking through the night on its journey southward. ". . . but someday I'm gonna be somebody . . . and you ain't gonna get to see me . . . 'cause I ain't ever coming back here again!"

* * *

Fifty years later, almost to the day, at the last minute Josephine canceled her engagement in St. Louis. She did not tell me why she was doing it. I did not need to be told. The city fathers had prepared a great event for her. It was to be Josephine Baker Day. They were devastated, then infuriated.

Instead, she flew first to Paris, then to Israel, where she was to be the guest of Golda Meir.

Yes, now Josephine Baker was *somebody*.

Chapter 4

"... In particular, a sort of colored Charlotte Greenwood caught the house. She is Josephine Baker, billed with the cast, and is an eccentric dancing comedienne, affecting a regulation boy's haircut, with her locks plastered so that she appears to have satin hair."

* * *

Surprisingly, as Bessie Smith's maid, Josephine had little to do. Bessie wore two gowns, one in the first act, and one in the second; and for Josephine, taking care of them was a snap.

"I had been taking care of piles of all kinds of wash for a long time by then, and those two little things were nothing. The big problem I had was getting her out of a gown when she came off stage. Usually, she would just fall down and go to sleep in them.

"I used to make a little extra money doing shirts for some of the musicians, and Bessie never cared. I had asked her first if she minded. She didn't care about anything then. She seemed to be unhappy all the time. I tried to cheer her up, and you know, when I was young I had a pretty good sense of humor, but not much of it took off on Bessie.

"The one I really had fun with was Benny. I used to stand in the wings and watch them whenever they were on stage. Benny would look out, and when he would see me he always did something that would make me break up. I just couldn't help it. He would cross his eyes, and walk pigeon-toed, or pretend to fall. He had two big rubber balloons that he used for his ladies' breasts, and I used to blow them up for him. I tried to get the same amount of air into them the first time I did it for him.

"I guess that's when I learned my first stage trick. It was pretty simple, and obvious too. He told me to blow more air into one than the other, then when he went out, his bosom would look lopsided. He was right, too. When he walked out and threw back his shoulders and showed that lop-sided balloon bosom of his, the audience would roar with laughter.

"You know who reminds me of him so much when he does that drag act of his? It's Flip Wilson. The way those arms go out, and the way he plants his feet apart on the stage. Benny was just like that.

"I watched that act so much that there wasn't a movement or gesture that I didn't know, and one night on the train heading for Memphis two things happened. I did that act, and I had my first drink.

"I had never had anything to drink before. Believe me, never in my life. And I didn't make the same mistake that others make when they have their first drink. They think if they feel good with one or two, what will ten do for them? They usually find out the next morning. But you know, then I didn't like liquor, and I still don't. Bessie gave me a little gin. I had a bad cold and was coughing my head off. You know, I only had that little coat that I ran away with, and one of the musicians threw his big coat over me to keep me warm.

"Bessie seemed to be real concerned and insisted that I have a slug of her gin. She gave it to me right out of the bottle. My God, it burned like fire. I wondered how people ever got that stuff down. But you know, it stopped my cough, and I even asked her for another. Everybody laughed. Some of the boys in the band were playing a Charleston number in the back of the car, and what with the gin in me, and the singing going on, I began to feel pretty good.

"Then Benny came down the aisle and did a real *number* on me. You know then, as now, my favorite position is to put my hands on my hips and spread my feet apart and throw back my shoulders. And that's what Benny did, and he was a great mimic. My voice was quite high-pitched then, and he had me down to a T.

" 'Bessie, you gonna wear the white one or the blue one for the first act?'

"Then he answered himself right away, just like I always did, 'cause Bessie couldn't care less what she wanted to wear, and I always chose them for her.

" 'I'll just get you the blue one tonight.'

"He walked down the aisle of the car slowly, swinging his big behind to one side and then the other as he walked, and he acted as though he was carrying a dress in both arms.

"Bessie screamed with laughter. I think that was the best time she ever had—that night on the train. The rest of the time she was just moping around.

"But by then I was ready, and I had Benny down pretty good, too. I jumped out into the aisle, and while Benny was going down one way, doing his imitation of little Josephine Baker, I was going down the aisle the other way doing my imitation of his drag act.

"I just started right out singing, imitating his high-pitched lady's voice: '. . . if you wanna make a nigger feel good, here's all you have to do . . .'

"By then I got to feeling real good, and a couple of the boys in the band who had been watching us started playing 'Chicken Pie,' and I really went into it.

"I swaggered, and I sang, and squatted down, and put my arms on my hips, and walked pigeon-toed, and tripped over my foot, and never missed a beat of the music or a line of the song or one of his movements. Right in the middle of it they started applauding me—and it was at the same place that they always applauded Benny in the theatre. I just knew I was good. I don't know why. I just was. I was always good with a song or material that I liked real well; but try to give me something I didn't like, and I just couldn't put it over. I don't know why.

"But then it came so natural to me. I even told those tired old jokes in the middle of the song, and Bert came along and played his part, and then he put his arms around me and we strutted down the aisle, and I wasn't Josephine Baker anymore: I was really Benny doing his act. Boy, it was wonderful.

"Then I wasn't really thinking about being in the theatre. I never really tried hard in all of my life to be on the stage; it just sort of happened for me. You know, people kill themselves and they never make it.

"For me, I just thought, 'Well, it wouldn't be bad, I could make a nice living out of it,' and that is just sort of how it happened. It happened that night on that train bound for Memphis, Tennessee. I never really said to myself, 'I think I'll go into show business!' I just never assumed that I wouldn't go into show business.

"When Bert and I finished, even Bessie started applauding me. Then the band started playing another real hot Charleston, and I got into that number with one of the musicians. Again nobody had ever showed me how to do the Charleston. Nobody had ever showed me how to do the cakewalk either. I just knew how to do them.

"In my entire career I never had a singing or a dancing lesson. Everything I did just came to me naturally. You know, they say colored people have a 'natural rhythm,' and have 'natural movement.' You know that that is crazy. I've seen some colored people who couldn't dance or sing their way out of a paper bag if they tried for a hundred years, but for some reason, it did come naturally to me, and the more I did it, the better I liked it, and that was it."

The show had been in Memphis for a week. Josephine said she did not suggest it, that Benny did. Benny suggested that Josephine had talked him into it.

At any rate, at a Saturday matinee, for a laugh, or for a reason, Benny stayed off stage, and hidden behind the curtains was Josephine in Benny's drag, balloons and all.

In the number, Bert always made his entrance first, and then his "girlfriend" appeared.

It must have been something when Bert took out his alarm-clock-size watch to check the time. There was some dialogue about ladies always being late, and that was the cue for Josephine.

"Bert just did a double take. But the funny part of it was that I got the same laugh that Benny always got when he made his entrance. He got his laugh 'cause he looked so outrageous in his drag outfit. I knew I looked crazy, but not crazy enough, so when I made my entrance, I walked with my toes turned in, and I could cross one eye and not the other. I just threw out my shoulders, got my pigeon-toed stance, crossed one eye, and out I went."

So much for American and French showbiz history. The audience screamed.

"You know, I was even better than Benny was."

It is entirely possible that she was. At that moment the die was cast. It was a perfect casting. No other star was better made for the theatre than Josephine Baker. She was never happier than when she was on stage, or in her dressing room.

When she came off stage, all the stagehands came over to congratulate her. She never forgot that little gesture. For the next fifty years, whenever she was to appear in a theatre, in any place in the world, before she started rehearsing she would walk over to each stagehand and say, "Hi, there. I'm Josephine Baker. Thanks for helping me do my show." They never forgot her, either. As I traveled around the world with her, old stagehands long since retired would come over and speak to her and remind her that she had played in such and such a theatre in such and such a city so many, many years ago.

She usually remembered the city and the theatre, and then she would say, "Oh, my God, you don't say. Of course I remember. Do you still have to walk up all those shaky steps to get to the dressing room?"

And usually they still did. She would never fail to ask about their families, and she would never fail to leave them with the word that if there was anything she could do for them just to let her know.

Then, when her "bad times" came — when "Old Man Trouble" came— she would receive envelopes from strange cities all over the world, and in them would be a few dollars, a few pounds, or some pesos, and they would be from some stagehand and his family wanting to help her out.

She, of course, rarely remembered the man, but she always remembered the city and the theatre, and she would partly close her eyes and with that faraway look she would think about her times in that city.

"Oh, my God, aren't they wonderful to think of me!"

Many times people would wait for her backstage, and when she would come out, some young person would come up to her and say that his father had been a stagehand back in Rochester, New York, or some other city she had played in long ago, and he had heard so much about Josephine Baker that he had to come to see her. She would take time and inquire about the father, or the brother, or the wife.

Sometimes the wife of a stagehand would send her food backstage; then Josephine would insist the next day that the stagehand bring his wife, and she would place a chair backstage where the wife could watch the show. Many times the wife would end up in the dressing room, and they would just sit and have a good talk about family, and friends, and dogs, and cats, and Grandma and Grandpa. Of course, Josephine Baker knew none of the family, but she liked hearing stories of family life.

"You know, Stephen, it's always the same. Grandma—or Mama, if Grandma is dead—rules the roost in colored families. She's the one who pushes the little birds out and makes them go on their own when they are ready. You know, that's my trouble. I don't think I'll ever be able to push my little birds out when they are ready. But the world is so much different now, isn't it?"

* * *

Josephine stayed on with Bessie Smith until the tour brought them to New Orleans. She always insisted that she and Bessie parted the greatest of friends. I have heard no stories to the contrary. Probably Bessie took some motherly delight in Josephine, having had no children of her own.

There are those who tell the story that Josephine left because Bessie's boyfriend was getting too close and was making too obvious advances. Josephine insisted that that was not true, and that Bessie said that if she would go to New York she might well find a career in the theatre for herself.

At any rate, regardless of the reason, one day after a Saturday matinee, Josephine announced that she was leaving for New York City after the final performance.

"I had about ninety dollars I had earned from Bessie and doing the boys' laundry. And that was a lot of money. I think they were sad to see me go, because I used to keep everybody laughing. They all pitched in and gave me a dollar apiece as a going-away present, and Bessie gave me one of her beautiful handbags. It was used, but I loved it. What little money I had always had in the past, I kept in my bra. It took me a long time to get used to carrying money in a purse."

When she finally got around to carrying money in her purse, it never bothered her to carry $50,000 or $60,000 at one time. She said that she had never had a penny stolen out of her purse in her entire career. "They stole it with contracts instead," she claimed. Of course, there are two sides to that story, for many a promoter has said that Josephine robbed him blind, leaving his theatre and city with everything, and him with the empty pockets. I do not doubt that many times it was the truth.

* * *

When she walked out of the stage door, she never looked back, as was her practice. Benny stood in the stage door a long time watching her go up the alley and to the station. He waited for her to turn around so that he could wave good-bye. She never did. It was to be many years, and countless thousands of miles, before his path would cross Josephine's again.

Josephine said that as they neared New York City she saw everyone on the train preparing to get off, so she did too. When the train stopped, she was the first one off. She stood alone on the platform, wearing her thin coat and clutching a small cardboard suitcase. A little carpetbag was flung over her shoulder.

But it was not Grand Central Station; it was the station at 125th Street, in Harlem.

Josephine, thinking she was in downtown Manhattan, wondered how she was going to get to Harlem. Bessie had told her to go to the Cotton Club and see if they could use her in some capacity. Bessie had advised her to try for a dancer's job. Josephine remembered that, but she also thought about what her mother had told her about going to Harlem to get herself a rich man.

She asked two girls on the corner how to get to Harlem. They laughed and thought they were being put on. Next she asked a black policeman. He took one look and knew that it was the first time this little girl had ever been in the big town.

"Sister, you are there right now. Where do you want to go?"

She was amazed that she was in Harlem. She couldn't figure it out, but told him she wanted to get to the Cotton Club, and he directed her. He pointed up the street, and she saw the sign.

Josephine insisted that this story was true. She also insisted that she then walked up the street and into the stage door of the Cotton Club, where they were auditioning for dancers, and—even though it sounds like make-believe, or too good to be true—that she got the job.

Now comes a confusing period in the life of Josephine Baker. She told the story one way to me, and always stuck to her version. She may well have told conflicting versions to others, out of a desire to throw people off the track if she was remotely suspicious that they might be thinking of writing her life story. "You know, we can't be too careful," she would tell me.

After a person becomes "someone" in the theatre, there are countless hundreds, even thousands, who claim to have had a part in making that person a star. They are all wonderful stories, and part of the theatre; without them, I suppose, the theatre wouldn't be the theatre. If you liked the person and were around him just before a particular incident "happened," then you related it your way. If you disliked the person, you related it another way. So it was particularly with Josephine.

I heard the stories firsthand from Eubie Blake, F. E. Miller and Ivan Browning. In all cases, they were either in complete agreement or totally different. But it was again a case of "remembering," and a remembering after many years. It is possible that the one who was really responsible for "discovering" Josephine was some long-forgotten choreographer of that period of the Cotton Club.

Josephine insisted to me that she walked in in the middle of an audition. She saw the other girls putting on tap shoes and changing into pants, or skirts, or any piece of wardrobe that would make them appear exciting and that would either add to their proficiency or cover a deficiency.

Josephine had no tap shoes. She pulled the blouse out of her skirt and knotted it under her breasts to "push them out a little." She sat down and retied her shoes as though they were tap shoes, and when the first line of girls was called she watched very carefully what they were doing.

The choreographer had shown them a dance combination, and they were learning it a few steps at a time.

"I just stared at what they were doing. He was shouting leap, shuffle, ball change, step, step, ball change, leap, shuffle, shuffle, and I thought he was crazy. I had never heard anything like it before. Of course, most of these girls had had training and lessons, and they got right into it. I didn't even try. I put the talk out of my head and just watched the feet, and when I thought I had it, I jumped up with five other girls. I tried to get in the center so he wouldn't notice me too much and see that I wasn't doing what the others were, but somehow I landed on the end of that line."

What happened next, Josephine insisted, also was an accident. Who knows? She gave a good kick when she saw the other girls giving a good kick, and her right shoe went flying out into the empty club. Undaunted, Josephine says she continued. She said that she couldn't have cared less. She kicked off the other shoe, and as it went flying after the first, she jumped in front of the other girls who were dancing away and started doing a hula number. Somebody laughed, and that was all she needed. Then came the cross eyes, and the pigeon toes, the fat lips, the strut and the shuffle. It was all Benny, only it was Josephine doing it. The choreographer loved it. He had seemed a little unconvinced until he glanced over and saw the club owner "laughing his head off."

"I didn't know who that big fat man laughing so hard was, and when I saw him laughing, I started all over again. You know, they were playing 'I'm Just Wild About Harry,' and there I was doing a hula number, with the crossed eyes and all. That man got hysterical."

In two weeks Josephine was a line girl at the Cotton Club. "I got me a room by myself around the corner, and boy, I worked in that room like I never worked in my life. I knew that I couldn't get along with that funny hula routine of mine, and I really tried. Fortunately, I had a basement room, and boy, I tapped away night and day on those cement floors until I got it in my head. When I got it there, you couldn't get it out with a team of horses.

"I always gave it a little extra, and since I was taller than the other girls I was always in the very center of the line or the tall one on the end, and people just naturally noticed me. Of course, I wasn't above giving them one cross eye or the other, 'cause I could do both eyes individually, or sometimes I gave them both, if I thought they weren't watching me. I knew how to get their attention if I wanted it."

Again, whether intentionally or unintentionally, Josephine gave a repeat performance of her by now famous hula routine. She figured if it worked once, it might work twice.

Actually it worked three times. The last time would be in Paris, for one of France's most prestigious impresarios and directors. But that would be sometime later.

That night, Josephine remembered, the "big guns" (as she called them) from *Shuffle Along* were in the club. These probably would have been Noble Sissle and Eubie Blake, or Lew Payton, or Julian Mitchell. Sissle, Blake, and Payton were the composers and writers, and Mitchell the director, of many popular black shows of that period. *Shuffle Along* was the first "accepted" black Broadway show. Rightly so, too, for it had the proper balance of elements that appealed to both blacks and whites.

For some reason Josephine felt she wasn't getting enough attention. At just the right time, the shoe went flying out into the audience. She tried, so she said lamely, to dance around in one stockinged foot. The audience started to laugh, and off went the other shoe. She tried a few more bars of tapping in bare feet.

Then out she jumped in front of the chorus line again. Her routine this time did not change much from the one she had done before. It was the hula, and it was the same cross eyes and pigeon toes, and it was Benny all over again.

Whatever happened, Josephine brought down the house, and she also caught the attention of the *Shuffle Along* table.

That was it, she said. In a couple of weeks Josephine was downtown doing a hot Charleston at the end of the line. It was the same routine. It was cross eyes, pigeon toes, fat lips, strut and shuffle. It was now *all* Josephine Baker, and blacks and whites alike went wild about her.

"You know, I was good in what I did. But if I had not gone to France, I believe I would have eventually ended up in Harlem, marrying some guy with money, or maybe without, and ended up having a bunch of kids to take care of. But for some reason I was happy and unhappy, and I couldn't figure it out. I didn't like being in the chorus; I felt I couldn't get my breath. A couple of times I felt like walking out, but I stayed."

Regardless of the talk of the early years of Josephine Baker, she did not really begin shining until she went into *The Chocolate Dandies* and *In Bamville.*

"They always associated me with *Shuffle Along,* but the show where they really started noticing me was *Chocolate Dandies.* I just loved that show. Then I never minded going to the theatre. I could hardly wait for the curtain to go up. I worked hard at it. We were on the road a long time, and the happiest day was when I opened up the theatre program and saw my name listed in the credits.

"The first time they put my name in the credits was in *In Bamville.* Boy, I used to laugh when they said that name. I laughed till I almost cried when they first offered me a little part in *In Bamville.*"

In Bamville was called (by the authors) a "Little Vaudeville." It was written by Noble Sissle and Lew Payton, with music by Eubie Blake. It was staged by Julian Mitchell.

Probably the first time the name Josephine Baker was carried in a theatre program was at the Illinois Theatre in Chicago. The cast was listed in this order: George W. Cooper, Ivan H. Browning, W. A. Hann, Charles Davis, J. Mardo Brown, Lottie Gee, Valada Snow, Josephine Baker, and Amanda Randolph.

* * *

"The first time I ever saw my name in print like that was in Chicago, and Mr. Browning was standing in the wings, and when I came off stage with the other chorus girls he showed me a copy of the program, and he had underlined my name. It just sort of bounced out at me. Josephine Baker, and it was before Amanda Randolph, too.

"You know, it had probably appeared at other times too, but that is the first time I remembered it so well, and I never forget that it was Mr. Browning that showed it to me."

Ivan Browning was a friend of Josephine Baker's for more than fifty years. Very likely he was the one truly great friend she ever had, and whom she recognized as such. He and his little family never once faltered in their devotion to Josephine.

I came to know Mr. Browning very well in his later years, and during the last fifteen or twenty years of my relationship with Josephine. He was —and, I should say, still is—a grand old man of the theatre. In his day he must have been brilliant.

"You know, when Mr. Browning used to sing, I would stand in the wings and watch him. Those notes would just float out of his mouth, and he would captivate that audience. When he finished, there would be a long pause, because the audience was so enchanted with what he had sung, and the way he had sung it. Then they would break out into cheers and applause.

"I always called him Mr. Browning; I don't know why. I guess in those days he sort of used to watch over me, and so did his family. I had to be careful what I did, too, and he wouldn't think twice about telling me when I had done something wrong, and when I could improve something I had done."

"Stephen," Browning once told me, "I've known Josephine for over fifty years. Sometimes I get so mad and she exasperates me so much I could kill her. But then, you know we love her so much that after I cool down, everything seems to be okay again."

There is little doubt that the foundations for the career Josephine was to have were built by Eubie Blake, Noble Sissle, Julian Mitchell, who was her director on several shows, and of course Ivan Browning.

* * *

More than fifty years from the time Josephine first met Ivan Browning, I went to a small concert in the Wilshire Ebell Theatre in Los Angeles. Eubie Blake, then over ninety, was the star of the show. It was incredible. How good he looked, and how well he played! The capacity audience was enchanted with Mr. Blake and his entire show. He recalled the great moments from his life in the theatre, and the house was spellbound. Then he talked of *Chocolate Dandies,* and *Shuffle Along,* and *In Bamville,* and he told the audience that the star of those shows was in the theatre, and asked if they would like to meet him.

The spotlight hit Ivan Browning, and he walked slowly up to the stage. When he hit the footlights and started to cross over, Eubie Blake started "I'm Just Wild About Harry," and they sang it together. It brought down the house.

Then Eubie Blake started a little-known but fabulous song. It was "If You Ain't Never Been Loved by a Brownskin, You Ain't Never Been Loved At All."

Somewhere a couple of smart and attentive electricians dimmed the stage lights and put a spot on Eubie Blake at the piano and another on Ivan Browning, who started singing that marvelous black ballad that was written so long ago.

I sat back in my seat, and it seemed that Mr. Browning was about twenty-five years old. I imagined that he was on stage in some theatre more than fifty years ago and that a young little Josephine Baker was in the wings peering out at him, and studying him, and learning from him.

When Ivan Browning finished, half the house were using handkerchiefs to dry an eye or blow a nose. He held that last note for ten seconds, and it was in perfect pitch and crystal clear. I would have given anything for Josephine to have been in the audience then. When I wrote her a detailed letter about the concert, she responded immediately, wanting more of the details.

"My God, Stephen, can you imagine Mr. Browning still singing so beautifully?"

They gave him a standing ovation that night, and he deserved every bit of the ecstatic applause and devotion. He was sending his love over the footlights to his audiences. After I saw him perform that night, I realized how much she had really learned from Ivan Browning. It was so obvious that she was still using the same tilt of the head, the same twist of the body, the same gesture with the hands that she had studied in Ivan for so many years in their tours during the early twenties.

* * *

Many people have taken credit for the "making" of Josephine Baker—some of whom she had never even heard of. In his marvelous book on the Folies Bergère, the great French impresario and Folies owner Paul Derval devotes a chapter to the "Terrible Josephine." He, of course, adored her. He says that he discovered Josephine Baker and put her into his theatre. But the only two people I ever heard her mention as having "discovered" her were Ivan Browning and Henri Varna. The basics she got from Benny, the solid foundation from Ivan Browning and her innumerable Sissle and Blake revues, and the final polish from Henri Varna. That is the way she told it. That is also the way I believed it.

If anyone really "discovered" Josephine, it was Ivan Browning. "Mr. Browning really did scare me, and if I saw him in the wings, I really watched what I was doing."

Mr. Browning watched over Josephine for her entire life. Through thick and thin he stood by her. When, during the late sixties, Josephine was going through her terrible ordeal, and he visited the Château des Milandes with his grandson, and Josephine had little time to give to him, indeed even seemed annoyed, he forgave her, and remained her staunchest defender to her last days.

Mr. Browning "scares" me too. When Josephine would do something that would exasperate me to the point of my considering severing all relationships with her, he would telephone me and say:

"Now, look here, Stephen"—he is very much like Josephine in his speech—"I know Josephine is acting up, and you know it too. But there ain't nobody gonna help her here in America but you and me, so let's just do it, and forget all that other stuff."

* * *

"Boy, I was really working then, and I couldn't figure out for what. I loved what I was doing, but even then I felt that I was going to do bigger things. I never dreamed what they would be. My God, how could I have?"

Josephine appeared in different versions of *Shuffle Along*, *In Bamville,* and *Chocolate Dandies* almost continually from the time she left the Bessie Smith company until she left for France.

In 1924, in Rochester, New York, on Tuesday, November 11, Josephine got her first important billing for playing a character in a revue. The show was *In Bamville,* and the character she played was called Topsy Anna.

"You know, I laughed when they told me they wanted me in *In Bamville* but I really laughed when I played Topsy Anna. I just fell to the floor."

In telling the story, Josephine almost fell to the floor again. She could not remember what she did, and the critics did not notice her. If they did, they did not write of it.

On May 27, 1924, in Baltimore, Maryland, at Ford's Theatre, a long-forgotten critic who used only the initials G.E.K. wrote:

> . . . In the Bacchanalia there is a cayenne girl named Josephine Baker, who simulates Ben Turpin eyes and who dances with all the abandon of a half a dozen eccentric girls of a harem. . . .

It was her first review, and one of the very few notices she ever kept. In her later years she would take it out and show it to some of her intimate friends. She would read the critic's description of the chorus and again literally fall to the floor:

> . . . there are the Jazzy Jassimines, the Bandanaland Girls, the Bamville Vamps, and the Syncopated Sunflowers.

"You know, I was one of the Bamville Vamps, and I did that part up good. Those Sunflowers would wilt when I was on that stage!"

Ivan Browning was in the same production. Very likely he was in the wings keeping his eye on little Josephine.

"Little Josephine" was growing up pretty fast.

* * *

Now the critics never failed to notice Josephine. Their praises for her were getting longer and more important. They were even ignoring the stars to write about her. She was hitting her stride.

Seeing *In Bamville* at the Metropolitan Theatre in Cleveland during the same tour, a critic wrote:

> . . . And then there's Josephine Baker, one of the funniest young ladies of the moment on the stage. And it is interesting to note that she's a chorus girl. She has been promoted to "principal" at times in various scenes; but even when she is back in the line, the audience is watching—and applauding her every movement. . . .

Regarding the show, the critic stated, ". . . and don't wait until next week, and then be unable to purchase a seat on account of the capacity sign."

"Sissle and Blake and Mr. Browning knew I was good. Eubie Blake wanted to sign a contract with me for a long period of time to stay in their shows in New York and on the road, and for some reason I didn't want to. I don't know why. It was that same thing that kept telling me. Like it did before . . . like it stopped me when it wanted me to go back to the Booker T. Washington Theatre and see Bessie Smith."

Now Josephine worked. It is probably true that they pushed her hard, for if they did not she tended to be lazy. If she did work, it paid off.

One other notice Josephine kept for more than fifty years was one from *Variety,* the show-business bible, as important then as it is today. It was dated September 3, 1924, and signed "Ibee." In those days, as today, the critics for *Variety* used this type of byline.

> . . . At least two of the chorus scored hits with dancing specialties. In particular, a sort of colored Charlotte Greenwood caught the house. She is Josephine Baker, billed with the cast, and is an eccentric dancing comedienne, affecting a regulation boy's haircut, with her locks plastered so that she appears to have satin hair.

She especially loved the line about the "regulation boy's haircut."

"You know, when I made my last tour with *In Bamville,* or *Chocolate Dandies,* I can't remember which, I didn't get along too well with the other girls in the chorus. One day I didn't like something one of the girls said to me, so I just moved down the hall to the boys' dressing rooms. I never moved out, and they loved it, and so did I. We used to have some real fun, as you know most of them were gay, and they would tell me all about their romances and all, and I loved those stories. I remember one of them had a complete woman's wardrobe, as well as all his men's clothes, and when he felt in the mood he would put on his women's clothes and go out in them. He was something, too. He would wrap his head in a towel, and with his back to you, you couldn't tell the difference between him and a woman.

"He used to conk [straighten] his hair. What a stink that used to make, and it was real long, and if he wanted to be a woman, one of the other boys would marcel it and wave it for him. Nobody in the company paid any attention. But I just loved his hair, so one day I asked them if they would do mine for me too.

"They did. Up to that time, I had only pressed it with a hot comb to straighten it, but one day after the matinee in New York—the Colonial Theatre, on Broadway—we all got into it, and they cut my hair short. They made a mistake and cut it too short, and when they put the conk on it it burned me like fire, but I took it. I didn't care. Then after they were through, it wasn't long enough to make those marvelous waves, or to marcel it, and the only thing I could do was to just plaster it down. I looked just like a boy, but I loved it. It was just like patent leather, it was so black and shiny, and that night when I went on in the show, I caused even more of a sensation. They even wrote about it in the papers the next day.

Probably painted about 1926 or 1927. "Everyone was scandalized when I had them release this photo of the painting. I can tell you it didn't hurt business any. It did for me what that photo of Marilyn [Monroe] did for her, only a long time later. . . . I wonder what ever happened to the original."

(Preceding page) "When I had this photo made, and I showed it to someone, they said, 'Why, you're the black Sally Rand,' and I didn't know what they were talking about. Then when I was in America in the thirties, I saw Sally, and I said, 'Boy, that was some compliment, 'cause I could never be as beautiful as she is, or dance as well.' "

Photo courtesy of George Hoyningen-Huene

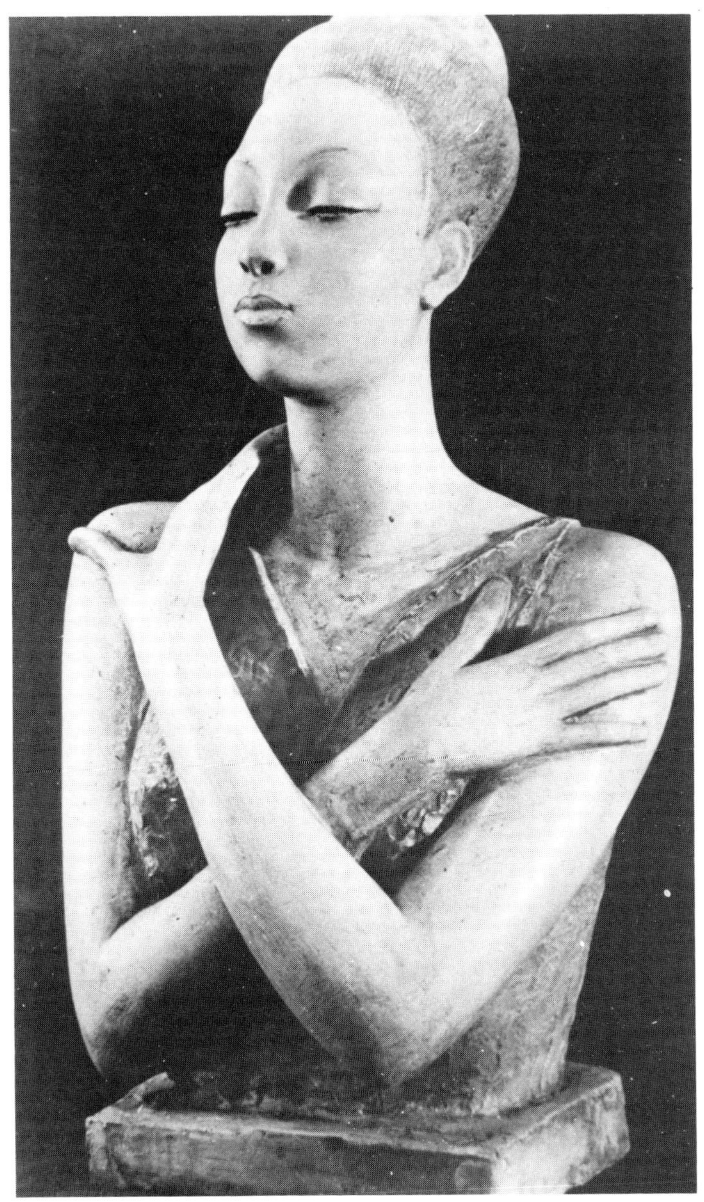

Josephine Baker, about 1928. ". . . She is no doubt the Nefertiti of now. . . ." (Picasso)

Backstage at the Folies Bergère with Mildred, who had replaced Sheik the panther. Mildred loved the movies but hated opera, and when Josephine took her to a performance of *Aïda,* she leaped into the orchestra pit and mauled the conductor, and the performance had to be stopped. "I should have known . . . Mildred only liked those jungle pictures."

Josephine Baker in 1927. "Our Entertainer—The Charleston Queen of Paris."

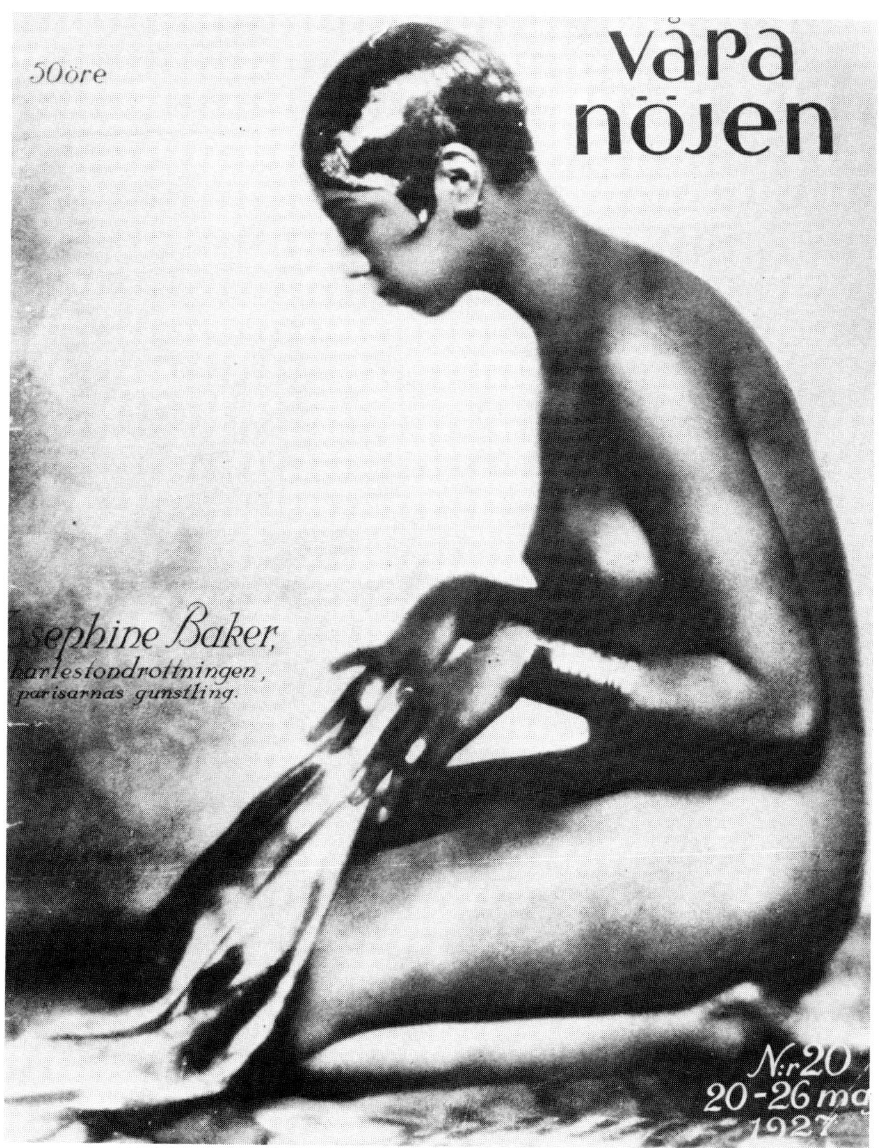

Abbè

Varna Collection

Josephine about 1928. It was in this year that she was first placed in a sketch in the Folies. She impersonated a sailor out on the town with some of "his" shipmates. The shipmates couldn't understand why their pal wasn't interested in all the girls. They ignored the fact that her sailor outfit was very abbreviated indeed. Finally the captain unmasked her, to the joy of the crew. "Can you believe that theme?" she said. "But those audiences loved it."

Varna Collection

Near the end of the twenties. The hair was slowly changing (note the ringlets), as were the eyebrows. It was the beginning of the end of her "madcap" period.

"When I walked out of the theatre, they didn't know if I was a boy or a girl. Then, when I got to Paris, that's what caught their attention first; it was my hair. They even said, when they first saw me, 'Are you a girl, or are you a boy?'

"I never would answer them. I would just laugh. Probably because then I didn't understand what they were saying to me. You know, when I began to lose my hair after I was poisoned, it was one of the things that always made me feel worse than anything else. Many times I would just sit and look in the mirror at those little wisps that were left of it, and I would almost cry.

"But then everything works out for the best, doesn't it? Then I started to wear my fabulous wigs, and it was a 'new' Josephine Baker, and if those things hadn't happened to me, I probably wouldn't have lasted as long as I did. And you know, I have lasted in the theatre almost fifty years. It seems like it was only yesterday that I started out straightening my hair and everyone said, 'Are you a girl, or are you a boy?' "

* * *

Sometime in 1925, *Chocolate Dandies* returned to New York City for a short layoff. Josephine happened to hear of a new revue being prepared called *Revue Negre*.

Josephine later insisted that she did not know the revue was being prepared to play in Paris, France. She of course got the job immediately. By now, she was beginning to be something of a "name."

"But my God, I'd never even heard of France, let alone Paris. For all I cared, it could have been on the moon.

"Oh, of course I had heard of it, but I didn't know anything about Paris and didn't care. A lot of people said that I went over because Ethel Waters didn't want to go. That isn't true. If that is the case, I would have known they were going to France.

"Then, when I heard the show was going out of the country, I went to the producer and said I wouldn't be able to go, even though I had already signed a contract. I tried to back out of it. I remember they were a tough bunch. I got warned that if I didn't go to Paris with this revue, I wouldn't be going out with any other one. Well, to tell you the truth, they did scare me, and I went into rehearsal with them.

"When I was in rehearsals with that show in New York before we went overseas, I knew it was a bad show, but I was stuck with it, and that was that."

Very likely it is one of the few contracts that Josephine did not try to break. In later years, she thought nothing of abrogating a contract to make other demands, or to get out of an engagement she did not want.

She did it with countless producers in the United States, and countless more in France and other countries. She gave it not another thought. And of course she always blamed her producer at the time. It was a strange quirk that stayed with her to the end. Just before her death, when she was appearing in Paris at the Bobino, she was in litigation with her last producers in America.

As Josephine tells the story, the *Revue Negre* was "horrible. I hated it; it was awful." Others tell the story that it was an exciting, brilliant, marvelous revue. It is difficult to determine. As usual, I will give her version.

"I knew it was bad in the rehearsals, I knew it was bad when we rehearsed it on the boat, and I knew it was bad when we opened in Paris. But it was that boat that was the worst of all. I hated that show, and I hated Paris, and I hated France, and I hated that boat most of all. I was as sick as a dog all the way over. Do you know that I was so dumb that I asked the doctor to have them take the ship back to New York and let me off? That's how dumb I was.

"And there I was, hating France and Paris, and I hadn't even got there yet. I regretted a million times that I had signed that contract. But now I was stuck. Stuck in the middle of the ocean, and I couldn't escape."

Josephine *was* stuck. It was either the S.S. *Europa,* or the S.S. *Berengaria.* "What difference does it make? They're all the same, I can't remember. They all make you just as sick.

"But now that I think about it, I don't ever think I would have been a star in the theatre if I had stayed in New York. I was lucky, I guess. Something was just guiding and pushing me along. I never had the vaguest idea of what was going to happen to me. All I know is that when we landed in Le Havre, I didn't hate France so much, because it was dry land, and I was able to get off that rocking ship."

Josephine Baker landed in Le Havre sometime in late 1925.

* * *

"The day I stepped ashore I was already thinking of how I was going to get back to America. I never made it back. I fell in love with France and Paris and the people, and they fell in love with me.

"Many times I thought I could go back to America and be a big star there too, like I was in France. It never happened. Oh, sure, I would come back occasionally and stay a few weeks in different cities, but after the first time, I knew I could never go home again.

"Then came that time in my life when they didn't want me to come home, and I couldn't even get into the country, except for the president [Kennedy] and his brother.

"But now look at me. [She was speaking about her final appearance in Los Angeles, California.] My God, how they love me! When I stand on that stage, and they are shouting and screaming and jumping up and down and clapping, I can hardly believe it. And oh, am I happy. And I forget all about those bad times, and Walter Winchell, and all that, and I think that it has all been worth it. I *know* it has been worth it. You have to face facts, and the people in the world have to face facts. *America is where it is.* You only have to lift your finger for anything you want—and the Americans did it all in two hundred years. In France and other countries, it takes them two hundred years to fix the toilet when it breaks down. And you know, too, America is where the money is. In my entire life I've never earned money like I have earned in America. And now maybe that things are okay with me and America again, and when I come back next year, we can maybe make some real money, and I can get myself straightened out."

Josephine Baker never returned to the America that now loved her. She never got into the "real" money she wished for. It is unfortunate. "You know, if we live long enough, that wheel of life makes the great circle, and you are right back where you started from."

Chapter 5

"My dear, don't ever do that to me again. Why, those people actually had pieces of iron on the bottom of their shoes. All they did was tap—what a racket! They tap one number, then they tap more numbers. All they did was tap for two hours! Why, everyone will absolutely run out of the theatre. Only you can fix this up if you want to use these Africans. I want no part of it. If you think there is something worth showing, then you get over there!"

* * *

There has not been a great deal written about *La Revue Negre* and its presentation in Paris. If one spoke with most people in that company, he was told that the show was a great success. If he spoke with Josephine and a few others, he heard that it was a disaster. Even the reports in France and in the United States were conflicting. Some raved of this "marvelous black revue from America"; others dismissed it as a "lot of racket."

When I first visited in France with Josephine, I met a newspaper-critic friend of hers who had dropped by to pay his respects. Over dinner I asked him about *Revue Negre,* as he had written a notice of it when it premiered. "There was nothing wrong with *Revue Negre;* it was with me. You see, I had only brought one pencil with me, and I needed two—one to stuff in each ear to keep out the sound and prevent me from going deaf!"

Strangely, he had not remembered Josephine in the revue; it may have been that she was disheartened and did not give her all. Not long after he reviewed *Revue Negre* (and after it had closed) the critic was called by Varna himself to review an act that he was putting into his new show.

When questioned about what kind of an act it was, Varna told the critic that it was an act from the old *Revue Negre*.

"I wasn't going to go. Imagine that! I wasn't going to go. It was such an evening when Josephine made her solo debut that it has remained with me vividly for my entire life. And I must tell you that I have seen many shows since that time."

* * *

The *Revue Negre* first played at the Théâtre des Champs Elysées, a vast house for such a relatively small revue. The producers thought that by moving it to a smaller house they might be able to extend its run and in some way make it catch on. It did not happen. The cast began slowly to leave; those that had the wherewithal returned to America.

Finally the revue closed completely, and, with a few others, Josephine was stranded.

"I mean stranded. I had about three dollars, and some fruit in my room, and that was all. The stage manager came by the little room where I was staying and told me that there was going to be an audition for some guy from one of the big theatres in Paris, and there was a chance we could get into that show. I didn't have anything to lose, so next day I went up to this rehearsal hall.

"We did several of the numbers, but I could see the little guy that was watching us didn't like it much. Some of the singers sang, but it wasn't much either, and then we did a few more numbers, and it was deafening, the roar from the taps in that empty studio. He left in about an hour. He asked us to wait and he would send us some word. I didn't care. I was figuring that I would write to Mr. Browning or Eubie Blake or someone in New York, and they probably would send me enough money to get back. As a matter of fact, I was starting to write that letter when the door opened and this little short guy who was kind of chubby walked in. He didn't speak any English, but he had a guy with him who could, and they asked us to do some of our numbers again. Everyone else really got into it. They thought they had a chance. I didn't really care, 'cause I wanted to get back to New York."

* * *

Henri Varna, then the great director of the Folies Bergère, had earlier in the day sent his choreographer to interview what remained of the *Revue Negre* troupe.

Monsieur Daven had auditioned the dancers in a dreary rehearsal hall above the Théâtre des Champs Elysées. It was Henri Varna who suggested to Daven that they might introduce a black act into the revue currently playing at the Folies.

Later in the day, M. Daven burst into Varna's office. He dropped into a chair and fanned himself with his hat. He had obviously had a most trying time.

"My dear, don't ever do that to me again. Why, those people actually had pieces of iron on the bottom of their shoes. All they did was tap—what a racket! They tap one number, then they tap more numbers. All they did was tap for two hours. Why, everyone will absolutely run out of the theatre. Only you can fix this up if you want to use these Africans. I want no part of it. If you think there is something worth showing, then you get over there!"

* * *

If there was ever an instance of a person or party being in the right place at the right time, it was Josephine Baker in Paris in the mid-1920s. A few years earlier Josephine had been doing laundry and trying to collect for it from the whites in St. Louis. By the time the decade of the twenties came to a close, she was worth more than a million dollars.

The explanation is simple. We are constantly seeking leaders and innovators. We look for them in every field—in politics, in sports, in science, in education. We also seek leaders in the theatre.

Josephine was ready. She needed only a little guidance and direction. It came from a brilliant director of the period, Henri Varna.

Henri Varna was a leader, an innovator, a searcher. He had the intuitive feeling that perhaps there was more to his choreographer's report—"*toujours des claquettes*" (all they do is tap)—than met the eye.

So he put on his coat, lit his cigarette, and ambled over to the dingy rehearsal hall over the Théâtre des Champs Elysées. As he opened the door, what he saw at first glance was not reassuring. The dispirited group of black dancers and singers was a pretty sorry lot.

However, for the dancers and singers it was one last chance, and as Varna seated himself to watch, they took off, hell-bent for election, on "I'm Just Wild About Harry." The choreographer was right. To the rather sensitive French ear, the tapping was horrendous. Quite true: they tapped one number, then they tapped another, then they tapped another.

All the while, however, Varna kept noticing "the little one on the end of the line."

Josephine said it was an accident. She also said it was an accident some years earlier in the Cotton Club. But if that "act" worked then, why wouldn't it work now for the Frenchman? Off came the shoe—then off came the other shoe—and before anyone knew it, Josephine was into her hula number. Hips swaying, eyes crossed, pigeon-toed. It was the whole Bert and Benny bit, but it happened to be in Paris, and it happened to be in front of one of the greatest theatrical directors of that period.

Varna thought it was part of the act. His eyes closed in on Josephine, and that was it. It was *magic time!* Even Varna the innovator did not realize at that moment how much of a magic time it was to be, or how long it would last.

For more than forty years, almost up until the time of his death, he presented Josephine. In that entire time, they had no contract but a handshake. It was a remarkable business relationship.

I witnessed one of these little ceremonies in the resort city of Enghein-les-Bains, outside Paris, where Varna kept a summer home. Meticulous contracts had been drafted, and were read in each other's presence. Very quietly they both looked over the fine print. Finally Varna said, "Okay, Josephine" —his only English—"*d'accord*." They shook hands as Josephine repeated the one key word. Agreed!

Then, without any hesitation, they toasted with a glass of champagne and dumped the meticulously detailed contracts into a wastebasket.

In her defense, I will say that Josephine never breached an agreement with Varna. The same cannot be said for her dealings with many well-intentioned American producers. She would abrogate an agreement at the drop of a hat if she felt it could be to her advantage. She did have one advantage: with Josephine, there was no such thing as an understudy.

* * *

On this particular day in 1925, Varna quietly thanked the group and walked over to Josephine. On the way, he picked up the slipper. I have heard the story a thousand times from Josephine but could hear it another thousand times.

It was near the end of the day. Josephine was tired. When Varna approached with his interpreter, he held the slipper. She looked at it a long time, then at him. She had no idea that he was Ziegfeld ten times over. She probably didn't care.

"Are you gonna be my Prince Charming?" At first neither Varna nor the interpreter understood. Then it came to both of them at the same time. What a shame that the scene was never recorded for posterity by a photographer, but perhaps it has been better in the telling.

Varna only kneeled down and put the slipper on Cinderella's foot.

The rest is history. He of course offered Josephine a job in his current Folies Bergère revue.

Josephine had never heard of the Folies Bergère. Undaunted (and, it must be noted, with understanding), Varna went to great pains to explain exactly what the Folies was. Josephine thought it was interesting. She made an appointment with Varna to see the Folies that evening.

Josephine never showed up. She did arrive at the theatre that evening, but something told her not to go in. She never was able to explain what that "something" was. Years later she thought that she might have had the idea she would be frightened by the awe and splendor of both the theatre and the spectacle itself. She had seen the photographs outside. She felt that she could never live up to the "class" of the revue. She went on her way.

However, next day at ten o'clock in the morning, she marched up to the box office and demanded to see Varna in his office.

Varna had been slightly miffed when she did not show up the night before, but it was an old experience for him, and he put it out of his mind.

Now, the gentleman in the box office demanded to know who was calling on *Monsieur le directeur*. "Tell him it's Cinderella."

Varna was delighted. As she walked in, he studied her closely. Underneath her rather shabby little outfit he was able to see the body. Her hair was slicked down, almost like a little boy's. That fascinated him. It looked almost as if it had been painted on. She was eating an apple.

He rang for the interpreter. "Tell her she's not Cinderella at all—she's Josephine!"

"I know," she replied, "and you're not Prince Charming either; you're Mr. Varna." They both laughed.

Varna studied the apple and studied her. He suspected that she was running low on cash. He didn't realize that she was, in fact, broke. Then he did something he had never done before.

He offered her a job as a solo dancer. Within two weeks she could go into the Folies as a featured artist. He would pay her the equivalent of ten dollars per day.

Josephine didn't quibble for a moment: she jumped at the offer. What Varna did then made an impression that was to remain with her forever. He called his treasurer and ordered him to pay Josephine her first day's pay in advance. The treasurer disappeared and returned almost immediately with a receipt book and her money. It was in gold.

Varna rose and held out his hand. "*D'accord?*"

"Do you agree?" asked the interpreter.

Josephine held out her hand, gave him one of the famous Baker knuckle-breaking shakes, and replied, "*D'accord!*" In her other hand she held the two gold coins very tightly.

Forever after, during the entire length of her career, Josephine Baker was paid daily for her work, and was paid in cash. In the United States and other countries she demanded and received cash in advance.

The next two weeks were hectic for Josephine. She did not speak the language, and the choreographer was having a difficult time conveying his thoughts and ideas to her. Even then she had a mind of her own. When the choreographer complained to Varna that she would not follow instructions, Varna persuaded him to let her do what she wanted. "But what can I do?" he said. "She acts like a little monkey."

"Is that bad?" Varna replied. "Monkeys can sometimes be very amusing."

Whether the ideas for the original costume for her debut belonged to

Varna, or to some unknown designer, or to Josephine herself, will forever remain a mystery. At any rate, it was a combination of a clever designer, Baker, Varna, and, of all things, a banana.

The particular number that was to be the vehicle for Josephine's debut was Hawaiian in motif. Varna probably got the idea from her little hula he had witnessed in the rehearsal a few days earlier.

But it was not the Hawaii of the Matson Line ships, or the Dole pineapple plantations. The designers had hardly heard of Hawaii, much less been there. It was something else, Hawaii designed as only it could be by a French designer in the 1920s who worked for the Folies Bergère. It was silver and white, and black and gray, and sand, and sea, and palms. But it was also art deco. An early form of it, to be sure, but art deco it was, unmistakably stamped on the set sketches.

The designers had prepared countless costume sketches for Josephine. No doubt they were stupendous—*anything* presented in front of that set would have been stupendous. Yet none of them seemed to satisfy Varna. Sketch after sketch was presented to him, but he nixed them all.

Josephine, watching from across the room, showed even more disappointment than the designers. She would have given a king's ransom to be in any of the sketches, but Varna knew that putting Josephine into one of these colossal gowns would kill her. She could not compete, not yet at least, with Mistinguett, the current favorite star of the Folies. He knew that.

Josephine's and Varna's recollections differ on the famous banana costume, which became the rage of the continent overnight. She maintained that it was her idea, saying that if she could not be clothed in something as dramatic as what the designers had sketched, then he should put her in nothing. Varna maintained that he had seen her eating a banana and thought of a "stack of bananas" costume. Very likely, though, it was one of the designers who came up with the final version. It was merely about twenty bananas on a string, with a few more around each ankle and each wrist, although this feature was omitted from time to time during the following year. It cost less than five francs in all, and it became the sensation of Paris. It was that banana that was the foundation on which her career was built. Bananas on a black kid from East St. Louis who was taught all she knew by a second-class vaudevillian. But what he had taught her was good stuff. Why was it good? Simply because it had never been seen in Paris.

Josephine became a great star because she was "greater than life." Everything she did was greater than anything we ever experience in our own lives. A lot of people can cross their eyes. The kid next door can do that. But can she also walk pigeon-toed at the same time? Josephine could. Plus all the other old outrageous ham actor, black vaudevillian, chitlins circuit comedian's gestures that she had been perfecting during her trial-and-error period in *Shuffle Along, Chocolate Dandies,* and *In Bamville.*

On her opening night, Josephine Baker sat in her dressing room doing something that immediately rocked the place from top to bottom. It was as if a huge thunderbolt had hit the theatre, and everyone came running to see if it was true.

It was. When Varna walked in to greet her before her appearance, she was sitting at her dressing table in her banana costume holding two bowls of cracked ice up to her breasts. She had noticed that when it was cold outside her breasts became very firm and pointed out "very delicately." So, she reasoned, if the outside cold would do that, wouldn't some ice applied directly have the same effect?

By the following night there wasn't a chorus girl in France who wasn't doing the same thing. But Josephine had started it, just as she started nearly everything else that happened on the continent during that marvelous, outrageous, madcap period of the late twenties.

* * *

Varna felt in his bones that he had something good going. A black had never been presented in a solo role on the French stage before—particularly with such daring. But he was *l'ouvreur*—the opener.

First he placed her in a strategic spot, the opening of the second act. He knew that most people who meant anything rarely arrived for the first act.

Then he personally telephoned certain important members of the theatrical press corps. And, to doll his audience up, he brought up the big guns. He invited Maurice Chevalier, already established as the great heartthrob of France, and Mistinguett, then the reigning queen of the theatre. He invited the Rothschilds, his bankers, promising them something special. He invited Pétain, then just becoming known in French politics, and who later was to become a turncoat when he collaborated with the Germans during World War II. Varna invited the cream of French society. And he invited two of the most important people he could think of: Paul Colin, the famous poster maker, and Yvette Guilbert.

At first Guilbert declined, saying that she attended openings only. But Varna persuaded her that this would be something special. Finally she agreed to come. From that time on, until the day of her death, she would never miss a Baker opening.

Also in the audience were De Gaulle, Hemingway, Piaf, the Fitzgeralds, René Clair, the future great film director, and Stravinsky and his producer, Rolf de Mare.

There was one other person of note: His Royal Highness Gustav VI, then Crown Prince of Sweden.

That night, as the prince entered the royal box and the audience rose to applaud him, he happened to be looking for a "divertissement." He was young and handsome, a true Swede. "And when he spoke," said Josephine, "it was like you poured warm honey into some hot butter." He was something!

Josephine was something, too. And when His Royal Highness saw her that opening night, he knew it.

Chapter 6

"Est-ce qu'un homme? Est-ce qu'une femme? *Are you a boy? Are you a girl? No matter. . . . Here, take my crown, and take my stage, you beautiful black queen of the music hall . . . and long may you reign upon it!"*

* * *

The music halls of Paris! The Alhambra, the Bobino, the Casino de Paris, the Olympia, the Moulin-Rouge, the Folies Bergère!

And those great stars of the music halls of Paris. Names long forgotten probably even by the French, and names that can never be forgotten, so much has been written and so much has been said.

Gaby Deslys, Jenny Golder, Regine, Flory, Yvette Guilbert, Mata Hari, Colette, la Belle Otere. There were sister acts, such as les Soeurs Broquin, the Dodge Sisters, the Dolly Sisters, and later even the Paris Sisters. There were twins of all sorts: Ryan and Burke, the Rocky Twins, and, again, the Dolly Sisters. There were names that only a great aficionado of the music hall can recall: Madame Fanny, Barbette (the great impersonator), Chrysis, la Nicolska, Spinelly and Valeska Gert.

They came and they went. Some played once, and never returned. Some were Americans, but not many: Sophie Tucker and, much later, Harry Belafonte.

Some created a lasting impression, and very likely if their own "wheel" had not stopped, they still would be there. First in one great hall and then in another.

And finally there were those who needed only one name, either their first or their last, or some single name, to immediately recall them. Then, if the person remembering was in his declining years, his eyes would mist, and he would think back, and he would repeat the name, carefully, delicately, not wanting to disturb the fond recollection of his great idols.

There was Fernandel . . . and Polaire . . . and do you remember Sorel? . . .

Then . . . those names that can never be forgotten. Chevalier . . . Mistinguett . . . Piaf . . . and finally Josephine . . . ah, *Josephine!*

* * *

"Are you a boy? Are you a girl? No matter. . . . Here, take my crown, and take my stage, you beautiful black queen of the music hall . . . and long may you reign upon it!" said Yvette Guilbert on Josephine's opening night.

Guilbert would never have been able to comprehend how Josephine would be able to reign upon that stage for fifty years.

"My God, is it possible that I have outlived all those others? Where on earth are they now? You know, it almost scares me when I think about it. Can you believe it, they are gone. Am I the only one left?"

* * *

Years before, Josephine, who was notorious for leaving the theatre late after a performance, was alone in her dressing room.

"I told them all to go on home, and the doorman too. I knew how to slam a stage door shut to lock it. I needed to unwind, to get out of my clothes and relax. . . . I needed time to take off my makeup."

> Then I heard it. At first it was sort of a shuffling and brushing, and I could hear people moving down the halls outside my dressing-room door. Goose pimples came up on my arms and on to my cheeks. I called out to find out who was there, if it was the cleaning woman.
>
> For a moment there was silence; then I heard those muffled sounds again, like it was the girls in the chorus laughing, and walking outside my door.
>
> I quickly changed my clothes. I was really frightened. I grabbed both dogs, and they were scared, too. Usually they ran way ahead of me as always, but this time I had to force them to go out in front of me.
>
> I walked down the hall and into the wings, and it was icy cold. But outside it was a warm summer night, and then I heard it, and I saw it all at once. I looked into the audience, and it was full of people, and they were standing there and cheering, and applauding, and gesturing with their hands. But I could not hear them; all I could hear was this shuffling on the stage, and when I looked I was terrified, for there was Mistinguett.
>
> But now she was bowing, and turning, and twisting her little head like she did, and giving that smile.
>
> And I looked around me, and there were the stagehands, and the stage managers, and the wardrobe women, and the other acts, the acrobats, and the dancers. Everyone was there. I was surrounded, but no one spoke to me. It was as if I didn't exist for them. And I did not know any of them, for they were there from a long time ago.

> And then I looked at Miss [Mistinguett] again, and she was so young. But her clothes were old, and the feathers seemed dusty, and the satin and silk had no sparkle, and the jewelry was like little pieces of iron, and then as she moved toward me she smiled.
>
> I had never been so terrified in my life. I didn't know what I would do. I thought I would faint.
>
> As she came toward me, she was removing her gloves, and she seemed to be swirling the dust on the stage, and I opened my mouth to say, "Who are you . . . are you really Miss?" And at the same time that I wanted to speak, I looked at that audience again, and they were still cheering and screaming. Then she turned around again, and I could see her bowing to them, and bending her left knee and sinking almost to the stage, and again I shouted, "Who are you . . . Miss, Miss, please speak to me, don't frighten me!"
>
> And as I shouted it out, she disappeared, and they all disappeared, and I stood there shaking. Then the dogs came out, and they ran across that stage, and I ran after them, and I slammed that heavy steel door shut, and I leaned against it trying to get my breath.
>
> I recovered myself and walked into the street.

"But you know I have never forgotten that incident. And many times I have seen the others too. I saw Chevalier. And Piaf came up to me in my dressing room, and all she could do was to wring her hands and cry and stare at me. But I never saw Miss again.

"And often I think, since I am getting older, that one day I too will be like them, that I will walk down those steps like I have done a million times, to stand there with my feet apart on that stage, and with my hands on my hips, and smile at those audiences. Maybe I too will be in all my faded finery, and my silk and satin will not shine, and my jewels will be like little pieces of iron.

"Oh, my God, it frightens me to think about it."

* * *

After a short overture of "*Aux Iles Hawaii,*" the second-act curtain went up slowly to reveal a Hawaiian Island scene at sunrise. There were leaves, mountains, grass, blue water, and sand. Palm and banana trees abounded. It was a scene that only the French designers of the twenties could have created—at once tropical and art deco.

In the center, surrounded by dancers, was Josephine in a sort of Hawaiian muu-muu. During the slow orchestral introduction, they moved rather sensuously and did some lifts with her.

The audience had taken a ho-hum, so-what attitude. There were a few coughs, and some asides among friends.

Then, in an instant, Josephine was lifted high into the air and, while being held there, suddenly broke out of her muu-muu. She was held aloft completely nude, except for the little circle of bananas!

The music quickened. Josephine was tossed high, only to land like a fabulous flying swan in the dancers' arms. The Hawaii set slowly rose out of sight, and reflected in a thousand mirrors were a thousand banana-clad Josephines.

The audience exploded into a frenzy. On stage she was reflected again and again as she passed from one mirror to another.

It was never intended that Josephine sing in her debut. And she did not exactly sing. But she abandoned the original choreography and moved out onto the ramp surrounding the orchestra.

"Then it just hit me all at once. I thought maybe they would like to *hear* me too. So I just started with my little 'do-de-oh-does.' I just kept them going over and over again. Then I had reached the end of my music. But the conductor knew what I had done, and the orchestra repeated it all for me. God, it was heaven that night. In all those years I never heard another audience go crazy like that till we went to Carnegie Hall. [This was fifty years later.] That night it was like that too. They were *crazy!*"

Then, at the end of this remarkable number, she rushed to the center of the stage, where one banana tree remained, and in an unrehearsed move, she performed an incredible leap and landed in the top.

Slowly she spread back the leaves to reveal herself. She was squatting down, and like a little monkey she started crossing her eyes, tilting her head, and waving to the audience. It was pure Bert and Benny of vaudeville days, but to the French it was *le jazz hot*. It was something they had never seen or heard. It was driving, it was ridiculous, it was mad. It was Josephine.

The curtain came down and went up, and came down and went up, and each time Josephine scratched and twisted and tilted.

Then, in an also unrehearsed move, some by now forgotten spotlight operator got a brilliant flash. He did what no other operator had ever before dared to do in the Folies: he violated Varna's lighting instructions, changing the pink spot to blue.

The blue spotlight turned Josephine's tan body into a true café au lait. Her slicked-down hair looked as though it were painted with tar, and the bananas took on the brilliant yellows of a Cézanne painting.

Josephine left her tree. She had stopped a show. But she could not just bow, so she did what she did best: she performed a series of frozen dance positions. In the eerie light and reflected in the mirrors, it was as if she were something from outer space. The music blared on.

In the audience, Paul Colin, the famous illustrator, had already started sketching on the back of his program.

Backstage, as the curtain was lowered for the last time, Josephine just stood there, breathing heavily, sweat pouring from her. She did not know if she had done right or wrong; all she was aware of were the screams and the wild applause of the audience.

Then Varna rushed to get her, and as a wardrobe attendant threw a robe over her shoulders, he led her into the dressing room.

She dropped into a chair and looked expectantly at Varna, certain that he was furious with her. She had changed almost every stage direction and had thrown the technicians backstage into chaos.

He leaned against the door. Already the important members of the audience had come backstage and were pounding on it. Through the noise he looked at her for a long time. Finally he said:

"Josephine, if you will only let me, I will make you one of the greatest stars that Paris has ever known."

It was exactly twenty-one words. She even asked the interpreter to repeat it. She never forgot them as long as she lived, and ever after, she considered twenty-one to be her lucky number. Josephine, still worn out, could not speak; she only nodded her head.

Varna kept his end of the bargain. So did Josephine. Fifty years later, long after Varna and the others were gone, Josephine was still the reigning queen.

* * *

Suddenly the door burst open. If it was bedlam in the theatre, it was a catastrophe backstage.

The revue had been interrupted for fully twenty minutes as the audience screamed for yet another appearance by Josephine. Finally a fabulous cape from the wardrobe department was thrown over her shoulders, and Varna personally led her out onto the open stage, where the curtain was still up. He left her there alone. The curtain rose and fell on the waves of screams, shouts, whistles and applause.

Then she created the gesture that would become known to stagehands and curtain men around the world who worked Baker shows. When she wanted the last curtain, she merely followed it up with her eyes, and down again. Then came a short snap of her fingers and a cutting gesture with her right arm.

That was it.

* * *

Josephine did not know the people who had come backstage to pay her homage. The Rothschilds, De Gaulle, Mistinguett were only strange names to her.

One of the people made a lasting impression. It was Yvette Guilbert. Slowly, the aged but elegant lady made her way across the stage where she herself had at one time reigned supreme, although she always felt that Mistinguett had never really succeeded her as queen of the Paris music halls. As she neared the dressing room, the others peeled back silently.

She was in black, wearing the same gloves, with the same topknot on her head. Josephine knew she was someone of importance.

There was silence as she spoke, and the interpreter spoke after her:

"In one night someone has finally come who can replace Yvette Guilbert!"

Everyone shouted with delight. It was not until years later, when Josephine was given a copy of an illustrated book, that she spied a photograph of Guilbert next to the famous poster of her by Toulouse-Lautrec.

"If I had only known it that night, it would have meant so much more to me."

Josephine wanted to leave the madness of the theatre. She needed to get out, to think. To try to sort out and understand what was happening to her. She had a thousand offers to be escorted home. She declined them all.

She looked at the furs, the jewels, the formal attire of the audience. She wasn't quite ready for all this. She knew it.

She crossed the dark stage and looked out into the now empty theatre. She thought she could hear the audience, and it frightened her.

After leaving the theatre, Josephine, in her confusion, began walking in the wrong direction, and after ambling along for blocks she found herself in the Place de la Madeleine. It was quiet and peaceful, and she liked it.

For a long time she stood and looked at the church of the Madeleine. She walked across the great courtyard to get a better view, and stood there for some time, looking up at the church.

She walked slowly up the steps, and halfway up, at a small landing, she put her little carpetbag under her and sat down, staring out over the Place de la Madeleine. She was thinking.

"My God, I was trying to understand what was happening to me. To me. Josephine Baker. I was thinking all kinds of things. About Mama, and what she was doing, and about sister. I didn't know much about time differences like I do now, and I thought it was night in East St. Louis too, and that Mama and all of them would be asleep.

"Then I thought about Bessie Smith, and Bert and Benny, and all those musicians, and I thought about Mr. Browning, and Sissle and Blake, and even Lottie Gee, and I thought about the *Revue Negre* and that awful trip on the boat, and about how Varna had come to the audition and had chosen me for the Folies.

"Now I thought about those people in the theatre, how they had been screaming, and all those people who had run backstage. I figured they were some big shots, but I didn't know too much about that sort of stuff, anyway. I thought, Boy, if Bessie and Eubie and Mr. Browning had been there to see me. That would have been something. Then I wondered. Maybe they wouldn't have liked me and the costume I had on which showed so much of me. I thought of Mama, and I said to myself, When I bring Mama over here, I have to remember to wear that bra they made for me to take pictures in.

"Then, as it always did when I thought about it a lot, it came very clear in my head. I wasn't scared or nervous anymore. I began thinking about how in the performance tomorrow night I would do even more crazy things. If they liked me tonight, they would really like me tomorrow."

She had been sitting there for hours. Slowly the first rays of the early-morning sun began to cast a glow on the Place de la Madeleine. She had thought it all out. She was ready for it. But only if they were ready for her.

She got up; her legs were a little stiff. She put the carpetbag over her shoulder and buttoned up the little coat that Mama had given her. Now that all seemed like so long ago. So far away, all those things.

She started humming as she went down the steps, then broke into her little "do-de-oh-does." She fairly danced across the cobblestones as the sun moved up swiftly behind the church of the Madeleine.

Chapter 7

". . . This funny little fat guy came backstage one night and wanted to make a sketch of me. I let him do it, but I made him give me twenty-five francs first . . ."

". . . Gee, what a great apartment. . . . Do you know if they have any vacancies?"

* * *

Marilyn Monroe once told me that it took her twenty years to become a star overnight. It is interesting to note that it took Josephine only one night.

She had, of course, a lot going for her. By her own admission, the greatest thing she had going for her was her lack of a formal education. In East St. Louis, she had managed to make it only through the eighth grade. She did not read much, and if her general schooling was inadequate, her knowledge of the world and what was happening in it was even more so.

As an example, she forever confused Haiti and Tahiti. When she performed (and eventually recorded) her famous song "Haiti," she kept thinking of Tahiti and the South Seas. "What difference does it make?" she once said. "They're all islands." Perhaps she was right.

This lack of worldly knowledge, this complete lack of sophistication, served her very well. Later, of course, she learned, and she learned quickly. By the time I met Josephine she was reading, and conversant in, six languages, plus a good smattering of Arabic and Swedish.

When she met the Rothschilds, Josephine, who had no idea who the Rothchilds were, was neither impressed nor awed. The same applied to her attitude toward the other celebrities of the period.

Josephine was amused when a "funny little fat guy" came backstage one night and asked to make a sketch of her. "I let him do it, but I made him give me twenty-five francs first."

The "funny little fat guy" was already well advanced in his own career, and had something of a reputation of his own. It was Picasso.

The story spread like wildfire. The French thought it was outrageous behavior, and a great joke. Josephine thought at the moment that she was more important than the "funny little fat guy"; she did not know—or care, perhaps—who Picasso was.

On the Sunday after her debut, Hemingway woke her early in the morning. He wanted to show her the famous poster now on every Paris kiosk. The banana poster was heaven, and very few, if any, exist today; the French ripped them off the kiosks to take home almost as fast as they could be put up.

He shouted, "Josephine, come down, I want to show you something."

"Who is it?"

"It's Ernest."

"My God, Ernest who? I don't know any Ernests."

"It's Ernest Hemingway."

"Well, I still don't know you."

Even then, Hemingway was well on his way in France. He had written *A Farewell to Arms* and was quite respected in literary circles.

And so it went for her. She was totally unimpressed by Chevalier, Mistinguett, Hemingway, and a host of other Frenchmen and expatriates living in Paris.

When she was invited to visit the Krupps, she had no idea that they were the munitions princes of Germany. When she entered the townhouse, which had to be one of the most sumptuous in the world, her first words were, "Gee, what a great apartment."

Then came the words that made everyone scream with delight: "Do you know if they have any vacancies?" It was thought a hilarious remark. Josephine was beginning to be considered a master of the "gay repartee." In reality, though, she was being serious. She could not imagine anyone owning such a house. After all, it was as big as an apartment building.

There, then, was the basis for the making of the *grande vedette* of France. It was her complete lack of sophistication, her complete lack of knowledge about worldly affairs.

* * *

Now came the great years for Josephine. The period 1925 to 1930 was made for her—and she for it.

Her very first important admirer was a sheik. It appears that he was Moroccan, but sometimes in the telling he was transformed into an Egyptian. It made little difference to Josephine; he was always her "Sheik of Araby."

"You know, Stephen," she told me years later, while we were on a visit to the Los Angeles Zoo, "one time a while back, I had a black panther just like that." She pointed to a beautiful panther in the compound. "I called him Sheik."

She had casually met the little man backstage. At the time she remembered him only as being kind of roly-poly, and promptly forgot about him. Then, sometime later, there were screams outside her dressing-room door, and when the maid opened it, they saw a baby panther being delivered to Josephine. Around his neck he wore a fabulous diamond necklace from Van Cleef and Arpels.

It was an attention-getter and a real show-stopper, and it certainly showed ingenuity on the part of the sheik.

Thinking it was someone else, Josephine made a date the next night for dinner with him at Maxim's. When he arrived to pick her up, she was devastated. She had gone to great pains to "get hot," meaning "look good." However, she took it all in stride, and went out with him that night and countless others.

"You know," she told me, "the problem was that when I was young I used to like to do it standing up, and if I had ever done it with him, he would have been jabbing me in the knees." Big laugh, always followed by a good elbow punch to the ribs of whoever was sitting nearest to her.

That night when they entered Maxim's, it was sensation number two. She put the panther on a leash, still with the jewels around his neck, and marched in. He sat beside her on the banquette, and she ordered caviar. Josephine was learning. Anyone could give hamburger to a panther, but if you gave him caviar, that was something else.

Not surprisingly, Sheik didn't like caviar. He was a little heavy at the time, weighing maybe thirty-five or forty pounds. It seems he wanted the waiter's arm instead. Panic.

A French waiter running through a restaurant with a bejeweled baby panther hanging on his arm is something to read about in the papers the next morning, particularly if it happened in Maxim's.

Another time the sheik gave Josephine a little monkey. The way she described it, it must have been a baby chimp—long arms, legs, and so on. She expressed her disappointment to the sheik that Ethel, as she called the monkey, came without jewelry. (Josephine always said the chimpanzee looked like Ethel Waters—an insult probably occasioned by some alleged slight, intentional or not, on the part of Waters.)

The next day Josephine met the sheik at the Hotel George V, and they strolled down to the Place Vendôme, the monkey between them. What a sight that must have been: "me, looking like some little American black boy; a monkey; and a guy in an Arab oufit."

Down the street they went, and into Van Cleef and Arpels. The manager of the establishment was certainly up to the occasion. Ethel the chimpanzee was fitted out with two diamond bracelets and a choker. It never occurred to Josephine to inquire about the price. Years later, during the hard times when Josephine found herself in the rooms of the Paris moneylenders, she learned their true worth at last. On the chimpanzee's jewelry alone she borrowed $20,000.

Probably the one thing that catapulted Josephine Baker to real stardom, and the one thing that would have earned her a medal, if one were ever presented for outrageous antics, happened a few nights later.

Neither the panther nor the chimpanzee was housebroken. When the dressing room began getting a little rank one night, Josephine decided that she would walk them after the show. "After all, you walk a dog, don't you?"

After the performance, the real show started on the Champs Elysées. Josephine never intended it to be the sensation it was. What the patrons of the sidewalk cafés on the Champs Elysées were treated to was something indeed.

Out of the long black limousine bounded the panther, followed by the roly-poly sheik himself, then Ethel and Josephine. Both Ethel and Sheik were enjoying themselves thoroughly. Ethel, now decked out in her diamond bracelets and choker, was leading Sheik, the baby panther, who was wearing his own diamond necklace. Josephine held the other hand of the chimp and tightly clutched the arm of "my Sheik of Araby."

Down the street they strolled. Oblivious to the patrons, oblivious to the world. Wrapped up only in themselves. "After all," she said, "we were just a little happy family out for a stroll."

That incident probably epitomizes Josephine at her most outlandish.

When they decided to dine at Maxim's, they were refused admittance: the management remembered well the previous incident. Undaunted, Josephine made for the restaurant of one Louis Carton. She made him famous overnight. Restaurant Louis Carton still stands as one of the elegant watering spots of Paris.

In all the years I dined there with Josephine she was never given a check, regardless of how large her party was.

Years later, when she was refused admittance to another famous restaurant, the Stork Club in New York, it was for a different reason. But that was a different time in her life.

* * *

So went the period from 1925 to 1930. The Folies presented two revues each season, and gradually Josephine became a power to be reckoned with.

Now she began to take herself a little more seriously. She dropped the "gonnas" and the "so whats" and the "ain'ts" and the "gees." She studied French and Spanish.

Slowly, even though her menagerie increased, she toned down the flamboyant behavior she had displayed in her early days in Paris, and took on the sophistication that was to be her great magic in her later years.

She moved from her little flat in the rue de Vignon (Hookers' Alley) into a sumptuous apartment across town. But she never forgot the hookers there, and they regularly visited her backstage. It usually made for a good gossip session. And at such times as one of them "outlived her usefulness," Josephine saw that she was taken care of, setting her up in a little business or hiring her to work for her own company.

For Josephine was now becoming the "businesswoman"; it was her first and, regrettably, her *only* successful business venture. When she had first come to France, Josephine's "conked" or straightened hair was a sensation. She attended to this rather smelly chore faithfully, using a compound she had brought from America that was sold in Harlem. It contained mostly lye, but it did the job.

Soon after her dramatic Paris debut, she was approached by a cosmetics firm that inquired into the formula. They analyzed a sample and made a contract with Josephine, and "Baker-Fix" was on the market. It too was a sensation. Thousands of women with kinky hair used the straightener, in imitation of Josephine. The product made such a lasting impact that *Paris Monde,* the prestigious Paris newspaper, even made mention of it in her obituary.

So when the hookers of the rue de Vignon "wore themselves out," they could count on becoming salesladies in the elegant shops. "My God," said Josephine, "you have no idea of how well they did. They would call up their old street customers, who would come in and buy for themselves and their wives." To the best of my knowledge, she was still receiving royalties for Baker-Fix in the 1950s.

Now, also, Josephine began to be better able to evaluate her worth. When she walked into Dior, Balenciaga, or Worth, she walked out with whatever she wanted. She always demanded a bill, marked "Paid in Full," but a penny never changed hands. She was a walking advertisement.

She knew it, and so did the couturiers of Paris. Even in the early 1950s she still wore the clothes and costumes prepared for her by Dior, Worth, Chanel, and others. She never paid a dime for them. But in America, she never failed while on stage to mention what house had designed them. Eventually most of the houses sold these same "models" to Ohrbach's in New York. They were then copied by the hundreds of thousands.

I tried desperately to persuade her to let me negotiate a royalty contract with the famous houses, but to no avail. She thought she had a "good deal" by getting the clothes for nothing. At that time, the houses would have paid any price for her endorsement.

A few years later, when times were really bad, we went to the House of Chanel. It quickly became obvious to me that now, when Josephine really needed it, it was much too late for a royalty contract to be negotiated.

Gabrielle "Coco" Chanel did not even come down to greet us. Another cruel blow fell when Josephine tried on a magnificent black silk faille suit, only to discover that the old deal didn't hold anymore. As we were leaving the shop, they approached me about payment. They would require a check for $500—which Josephine did not have. I wrote my own check for it.

Josephine never mentioned the incident; it was one of the things that were too unbearable to dredge up. But in her last years, when "the wheel had come around again," as she would say, she never failed to bring me or send me the latest fashion from Cardin or Brioni. I still wear them today.

* * *

But it is 1929; it is Josephine's year. When Josephine's auditors called on her near the end of 1929, they reported her assets to be in excess of one million dollars. Josephine was dumfounded. While a major portion of her wealth was in jewelry and properties (the sheik had bought her the first of several townhouses she now owned), she was still a millionairess. In New York City, men were jumping out of windows, their fortunes having been lost on Wall Street. But Josephine Baker, the little black kid from East St. Louis, a washerwoman's daughter who started out as an ironer for her mother, was "haute Paris." She was "it." She had box-office muscle, and for the first time she used it.

Chapter 8

". . . He was my cream, and I was his coffee . . . and when you poured us together, it was something!"

* * *

Melba, the long-reigning queen of the Covent Garden Opera in London, stood on the tiny stage of the Folies Bergère. Moments before, she had swept Josephine Baker into her arms, and they had kissed like old friends who had not seen each other in years.

To Josephine it was the ultimate compliment. Very likely, a few years earlier she would not even have known who Melba was.

The time was the late 1920s, and Melba had been persuaded by her conductor to attend a performance of the Folies Bergère. As she watched the revue, she marveled at how Josephine could negotiate the complicated steps. She marveled even more when after the performance she came on stage and commanded Josephine to repeat for her what she had seen while sitting in the audience. Josephine fairly flew to the top of the steps, and without ever looking down, head held high and eyes on the balcony, she moved down them one by one.

"If only you could teach me to do that," Melba cried.

"And if only you could teach me to sing," Josephine replied.

Perhaps both meant what they had said. For while Melba was considered to have the greatest voice of that age, she moved about the stage very little, preferring to stand in one spot to deliver her arias and to hit the famous high Cs which floated out over her adoring audiences. Josephine, of course, moved like a gazelle.

Josephine had been thrilled when she received a message backstage, delivered by Henri Varna himself, that Melba wanted to call on her. "Oh, my God, how wonderful!" she had exclaimed. "Do you know she's so famous they named a dessert after her?"

Of course Melba was famous, and of course they had named for her a dessert that a chef at the Ritz had created—*pêche Melba.*

For years afterward, whenever Josephine would be dining out and *pêche Melba* appeared on the menu, she would order it and comment, "Did I ever tell you that I knew Nellie Melba?"

Actually, her claim that she "knew" Melba was somewhat farfetched. If she did know her, she came to know her in that one night, for that is the only time they ever met. Not long after this meeting, Melba returned to Melbourne, Australia, where she was spending her remaining years in retirement.

"When Melba died, I felt like I had lost an old friend. You know, if it had been now, I probably would have jumped on a plane and gone to her funeral. But you know, it took weeks to go by boat to Australia, so then it was impossible."

On that one evening long before, in the late 1920s, the two ladies walked arm in arm out of the stage door of the Folies Bergère.

Melba insisted on leading one of Josephine's wolfhounds, and Josephine led the other. She had been enchanted with Josephine's menagerie. One wonders what had come over Melba, who was usually extremely reserved and had few kind words for other artists. Perhaps it was because she realized that Josephine was not a rival. Melba guarded her stage at Covent Garden like a tigress, and she warned Josephine to do the same.

Josephine did not heed that advice. Neither did she take the second piece of advice Melba offered later that evening.

The aging diva and the beautiful Josephine went to Maxim's that night, where they sat in a banquette. One of Josephine's wolfhounds rested her head in Melba's lap as Melba fed her pieces of chicken. The other slept soundly next to Josephine, oblivious to these two great ladies and to the surroundings. The restaurant was nearly empty, but they talked on and on.

There was at this time a then unfounded rumor concerning Josephine which Melba had obviously heard. The second piece of advice she gave Josephine was in regard to this rumor:

"Stay away from royalty, my dear. It will lead to a broken heart, and unless you are very strong, it will lead to a broken career too."

Melba was referring to her own affair with Louis Philippe, Duke of Orleans, in whose veins ran the blood of the Bourbons. She had been mad about him, and he about her. But the affair had almost ruined her—and her career. It was a scandal that had closed every important door in London and on the continent to her—the very same doors she had spent years attempting to pry open.

Very likely because of Melba's age and status, Josephine became the listener and Melba the talker. Melba may well have poured out her heart to Josephine that night—and Josephine certainly would have been an interested listener, because she always loved hearing of a good affair of any kind. It might well have been then that she decided to embark on her own matchmaking career. She brought many people together during the years, even though she herself had no outstanding love affairs, even with her husbands—with the exception of one person.

That was the rumor that Melba had likely heard. Perhaps she had wanted to see Josephine that evening primarily because she admired her as an artist. But perhaps she also wanted to counsel her, to warn her.

"You know," Josephine said later, "I'm glad I didn't take her advice. When sometimes I'm at my lowest, I think about those days and I get happy all over again."

As they left Maxim's, again arm in arm, Melba turned to Josephine and whispered in her ear: "Remember what I've told you. Take my advice. Don't do it . . . and also breathe from here, child," she said, smacking Josephine's diaphragm. Josephine never took that advice either. And perhaps it was a good thing, for the charm of the Baker voice was that it came from the throat, pouring out in a rich tremolo. Over the years, as she grew older, it also grew more mellow. It was one of the few things that Josephine did not lose in later life; her last recordings attest to that.

As Melba dropped off Josephine at her home, one of the dogs refused to leave the car. Nothing could induce her to move, and she cried piteously and licked Melba's hands when the chauffeur tried to pull her out.

"Then let her stay," Josephine told Melba. "She loves you. Keep her with you always."

"But what's her name?"

"Call her Josephine. Then you'll always think of me."

"But how will you remember me?" asked Melba.

"Every time I have raspberry sauce over my peaches and cream, I'll think of you."

Melba was delighted. She said good-bye and ordered her chauffeur to move on. As Josephine stood in the street, she saw the great Melba turn to look at her through the rear window of the car. Melba smiled and gave a little wave.

Not many years were to remain to Melba. She fell ill soon afterward, and early in the next decade she died in Australia. Of course, by then Josephine was well established in the music halls. Melba and her advice were far behind her; so was the one great love affair of her life.

Perhaps at the time, Josephine had forgotten Melba's warning. If she had not forgotten it, she obviously did not intend to heed it. Perhaps she did take it eventually; but if she did, it was after the first few weeks of the affair.

Josephine told the story of her affair only rarely. She preferred not to share it with anyone. It was her own little private thing. Perhaps she regarded the story as her only private possession, and felt that whenever she told it, she was giving part of it away.

Very likely I was told more of the details than any other of her few intimate friends. It took more than three hours to tell. Regrettably we were in a Canadian prison at the time. But perhaps if we had not been in that prison, none of the details of that beautiful romance would ever have been recorded.

* * *

On June 15, 1960, in Montreal, Canada, Josephine Baker was apprehended by the police, a federal warrant having been issued for her arrest, and for mine as well. The charge was possessing stolen property and transporting it across the Canadian border. I must say that while I myself did not resist arrest, it took four policemen and a policewoman to get the handcuffs on Josephine.

"How dare you arrest Josephine Baker!" she shouted as they pinioned her arms behind her.

"I am not arresting Josephine Baker, madame. I am seizing a felon," replied one of the policemen.

"Times are changing, Stephen," she said to me in the police car. They were indeed. It was the wind whispering to Josephine, warning her of the storm that lay ahead. Her words were prophetic too in that she would later perform Bob Dylan's "The Times They Are a-Changin'" during what can only be termed her incredible comeback. But all that was still years ahead.

On that night, the bars of the federal prison slammed shut on both of us. The only concession the prison authorities made to her was to place us both in the same cell; to their credit, they did not undress her and throw her into the women's tank, as was the usual practice. By this time, Josephine had changed much; from the girl who had danced nearly naked in the Folies and gave not a second thought to posing in the nude, she had become rather matronly in her thinking about her body. She covered herself constantly, and the only one, to my knowledge, ever allowed in her room while she was changing was a personal maid. So the police did spare her this indignity. The only one.

"What do we do now, Josephine?" I asked.

"I don't know. I don't know, Stephen. . . . I've never been in prison before. What do they do? They talk, I guess. Talk about happier times, and better things."

For over three hours Josephine talked and I listened.

* * *

It was the end of one of Josephine's performances late in 1929. That night there was more excitement than usual. From her dressing room she could look out and see the stage. All the artists—the chorus, the acrobats, the jugglers—were waiting. Varna himself paced back and forth nervously, chatting briefly with members of the chorus.

Then all conversation ceased. Josephine could hear the stage manager introducing *him* to the members of the cast—the future King of Sweden, Crown Prince Gustav VI—Adolf.

"Ladies and gentlemen, His Royal Highness!" shouted the stage manager. Josephine stepped back; she didn't want the prince to see her watching.

A year or so before, late one night in the rue de Vignon, Josephine had come upon a fabulously beautiful young girl leaning against the damp walls of the "street." Knowing that Josephine was always good for a handout on a not-so-good night, she stepped out of the shadows and spoke with her. Her name was Vera, she said; she had came up from Dordogne. A job had been promised her by the owner of a bakery; however, when she arrived—alone, and with only a tiny bag that contained all her possessions—she had been thrown out of the shop by the baker's wife, literally into the street.

Josephine, who knew something about hookers, befriending many of them in her time, sensed immediately that Vera was not cut from the hooker's piece of cloth. Perhaps also she was taken by the sentimental fact that the girl was from Dordogne, where Josephine had already paid several visits and where she eventually made her home.

Josephine asked the "street madam" to bring the girl backstage the next night, and before little Vera knew it, she was a showgirl in the chorus of the Folies Bergère.

But, as these things happen, her parents, who had sent her to the city to learn the bakery business, were horrified that she should end up in the theatre instead of behind the bakery counter. Sometime later her father, just off the train from Sarlat, came bounding into the theatre demanding to speak to Varna, Josephine, and Vera, in that order. Vera was on the stage and Varna was out, so he ended up in Josephine's dressing room.

By the time Josephine was through with him, he would have taken off his own clothes and paraded around that stage. He returned home with glowing reports of Vera's success. Nevertheless, shortly afterward Vera's mother arrived late one night. Asking for Josephine, she was immediately received in her dressing room.

"I just told her that if it was good enough for Venus de Milo, it was good enough for Vera. I never mentioned, though, that I had picked her up in the street. Besides, I told her that Venus de Milo got nothing, and Vera was making several hundred francs a day."

Apparently, to Vera's mother, this was a logical argument. Soon, thanks to Josephine's friendly persuasion, Vera became the most talked-about girl in Sarlat. On those few occasions when she returned home for a visit, she was a celebrity.

Sad to relate, Vera, in the prime of her youth, fell victim to a fatal illness. Josephine called on her several times a week, telling her that she must return to work immediately. She insisted also on sending her solicitor to the bedside to draw up a contract. Very likely Josephine had heard of such a circumstance from another impresario of the Folies who had played the same deception on a dying friend of his. It seemed to work, and little Vera died happily, sure that she was soon to return to the Folies.

But on that night in 1929, Vera stood on the stage showing a little more décolletage than would seem appropriate for a chorus girl about to meet royalty.

Varna approached her. "Cover yourself up. Let's face it, it's not you he's come to see."

"What's wrong with showing him a little sample?" She squared her shoulders, and under her thin dress could be seen a great pair of alabaster breasts such as are seen only on French chorus girls. "He might even remember them after she dumps him . . . like she's done all the others."

And according to Josephine, the prince did indeed do a double take on those wonderful alabaster breasts, and little Vera gave Varna a good right to the ribs to bring her point home.

Josephine had been watching through the crack in her open door. "You know, the young people today call someone we used to call 'hot' a 'fox.' Well, I can tell you, he was a real 'fox.' He had a gorgeous smile, and when he flashed it on you, you got knocked about two feet back. But the best part of him was that uniform—it was the best of any operetta I'd ever seen."

The prince thanked the company for his enjoyable evening, and Varna led him down the hall to Josephine's dressing room. She ducked back when she saw them coming.

Josephine was standing in the middle of her dressing room. Now she had "made it." Her dressing room was white and silver and black. It was stripes and circles and running lines. The furniture was in silver and black satin. On the chaise the cheetah, Mildred, was coldly eyeing the prince. Perched high on the back of a Bergère chair, Ethel the chimp fingered her bracelets and choker. There were love birds in cages hanging in a little garden on one side of the room, and Black and White, the two Persian cats, were grooming each other. Sleeping under the dressing table were two champagne-colored wolfhounds.

"But you know, I was something, too! I had my hair plastered down as though it had been tarred on. I think they invented the 'bias cut' for me. My dress was a silk satin in gray, and on the front were two wide rhinestone straps that just covered me up, and they crossed over and ran over my shoulders and down my back to the waist. In my belly button I had glued a real unset diamond, and that was the first thing he looked down at. But I just kept staring him in the eyes. And you know, that was something.

"For a minute everything was so still you could hear a clock tick. Then all my little animal family went crazy. Mildred jumped down and started rubbing herself against his legs, and that Ethel, she went crazy jumping up and down and chattering, and screaming like a monkey—well, that is what she was, but I had almost got to thinking of her as a person—and even Black and White stopped washing each other to look at him. He made that whole room turn into electricity. You could have lit up half of Paris on me and him alone."

Josephine bowed ever so slightly. "Good evening, Your Highness."

The prince gazed at her for a long moment. "This is my fourth visit, and it seems that you become more exciting each time."

"Your fifth, Your Highness."

The prince laughed. "Well, whatever—I am delighted that we can meet personally."

When he spoke those words to her, there was not another person within a thousand miles, as far as Josephine was concerned. "God, I just looked at him. He was my cream and I was his coffee, and when you poured us together, it was something! This had never happened to me before. When he looked at me, I thought I was floating a foot off the floor, and for the first time I heard music. I could hear a thousand violins playing. The other people were there, but they were blurred, like in the background of a movie, and he just stood there smiling at me in that uniform. Even when he was saying good night, I could still hear those violins playing."

"Thank you, Mademoiselle Bakhair," the prince said. "*Au revoir.*"

"He started to leave, but I just kept my eyes fixed on his. Even when he turned his back and started for the door, I knew he would turn around once more.

"He did too."

"Perhaps, sometime," the prince said, "you could honor us with a visit to Sweden?"

He stared at her for a long moment, taking her all in. Then he slowly turned to follow Henri Varna out of the dressing room.

Just as Varna walked out of the room, he glanced at Josephine and shook his head slightly from side to side. He arched an eyebrow. Varna knew.

"God, it was love at first sight. It had never happened to me. I just threw my arms around myself and started to dance in my room. I could hear that music again. So could the animals."

Josephine went to her dressing-room table, picked up a telegraph blank and a pen, and started writing. Ethel jumped down as if to see what Josephine was putting down on paper.

"Honest to God, I didn't give a damn about anything then. I knew he was married, but at the time I didn't know it was Louise Mountbatten. I just knew it was some big English lady. I didn't care. He could have had ten wives, like my sheik did. My sheik offered to get rid of them for me; why wouldn't the prince?"

Who knows? Very likely he might have. Not many years later a king was to give up his throne for a commoner. It could just as well have been Josephine and her crown prince.

After filling in the address, Josephine wrote one word: "When?"

Ethel the chimpanzee screamed and bounded around the room, as though she knew what Josephine had written. Then Josephine signed her name with a great flourish.

Josephine said that the answer to her cable came next morning. It also was only one word: "Tonight."

There was no signature, but she knew who had sent it.

* * *

It was a cold wintry December day as Josephine's huge black Daimler limousine pulled up to the dimly lit Gare de Lyon.

Her chauffeur opened the door, and the first out were the two wolfhounds. Then a plump, agitated little man stepped out to help Josephine down. From inside the car the chauffeur handed out to the attendants piece after piece of her fabulous Vuitton luggage.

From the time when she could first afford it, Josephine always traveled with the most handsome set of luggage Vuitton could create for her. "I remember not too many years before," she told me, "when Mama and I went back to Boxcar Town in East St. Louis and I carried an old potato sack to take away anything we could find from our burned-down shack."

Now it was hatboxes and secretarial cases and shoeboxes and gloveboxes. From a small truck that had followed the limousine, the railroad attendants were removing several huge wardrobe trunks.

Satisfied that the luggage was all there, Josephine made for the station entrance. Her plump little accountant threw open the door for her, and the unleashed wolfhounds raced ahead, then back, then ahead again, anxious for her to move along. They knew something was up.

"If ever I looked good, I looked good that night. I wore my new fox cape. I'll never forget it. It was built on chiffon, and under my throat a little fox's head started, and then fox after fox just kept wrapping around me all the way to the ground, one fox grabbing the other's tail. God, it was fabulous. It started out as the palest lavender, and by the time it reached the bottom and dragged on the floor they were dyed the deepest purple. You couldn't help but stare at it. Yes, it was fabulous."

* * *

She paused a long time. "My God, Stephen, where is it now? Where is my beautiful purple fox cape?"

I just looked at her. I did not answer. She started looking at the bars of the prison cell, unable to comprehend.

"My accountant was pleading with me not to do this crazy thing. To go on a holiday in the middle of the winter and in the middle of the season. He thought they might even have to close the Folies. I didn't care. I really didn't.

About 1932. Rapidly leaving the "tarred little head" behind. Note the matching lace on the shoes. It was one of her manias: everything had to match. She would send her slippers back half a dozen times before she found a color match that pleased her. This gown was by Dior.

The Crown Prince Adolf of Sweden, Gustav VI, probably about the time he first saw Josephine in the Folies Bergère. Not long afterward they met formally, and the little-known affair took place, despite the warnings of Melba.

Josephine as she looked at the time of her affair with the Crown Prince. "I'll never forget when this picture was made. I had Ethel [the chimp] with me, and she was frightened to death of the tiger rug I was lying on. Then when she was mean or did something I didn't want her to do, I'd just say, 'Now, Ethel, if you don't behave, I'm going to have you made into a monkey rug,' and you know, she straightened right out. Other times when she was mean, I would take her jewelry away from her, and can you believe it, tears would come into her little eyes, and I had to give it back, I felt so bad. . . ."

". . . He was the cream, and I was the coffee. . . ." The Crown Prince of Sweden, as he very likely looked at the time of the affair.

Casino de Paris Archives

(Left) In the early thirties. "This was Pepe's favorite photo of me. One day I took a pencil and blacked out a tooth, and autographed it for him. I wonder where that is—a real collector's item, no?"

(Below) About 1931, from one of the Casino de Paris revues. ". . . Those costumes were so huge and so heavy that they stood up by themselves, and I just walked in and out of them. Some were so big I never moved; I just stood there and looked hot."

Probably about 1930. "You know, Stephen, I could not for the life of me—even if you gave me a thousand dollars—tell you when this photo was made, or where. But let's put it in the book, and somewhere maybe one of those dancers will see it, if they are still here, and then we will know, won't we? Is that Tommy [Ladd] on the left?"

Casino de Paris, early thirties. Costume for a "trick" number staged by Varna. It was a huge introduction to Josephine's entrance, with twenty-four boys in top hat and tails. She was one of the chorus boys who waited for the star who didn't enter. Then she would reveal herself from the middle of the chorus. "It didn't work—though I don't know why—and we dropped it in a week or so."

About 1935 or 1936. Still the brightly painted lips. At this time she was experimenting with henna around the eyes and also on the palms of the hands. It did nothing but run during performances, and the hennaed hands dirtied her gowns. Note the hands. Even during her most trying times they were beautifully manicured. She considered them her best feature.

Air France

Josephine and Henri Varna.

Josephine, Varna, and Mildred the cheetah.

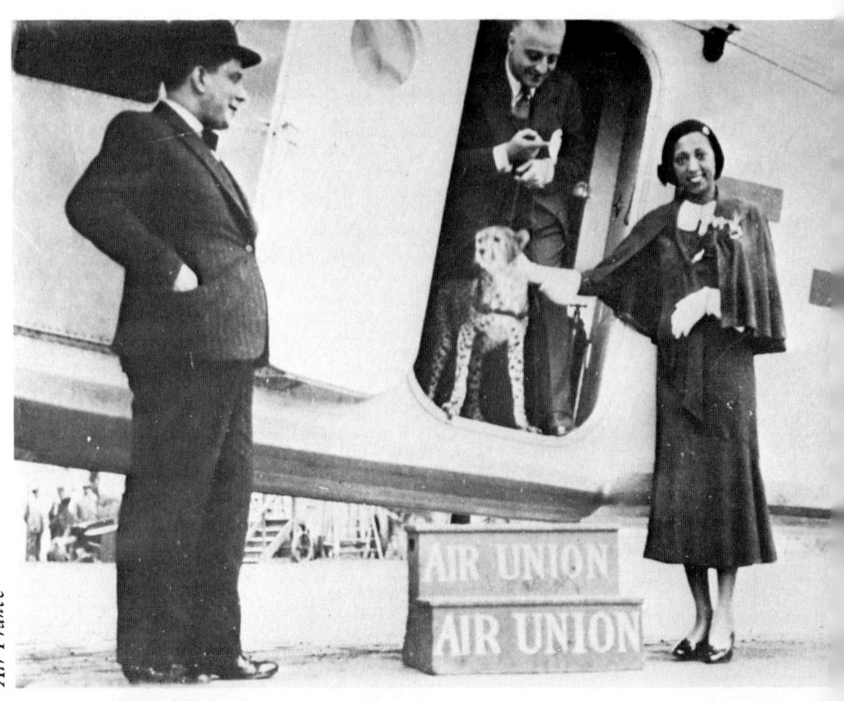

Air France

"I told them I had to have a rest and that I was going to Lyon. Imagine, I thought they would believe that story. He kept begging me to postpone. To go to the south of France when the weather was better, to go to Monte Carlo to follow the sun. Inside I was just laughing.

"He tried to tell me that I was causing a scandal. He said that one scandal leads to another. What a scandal it would have been if he really knew what I was up to!

"You know, years later in London I met Lady Mountbatten backstage at the Palladium. Now I wasn't young anymore. I thought she looked at me kind of strangely, although she was very pleasant. I asked her to have supper with me. She refused. I would have talked to her about it, too. I didn't care much by then."

* * *

But on this night her accountant pleaded in vain.

"Monsieur," she informed him, "the Folies was open long before I arrived here . . . and it will undoubtedly stay open long after I am gone."

"But, Madame, you must consider. The millions of francs that will be lost. You must consider that Monsieur Varna and the Folies have been good to you."

After a long pause, Josephine replied, "And I to the Folies, Monsieur. For every franc I earned, they made ten, and I am delighted."

They had reached the flight of stairs that leads to the famous restaurant of the Gare de Lyon. Then as now, it was unchanged from the way it had appeared during the great Mauve Decade. Josephine swept in, unhooking the little fox's mouth where it held her cape, and letting the fur fall across her right arm and trail on the floor behind her.

Josephine Baker had many great moments in her long life. She was at ease with kings and queens and presidents and premiers, with actors and dancers—with everyone who spoke to her. But it is very unlikely that she ever was more glamorous or more carefree or more at ease than she was on that night in the restaurant of the Gare de Lyon.

Under her fox cape, as it fell from her shoulders, she wore the most severe cream satin gown. Around her waist she wore a simple diamond-and-emerald belt about a half inch wide. Her hair, still plastered down, still looked as if it had been painted with tar. Her only makeup was a slash of fire-red lipstick.

Everyone in the restaurant rose and applauded.

"I can't remember who all was there. I know Picasso, and Ernest [Hemingway]. Piaf was there, and Maurice [Chevalier], and Miss [Mistinguett]. I think Foujita was there too, and I thought he was having an affair with Miss. You know, Miss wasn't young anymore. But that night she danced with her partner, Ladd [Tommy Ladd, an American dancer]. God, they were fabulous. No one could beat her. Piaf had her usual prizefighter. She loved those boxers. I remember when Marcel [Cerdan] was killed, how she came to me and we cried together. We talked about my affair with the crown prince. I told her everything. We both had a good cry and felt better afterward. She understood everything. She said later I was a fool to ever have come back. She told me to grab every chance for love I could. But you know, it hasn't been that way anymore. At least not now, with Jo [Jo Bouillon, her husband at the time].

"When the music stopped, they wheeled out this huge bottle of champagne. I think you call it a jeroboam. Do they still make them, I wonder? You tilt it over . . . it must be enough to make an army drunk."

Then Varna proposed the toast that electrified the room. "To my newest star in the Casino de Paris."

Even Josephine was stunned. She had had no idea that Varna was planning to leave the Folies Bergère for his own theatre.

It was a good hand that Varna had been dealt, and of course this was his lead, and he led well. That night Henri Varna hitched up the famous troika that galloped, in one fashion or another, for the next forty years. It was Varna, Josephine, and the Casino de Paris. It is doubtful whether more exciting theatre will ever be created.

Varna continued. "Enough, enough. She has just three minutes to catch her train. There is no changing her mind. If I cannot do it, no one can."

He was right, of course.

"Go on your holiday, Bakhair. Come back to me rested. We are just starting."

Raising her glass, Josephine downed the champagne without stopping, then threw the glass high into the air. A waiter caught it and ran up to Josephine, and she kissed him on both cheeks. The patrons in the restaurant roared their approval.

Then, as she had entered, she swept out. She was followed only by Varna, and he led her down the steps across the empty platform to the track where the Lyon express waited. He held her hand a long time. Then he kissed it.

"Josephine, play your games. But when you are finished, you must come back to me."

"I will, Henri. But for now, let me go for a while."

Varna disappeared down the track, and as he did so a small man in black came quickly to the car. He whispered to Josephine, and out came the baggage and out bounded the dogs.

Josephine and the dogs followed him silently to the end of the platform. Just over the top of the wall she could see the stack of another engine, smoke and steam blowing out of it.

Then, as they reached the end of the wall and came to another platform, she caught sight of the engine and its luxurious car. Attached to the front of the engine was a snowplow; on one side of the brilliantly lit lamp, Josephine saw the flag of Sweden; on the other side was the flag of the royal family. The engine had a full head of steam and was breathing heavily.

Josephine and the valet moved down to the private car. She remembered that it was gold, and on the side was the crest of the royal family of Sweden. The curtains were drawn.

If Josephine was something in her lavender and purple foxes, so was the interior of this private car. It was Louis XVI. It was silk and satin and Aubusson carpets. In the center of the salon an elegant table was set for a late supper. On the sideboard were silver salvers and serving pieces. Champagne was icing in a silver cooler.

After a solitary supper, Josephine stood up and walked down the passageway to the private compartment.

"I just looked inside after I opened the door. It was really something. I'll never forget that bed. It was like something out of a Hollywood movie. It was like a dream. It was a bed shaped like a swan. And it had its big wings spread out almost covering you when you looked up at it. I had heard of satin sheets, and was always going to get some for myself, but I never got around to it. Now here they were. All I could think of was getting into them.

"I just dropped my dress. I didn't have anything on. I was ready for anything. I picked it up and threw it over a chair, and I steadied myself against the rocking of the car, 'cause it seemed we were going so fast. I thought, boy, he must really be anxious. I said, 'What does he see in me?' I looked at myself in that mirror, and I thought I looked like a little boy with my slicked-down hair and my hard little dancer's body. I wondered if he'd like me when he really saw me. I even wondered if he knew that I was a colored girl. That threw me for a moment. I thought for a long time, then I remembered that song from *Chocolate Dandies* . . . "If You Ain't Never Been Loved by a Brownskin, You Ain't Never Been Loved At All." I laughed out loud for a long time. Then I thought, if you don't know it now, you're sure gonna know it when you see me like this. Then I really laughed and I just fell over on the bed laughing and covered myself with those satin sheets. Boy, were they cold; but after a while my body started to get all hot under them, and I could see every muscle in my legs and stomach. That sheet just covered me in the right places."

Josephine snuggled against the satin sheets. She turned out all the lights but the reading lamp, and settled down to read a magazine before falling asleep. First she took a buffer and went over her nails. It was something she had done for years, and she did it even to the last. She prided herself on her beautifully manicured hands.

Then she heard a slight knock at the door, and thinking it was the valet, she said, "*Entrez.*"

Slowly the door opened and the light from the corridor came into the room. The first thing she saw was the uniform. Then she looked into his face, and he was smiling.

"All I could see," she told me, "were those fabulous teeth, and the first thing that crossed my mind was that pretty soon I'm going to feel that mustache on me."

Josephine lay there, unsure of what she should do. Finally she just fell back into the cushions, threw the magazine down on the floor, and said, "I don't think I can stand up right now—" but he interrupted her before she could finish.

"Then maybe you will invite me to sit down."

Ignoring the chair, the prince sat on the edge of the bed. Josephine, noticing the way he kept glancing down at the satin sheets that followed the contours of her body, twisted and turned a little so he could get a good look.

"I didn't expect to see you until tomorrow," she said.

"Should I leave, then, and come back later?"

"Oh, no, don't do that. I'm just surprised. But I'm glad. I'm really quite glad."

Josephine shivered. His body felt warm as he leaned over her. She snuggled down and shivered again.

"Are you cold, Josephine?"

"I'm always cold, Your Highness. I guess that's why I'm a dancer. When I get cold I can jump up and dance, and it always warms me up."

"Would you like to jump up now and dance a little to warm up?"

"No."

"Would you rather do something else?"

She looked him straight in the eye. "Yes."

"Then perhaps I have something here that could warm you up a little."

Josephine knew it was coming, but she didn't expect him to make his move so fast. He took hold of her arm, and as he pulled her toward him he reached his free hand over and pulled open a drawer in the bedside chest. In an instant he had clamped a three-strand diamond bracelet onto her arm. Then he looked for a long time into her eyes before he kissed just the tips of her fingers.

"That's what I was thinking of when I said I had something that I thought would warm you up. Is your arm feeling better now?"

Josephine was in a situation she had never been in before, and it confused her. She had been grabbed and pinched and made love to before, going way back to the days in the Bessie Smith company. But this was a strange sort of lovemaking—lovemaking with class. It was class she wasn't accustomed to—not yet, at least. It was also a type of lovemaking she would never experience again.

"Is your arm feeling better?" he repeated.

"Yes."

Then, purring like a tiny kitten, she tilted her head to the side, laid her own smile on him, and said, "But my other arm is cold now."

The prince roared with laughter.

"You know," she told me, "he almost fell off that bed. Then he got that box out of the drawer and fished around in it for a while, and found another bracelet and clamped that on my arm too. Now, you know I wasn't unaccustomed to getting jewels by now, but this way was different, and it was a way that I liked."

Josephine did not look at the diamonds. She just looked straight into his eyes. The bracelets could have been made of cardboard. She held out her arms, and when she did the sheet fell to her waist. His eyes were still riveted to hers.

Then he slowly stood up and began to remove his jacket. Neither of them spoke. He sat down again and pulled off his boots one at a time, then removed his stockings and wiggled his toes. He took off his shirt. He wore no undershirt. He stood looking at her for a long time, and she could only stare back.

He reached over and turned off the reading light. The blue night-lights in the compartment stayed on, and they gave his chest and arms the look of a marble statue. Slowly he removed his pants. She noticed that his linen undershorts had a drawstring, and that they fit him tightly. He pulled the string and slipped them down his legs.

Then he reached over and slowly lifted her arms and pulled down the satin sheets, revealing her body in the blue of the night-lights.

At first she could only stare at him, and he at her. He dropped to his knees, and the first thing she felt, as she had imagined she would, was his mustache as it brushed her stomach. He kissed her stomach softly; his mouth then moved up to her chest, and he kissed first her left breast and then her right.

He rose up and put both arms over her and then both legs, keeping his body off hers, until he was on the other side near the window. Then he lay down very gently, put his arm under her shoulders, and pulled her tightly to him. He threw his leg over her body and slowly covered her mouth with his. She threw her arms over his back and shoulders.

It was everything she had ever thought about but had never had. She thought of what she had done in the past, backstage in dressing rooms and in cheap hotels. She thought of what she had done with other men whom she didn't even want to see the next morning. She remembered that many times she had left in the middle of the night, hating herself for what she had done.

Now it was different. This was something else. Breathing heavily, and never taking his mouth from hers, he maneuvered his body over her, put his free arm under her waist, and pulled her body up to his. Then he slowly pressed against her, and she was forced back onto the bed. They lay there for a while, letting the swinging and bumping of the railroad car do their work for them.

The train streaked through the night. The wind and the snow tried desperately to penetrate that compartment through the window. The whistle shrieked, and the little flags fluttered crazily in the wind and snow. In the cab of the engine the fireman threw shovelful after shovelful of coal into the roaring fire. The train sped northward, toward the ice and the snow and the birches of the north of Sweden. It sped to the country that would hide the lovers, even if only temporarily, from the outside world.

Inside the private car, they rested. Josephine ran one beautifully manicured finger up and down his arm, and he wrote his name with his finger on her back. He drew a heart with an arrow and put their initials into it, and she repeated everything he drew. He was no longer a prince, and she was not Josephine. They forgot who they were. They were lovers. And they began to make love again as the train sped through the night.

Outside, the dawn began to break. The snow had stopped. Josephine parted the curtain only slightly and glanced out. There was snow everywhere, and in the distance she could see the great stands of white birches, their branches covered with snow.

* * *

Gustav VI, Adolf, Crown Prince of Sweden took Josephine Baker, singer and dancer from East St. Louis, to Sweden. He took her to the summer palace in the dead of winter. They were alone for a month, with only three servants to wait on them.

Sometime in the late afternoon, the train came to a stop at a tiny railroad station. Josephine looked out the window and saw a pair of matched horses standing in front of a little sleigh. Steam came from their nostrils, and they pawed the ground impatiently.

Josephine and her prince stepped off the train and climbed into the sleigh, covering themselves with a huge polar-bear rug against the cold. She had wrapped a great scarf around her head and neck. The luggage was piled high into a second sleigh, and with the quick crack of the driver's whip, they pulled out of the station.

It was a still, gray day. Under the bearskin rug she cuddled up against the prince as the sleigh flew over the frozen road. The bells of the horses jangled; the harness creaked and the runners sang.

The prince gazed at Josephine for a long time. Then, like a little boy who must hide something from the world, he pulled the bearskin over her head and kissed her softly. The driver stared straight ahead as the sleigh flew along.

Soon the horses slowed to a trot as they entered a long avenue of birches leading up to the front of the summer palace. The fountain and the statue in the courtyard were covered with straw to shield them against the terrible cold. Smoke from the chimneys drifted straight into the crystal-clear sky. Josephine could see the closed shutters at the windows.

As they pulled up, a servant ran out to welcome them. When the prince took her out of the sleigh, she saw what was perhaps originally an elegant royal hunting lodge. It sat in a huge park, surrounded by leafless birches that cast long shadows over everything.

"My grandfather built it for a hunting lodge," he told her as they walked up the steps. "It was originally supposed to be that and nothing more. But my grandmother couldn't bear to be separated from him even for a night, and when she came she brought her own furniture. It has been here ever since."

Josephine remembered its formal rooms. The furniture was covered with linen to protect it against the cold, and even the chandeliers and wall sconces were covered with linen cloths.

They walked across a hall, and he threw open a door to reveal a luxurious dining room. A fire roared in the enormous fireplace. A massive table dared anyone to spill even a drop of soup. Elegant chairs sat around the room on the parquet floor. The table was set with two chairs, one at the head and one to the right.

Josephine ran to the fire and dropped her coat and scarf. She looked around the room and saw two French doors with cut-glass panes which were partly frosted on the other side. She walked over, and cupping her hands to her eyes to hold back the light, she peered in.

"The ballroom. Grandmama couldn't bear to be without one. She loved to dance, too."

Josephine moved toward another heavy mahogany door. She looked inquiringly at the prince. He motioned for her to open it.

She walked into a massive bedroom, with another roaring fire and a huge canopied bed with heavy velvet draperies that could be drawn against the winter cold.

"My grandmother brought it with her too. Even in the hottest summers she would be bundled up against the cold when she crept into bed. My grandfather slept with nothing, and in the mornings he would dash out those doors and rub himself down with snow, and Grandmama would watch through the window and scream with delight.

"Tomorrow, if you like, I'll take you on a tour. Or the next day. Or the next. Whenever you want. We have plenty of time. But these two rooms and the kitchen were all that they could get ready on such short notice. This is the only place I knew where we could be alone. Really alone."

He had moved Josephine back toward the fire, and as he stood there he kissed her again. He told her that he was afraid she would think he was foolish. He told her that he was jealous of her and that, even though he had known her for only one night, he was mad for her.

"Let's never leave here," he said. "Let's stay forever. In the winter we can hide in the snow and in the summer we can run away to the forests. My family will never find me, and your Paris friends will never find you."

He told her that he had never met anyone like her before. He had forgotten that he was married and that he would one day become King of Sweden. Josephine felt that no man was ever more sincère than he, and she knew that she could never be more serious about anyone than she was about him at this moment.

"What will we do?" he asked. "What can happen to us and for us?"

Nothing like this had ever happened to Josephine, either. For once, she could not think her way out. She tried. She pulled him down to the floor, and they sat on the hearth looking into the fire.

He got on his knees in front of her and put his hands on either side of her face. Then he pulled her to him, and kissed her softly again, and for the second time Josephine heard those thousand violins playing for her. Playing her favorite music and her favorite songs. She thought she would scream, their sound was so loud in her ears. Then, when he let her go and she looked into his eyes, she knew she had been hearing the wind roaring up the chimney. No matter. Even the wind was music to her. Josephine, too, was in love.

That night the prince, standing on one side of the great bed while he undressed, spoke to Josephine, who stood on the other side. They were hidden by the drawn velvet bed curtains.

"When you were a little girl at home in East St. Louis, did you have draperies like this around your bed to keep out the cold?"

Josephine thought of Boxcar Town and Mama and the steamy laundry piled high.

"Of course," she replied. "And every night my maid would come in and turn down the covers and warm up my bed with a great big pan of hot coals."

Meanwhile, Josephine had removed her clothes and put on a chiffon dressing gown. On the opposite side of the bed, the prince continued undressing and listening to her voice.

Josephine parted the curtains on her side of the bed, and as she quietly crawled across, she continued:

"One night she got carried away, and the coals got too hot and burned up the bed."

Now she was on his side, and she separated the curtains. With only her head sticking out, she went on:

"As a matter of fact, it not only burned up the whole bed . . ."

At this point the prince was just dropping his linen undershorts, and she was getting a good look at his alabaster bottom.

". . . it burned the house down and the whole town with it."

The prince turned suddenly and saw her looking at him through the curtains. Tossing his underwear onto a chair, he gave a great shout, and as Josephine ducked back into the bed, he leaped through the curtains.

"You're lying to me—and when you lie, you have to be spanked. What's this? What are you wearing that for?"

"To keep warm. Just like Grandmama," she said.

"Ah, but I never told you the best part. How he used to warm her up at night."

Josephine heard her thousand violins again. For the next few weeks she was to hear them often.

When she awoke in the morning, a blinding sun, reflected from the snow outside, was streaming through the windows. The prince leaped out of bed, threw open the French doors, and, with nothing on, threw himself into a huge snowdrift, yelling with delight and rubbing the snow all over him.

Josephine ran to the window, holding one of the linen sheets around her. She stood laughing at him, until he threw a handful of snow at her through the doors. It struck her face and shoulders, and she screamed, dropped the sheet, and ran to the bed. Too late. He rushed into the room carrying huge handfuls of snow, and leaped into the bed. She screamed all the more when he rubbed the snow over her body.

Josephine said that those were the happiest days of her life. Undoubtedly they were. They were like two children. She had escaped temporarily from the grind of the theatre, and he from his family and the affairs of state.

They rode during the daytime in a one-horse sleigh. He held the reins and she sat directly behind him, holding on for dear life as they raced through the snowy countryside.

And at night, they sat in front of the great fireplace. She roasted chestnuts and tiny pieces of apple and fed them to him.

One day he took her on a tour of the hunting lodge. He led her outside and told her how beautiful the estate was in the summer. He pointed across the water and said that if she looked closely she could see Elsinore. When they returned indoors, he told her more of the history of his country and showed her paintings of his relatives. He mentioned that one of his ancestors, Gustav I, was one of the last of the great knights.

Some afternoons they would go and hide in the birches. They would lie in the snow, heavily bundled against the cold, and stare up at the blue sky. On days when the sky was overcast and leaden, Josephine did not like it and asked him to take her back inside.

Christmas Eve came, and they had a little tree covered with candles.

Tucked in the branches was a small jewel case, inside of which was a beautiful diamond-and-emerald pin he had designed for her. It was a knight in shining armor astride a white charger, his sword of tiny pearls held high; the horse's eye was a flashing red ruby.

The prince promised to be *her* knight in shining armor. Whenever she needed him, he told her, she had only to call and he would be there to rescue her from any peril.

Years later, when the time of peril did arrive, he did not come. Very likely he did not know the desperate situation that had arisen. If he had, perhaps he would have come. But by then the pin, her little knight in shining armor, was gone—dropped with the rest of her jewels onto the black velvet jeweler's cloth of the Paris moneylenders. . . .

Josephine and the prince stared at each other for a long time. By now they had begun to understand each other and, more important, their situation. He was married. He was a prince—soon to become a king. She had begun to realize how hopeless their situation was. She knew that her great love affair could not last.

Josephine told me that he would have left his family and his throne for her. It was not unbelievable; by this time another king had left his throne for another woman.

The prince sensed and understood the problem as well as she did. "It doesn't have to be the last night," he said.

She smiled at him. As a woman, she knew the cold facts better than he did.

"We could leave, you know," he went on. "We could run away together. I can jump on my white horse and take you to some family palace, and we can live there happily ever after."

She kept looking at him, longing for him.

"Let's see . . . I'll kidnap you. Yes, I'll kidnap you from your theatre one night and hold you hostage in a cold damp garret in Paris. And you'll have to shout for me to come and hold you in my arms and keep you warm."

She loved his little fairy tales. They appealed to her sense of the theatre.

"Adolf . . ." It was the first time she had called him by his name. "It isn't going to work, is it? You see, when we run out of that door, you know who'll be waiting? It'll be Old Man Trouble. He's always been waiting for me. He just stands around waiting for times like this. I know . . . my Mama told me.

"She also told me to go up to Harlem and find me a good man with a little money. She said I should settle down and have some babies. She never told me, though, if I'd live happily ever after."

"Harlem? Where's that?" he inquired.

"In New York City," she said.

"Ah, yes, but you see, there are no more rich men left in Harlem. They have all lost their fortunes in Wall Street and then jumped out of the window. I know that. I read it in all the dispatches from America."

For a moment Josephine thought he might only be joking. Then she realized that he was not. What could he know of Harlem, of its people? What could he know of her and her background and the people of East St. Louis?

"No, baby. Ain't nobody ever jumped out of a window in Harlem, 'cause he lost a fortune in Wall Street."

Then she spoke very quietly to him. She wanted to explain her feelings, but it was difficult.

"And if we lived together for a lifetime, I'd never be able to explain all that to you. I'm Josephine, from East St. Louis. And sometime soon you will be the King of Sweden. And regardless of what you and I want, there are a million people who would keep us from getting it. Not just one Old Man Trouble, but a million Old Man Troubles.

"Tomorrow I must go to Paris. They're waiting for me there, and you must return to your home. They're waiting for you, too. And someday, when I need you, I'll just call, and you'll put on your armor and jump on your white horse and you'll come and rescue me. And we'll run away . . . to somewhere . . ."

". . . And we'll just live happily ever after."

Josephine walked over to the cut-crystal doors of the ballroom and peered into the darkness, trying to hide her tears. She stood there shivering, with her hands cupped against her cheeks.

The prince walked over to the table and from a huge box he took out a magnificent floor-length sable coat. He moved toward her and put it over her shoulders.

Josephine wanted to be a million miles away. She twisted the handles of the ballroom door and rushed inside. She stood in the middle of the room; it was dark and cold, and the prince took up a lighted candelabrum from the dining-room table and walked after her. He placed it on a marble table and took her into his arms.

She heard those thousand violins again. She pressed herself close to him, and he held her tight. Then, as though he too heard the music, he began a silent waltz in the empty ballroom. She threw the sable over his shoulders, and it covered them both.

The candles had burned far down when they quietly left.

The next day at the little station where she had arrived, Josephine entered the same private car that had brought her there. She sat in the salon and gazed from the window. The last sun of the day was streaming through the cold birches. She heard the screaming of the train whistle, but now she hated it. It was a mournful sound.

Then she heard music coming from somewhere. She looked out again on the platform and saw several musicians playing. The prince had assembled a colorful little band to help bid her good-bye. It was a happy song. She stood and moved closer to the window.

The wind began to whip up the snow again. The train jerked, then moved slowly out of the station. The music continued, only now it was her thousand violins that were playing. Tears ran down her cheeks.

Then she spied her prince. He sat astride a tall, nearly white horse. He was in full uniform, and as the train passed he raised his arm in a salute. He held it until the train was out of sight.

It was the end of the affair. She knew it would never happen to her again. For her entire life she tried to fathom what act of fate had cast her into the role she played in that fabulous love affair. She never could.

But that day, she tried to think again as she sat down in the salon of the private coach. She leaned back. Then she saw the jewel casket on a *bombé* chest at the end of the car.

When she left the summer palace she had left the jewels behind. She had forgotten them. Her prince and her affair had been more important to her than any jewels.

But he had had them placed aboard the train for her. She walked over and raised the lid.

On top of all the other gifts sat the little Van Cleef and Arpels box. When she opened it, she saw her knight in shining armor. His sword was held high, and the horse's red eye gleamed in the last light of the day.

* * *

Years later, in the early 1970s, in her suite at the Beverly Hills Hotel in Hollywood, California, I opened up the morning paper to read her the notices of her opening the night before. I saw the front-page story and paused. I glanced over at her sitting in her chair. She sensed that something was wrong and asked me what it was. I said simply, "The King of Sweden is dead."

She did not answer. She stared out the window toward Sunset Boulevard for some time, then excused herself and walked into her bedroom.

That afternoon I asked the switchboard to shut off all telephone calls. I knew what she must be thinking, and I wanted her to think without interruption. Undoubtedly her thoughts took her back to that one really wonderful time in her life. She was recalling the full moon fading as the dawn appeared, the screaming whistle of the train. . . .

She emerged much later, at dusk, and we prepared to go to the theatre as if nothing had happened. She never spoke of it, or him, again.

The High Noon

Chapter 9

". . . I was in black. It was jets and egrets and shiny black rhinestones, each sewn individually onto the chiffon. But the egrets were something! It was also when I first started to put diamond dust on my face —real diamond dust—and it took me hours to remove it later, very carefully so that it would not cut me. It was also my first big headdress, and those egrets reached to the sky . . . my cape was a thousand feet long, it seemed . . . it was . . . swansdown and peacock feathers . . ."

* * *

Sometime in the early 1930s Colette, the queen of the literati, wrote: "*Elle est la plus belle panthère*"—"She is the most beautiful panther."

By the merest chance, on the same day Josephine Baker had placed the following advertisement. It appeared, not in the theatrical section, but on the front page:

> I beg to take this opportunity to extend my heartfelt thanks to the hundreds of thousands of people who have taken of their valuable time to wish me so well. I would love to have been able to write to each of you individually, but as you can see that is impossible.
>
> And . . . to the 2,000 fabulous Frenchmen who proposed marriage to me, I personally accept; however, that would be breaking the law, for we unfortunately are allowed only one spouse. Therefore, by law I must now decline, but forever I will dream of how marvelous it would have been to be married to all 2,000 of you.
>
> Here is my kiss.
>
> Josephine Baker

Years later—for being with Josephine was never really *now;* it was always years ahead or years back—Josephine and I were sitting in the little park at the Milandes. It was during what I called the "period of hell," and we had been discussing the finances.

As we talked, an old Frenchman and his wife quietly approached. As he greeted her, he removed his hat. Then he took from his wallet a tattered news clipping he had carried for almost forty years. It was the advertisement she had placed years ago.

"I was almost one of your husbands, Josephine."

Josephine, looking at the little wife, replied: "And how lucky you were that you got him, Madame. Had I married him, my life might have gone for the better."

Only Josephine and I knew what she meant.

* * *

But now it was the thirties, and it was the Renaissance for Josephine. It was to be her fabulous decade—with two exceptions. The first was a cable she received from Florenz Ziegfeld. The second was the not-so-far-off sound of German boots marching on the pavements of the Champs Elysées, and the sound of Hitler's feet tapping their little jig in front of the Eiffel Tower.

She was ready. Her initiation, her trial by fire on the French stage, was over. It had not even been a little match blaze. Where others had struggled for every foothold in the theatre, she had merely leaped from one version of the Folies to another.

But she knew that wearing bananas, and holding ice to her breasts, and walking with diamond-bedecked chimpanzees were part of the past. She knew that she had to hibernate temporarily, that the cocoon had to rest to build the splendid butterfly.

When it emerged in that year, it was some butterfly. Henri Varna knew as well as she that she was ready for more than bananas.

Paris qui remue was without doubt Henri Varna's most splendid contribution to the French music hall. It marked the debut of both Varna and Josephine in that venerable house, the Casino de Paris.

It was another momentous occasion. The real aficionados of Josephine knew when they heard "*J'ai deux amours*" they would see their "divine one."

Her theme song, "Two Loves Have I," was written principally by Vincent Scotto and Varna himself. Varna had based it on countless stories Josephine had told him about America, which he had never visited and with which he was fascinated.

Josephine, who was yet to experience her painful "American trial by fire," really was as much in love with her native country as she was with Paris. After all, she was still an American.

"Two loves have I . . . my country and Paris." It was a song that took the continent by storm. Regrettably, only those who "knew" Josephine "knew" the song in America.

It was a strange enigma of her life and her career. When Josephine Baker was mentioned, you either knew and adored her, or you had no idea who she was. That was the way it had always been in the United States.

Only forty years later did the song suddenly catch on to some extent, but that was after her last triumphant tour in America. Had she lived to complete the final tour that was being prepared for her, there is no doubt that in the United States it would have carried the impact that it had always carried on the continent and throughout the rest of the world.

* * *

So in *Paris qui remue* the famous "troika" was hitched up. It galloped in one form or another for the next forty years. At that time the troika was Josephine and *"J'ai deux amours,"* Henri Varna, and the Casino de Paris itself.

To say that Henri Varna pulled out the stops is to put it mildly.

Josephine was ready for hard work. She had just emerged—and not unscathed—from the really only great romance in her life. In order to "forget," she threw herself into a romance with Pepe d'Albertini. She denies having married him; she supported him for years, until 1937, when she married a French industrialist. She always said that *Pal Joey* was later written and based on her experiences with Pepe. Perhaps.

But Pepe did afford her a little relaxation between rehearsals. One weekend he took her for a drive in her new Bugatti. They traveled through the countryside of southern France, through the valley of the Dordogne, where the French (who love fairy tales) say that the King of the Castles picked up bunches of extra ones he had, and flung them along those mighty banks.

One that he flung there was the Château des Milandes. The Sun King, Louis XIV, *"Le Dieu donné,"* had spent the night there with his mistress Louise de La Vallière on a similar journey.

But that is getting ahead of our story.

Now it was work, work, and more work. It was the most incredible revue that was ever presented. It was the revue that presaged *"l'escalier"* steps. Varna and Josephine threw themselves into it.

Worth, Balenciaga, and Erté did the gowns. Varna designed the set for her first entrance. He also designed the machinery.

It was the most complicated set ever devised. And the set itself is a strange story: it has *never* been duplicated. For, like Toussaint in Haiti, who murdered the architect of the citadel so that it could never be duplicated, so Henri Varna destroyed the original blueprints. But let Josephine tell the story.

* * *

"The entire design was in red, white, and black. I waited high up on a platform backstage, and my costume was so elaborate that it took two maids and two stagehands to assist me and help maneuver it as I descended.

"I was in black. It was jets, and egrets, and shiny black rhinestones, each sewn individually onto the chiffon. But the egrets were something. It was also when I first started to put diamond dust on my face—real diamond dust—and it took me hours to remove it later very carefully so that it would not cut me. It was also my first headdress, and those egrets reached to the sky, and were dyed gray.

"My cape was a thousand feet long, it seemed, and was constructed of swansdown and peacock feathers.

"The orchestra had been augmented, and there were over sixty men in the pit. And when I heard that music on that opening night for the first time—when I heard *"J'ai deux amours,"* "Two Loves Have I, My Country and Paris"—even I got goose bumps, for at the time I *really* meant it.

"I was hidden up high, and I could look down and see what was happening to the set as the curtain came up.

"It was a huge, old-fashioned, gay nineties sort of valentine that just kept opening up. One layer after another, then another and another, and as each opened up, it showed all those little cupids and angels and hearts that the old valentines showed. Then when the last one opened up, the stage was still empty, incredible as that seems.

"Then it seemed that in an instant I was seen at the top of the huge platform and I started to walk forward into nothing. I had rehearsed a thousand times and I never once looked down. The audiences gasped, both at me and for fear I would drop fifty feet. But in another instant, it seemed something from the flies flashed in front of me, and in that split instant the dressers changed my gray egret headdress to a brilliant green, and somehow, the thing that had covered me only for a moment opened up and it was about ten steps, and without looking down and as they were hanging in midair, I started down. Still at least forty feet between me and the stage.

"Then the same happened again, and in the same instant, my headdress became a beautiful lavender, and again of a different design, and I just kept walking, down, down, looking at the audience.

"Now they were screaming. Never had they seen such a sight. Never would they again. Twice more the steps flashed in front of me, and as I reached the bottom one—and when it appeared that I would drop to my death—they opened up for me. It was the *real* magic, the greatest magic! The magic of Henri Varna.

"Now my huge cape of peacock was behind me and covering all the steps I had come down, and from way below on the stage elevators, more steps were rising out of nowhere to meet me. When I reached the bottom I could not continue. I had to stop. The audience was screaming and jumping and applauding and whistling. It was truly incredible.

"Then I started singing—my song—and it came up from inside of me, and I meant it and I loved it. I never thought that times would change for me as much as they did. I never thought America would hurt me so much. I wanted them to love me too. I wanted to go back to my own country. Now I knew I was a great star—I wanted to show them something. It never happened for me. When it did, it was all different, just me alone—all alone—on that big stage at Carnegie Hall. That night they made more noise than they did at my debut at the Casino."

* * *

"They were standing that night in Carnegie Hall, and their arms were raised and their fists were clenched, and they were chanting 'Right on, sister, right on, sister. . . .' It was new to me. I never had heard those words. I guess that at that moment I stopped regretting all those things I had said years earlier."

* * *

"But that night in Paris I knew that what we had all accomplished was something . . . "

Josephine just looked at the wall.

A long time later, a friend of Josephine's came backstage in Los Angeles to see her. While a young medical student in France, he had been in the audience at her Casino de Paris debut.

He had just returned from seeing the new MGM revue at the Casino in Las Vegas. He told her of the Vegas revue, and then reminded her of the Paris debut in 1930. She loved it. She invited him to stay in her dressing room, and they talked until after midnight. "Do you remember this, do you remember that, then it was green, then purple . . ."

"But how in the hell did they ever do it, Josephine," the man finally asked.

She did not know. It was then that we learned that Henri Varna had destroyed the plans and blueprints of his one really great masterpiece.

It seems criminal that no film record remains for us to see.

* * *

They didn't tell Josephine until the morning following the Casino debut that one of her favorite stagehands had been crushed in the complicated machinery. He had died almost instantly.

She attended his funeral, and for the rest of her life, until she could no longer do so, she provided for the widow.

Then one day, during the hard times, the widow approached her on the streets of Paris. She opened her purse and gave Josephine 1,000 francs. Josephine took it. She needed it. And in taking it, she gave that poor Parisian widow one of the happiest moments of her life.

* * *

Now the funny little caterpillar was the fabulous butterfly. And it tried its wings—and it flew—and it was truly something to behold.

She took a stab at motion pictures, but they were not particularly successful. Probably her best was *Zou Zou,* the story of a washerwoman's daughter who makes good. So much for movies in the story of Josephine. She realized she was not cut out for the cinema; the concert halls and music halls were her métier.

She opened the first Chez Josephine, her intimate supper club, "to give me something to do after the show."

Josephine invited Jean Gabin, with whom she had just made *Zou Zou,* to perform at Chez Josephine. To the end they were the greatest friends. They sang and danced and were together constantly. Their favorite dance song was "Dengoza," a little melody that few people recognize by the title but which almost all people recognize when they hear it. These were, as Josephine called them, "my nights of gladness."

Now, whenever I hear "Dengoza," I think of what it must have been like at the Chez Josephine.

Josephine also decided to try her wings elsewhere. She knew she was a huge success in France—but that was only one country. She wanted to see what they thought of her elsewhere.

So, early in 1933, as Roosevelt was slowly leading the United States out of the Depression, Josephine accepted an offer to sing in the Opera of Parma, Italy.

Parma, of all places. It had never occurred to her to go to Italy first. Parma was famous for its ham, and for the finest in opera. It is Parma where to this day the audience brings rotten fruits and vegetables along with its operatic scores, and woe to the tenor who sings off key!

The day after the concert, the headline was a half page high: *"Divina"*—divine. They adored her. And they did many things the Italians do best. They screamed for her; they pushed her chauffeur out of her car and drove it down the streets themselves; they carried her into their restaurants. And all the while she was on the arm of Pepe. What better? An Italian in Italy, and the lover of the Divine. That was something the Italians liked. They could appreciate that. And if one had to confess the next Saturday morning, so what?

Then they did for her what the Italians are really best at. They wept.

They wept for her in the Opera at Parma. It was only one night, and she stood on the stage where Caruso and her friend Nellie Melba had stood.

At the last minute, she decided to include her favorite song, "Haiti," in a group she wanted to do as an encore.

At the end of the concert, she came out quietly. The stage lights came down, and with only a spot on her face, she sang. She recalled years later that she sang as she had never sung before. And it must have been beautiful.

Later she recorded "Haiti." When one listens to it now, one can imagine what the Italians thought. They had not expected an opera singer, but what they heard, they seemed to like better. It was a soprano voice, filled with trills and highs and lows.

And Josephine did one further thing the Italians could appreciate: she sang from the depths of her soul. Undoubtedly she was recalling that night not long ago when she had sung this same song for a prince in a private railroad car as it sped through the Swedish winter night. She remembered that shrieking train whistle, that walk in a dark and icy ballroom when they were wrapped in sable. . . .

When she finished, tears were rolling down her cheeks. The audience was stunned. The thunder was heard around Italy and throughout the world.

It was not heard in America.

* * *

When word of her triumphant debut in Parma reached London, the managers of the Palladium sped to France to meet her.

In the summer of 1933, Josephine Baker walked onto the stage of the London Palladium. Forty years later, in 1973, she was still there, making her twentieth appearance at that theatre. She played for two weeks; the tickets sold for as much as $100 each, and there was never an empty seat.

In forty years, she played the Palladium twenty times. She also stayed at the Savoy twenty times, and always in the same suite. A Turkish prince once vacated it so that it might be available to her; even the President of Italy once moved out a day early so she could occupy it. She was now accustomed to the best. She expected it. And she could afford it.

A few Baker stories from the 1920s were still flashing around in the 1930s. Was it true that she ate plover eggs for breakfast? "Of course." Next morning the management somehow arranged to secure and serve her real plover eggs. "My God, I didn't know what they were. I thought they were little robin's eggs."

It was a love affair that lasted forty years. When she died, the managers of the Palladium displayed a photograph of her in the lobby and draped it in black.

Chapter 10

". . . but remember, Stephen, we must be careful what we write, anyway. Billie Burke is still a great star in America, and even though the story is true, and she treated me as she did, we must think about whether to write it or not. You know, I don't want any more scandal . . ."

* * *

Billie is gone. Flo is gone. Josephine is gone. When Josephine told me the Billie Burke story, Billie was still living, spending her last days in a rest home in Los Angeles. I had gone to visit Pearl Felix, who was there recovering from a broken hip, I believe, and as we were going down the hall she nodded toward a little lady sitting and staring idly at the wall. When we were out of hearing range, she said, "Billie Burke."

I could hardly believe it. The first thing that flashed into my head was *Dinner at Eight*. The second was the time Josephine told me of her horrible experience with Billie.

It is interesting to note that Pearl Felix was the wife of Seymour Felix, the brilliant choreographer and director who had staged the numbers in *The Great Ziegfeld*. His big production number in that film was a masterpiece.

When I looked at poor Billie Burke, I was reminded of Mae Murray. At that time, I believe, Mae was in the beautiful Motion Picture Country Home, and I had gone to see her several times.

One day I mentioned to Josephine that I had seen Mae Murray out at the home. She had seen *The Merry Widow* a number of times as well as several other Mae Murray films. She thought Mae was divine, and she wanted me to take her out to the Country Home to see her.

I told her that it would be best to remember Mae Murray as she had appeared on the screen. I told her about Mae's condition, that she was partly paralyzed. Josephine hated hearing it.

"Please, God," she said, "don't ever let that happen to me. You are right, Stephen. Better to remember Mae Murray in that fabulous dance number, when she did the Merry Widow Waltz."

Josephine Baker got her wish. It did not happen to her the way it happened to Billie Burke or to Mae Murray.

* * *

The first cable Josephine ever received from Florenz Ziegfeld came in the late twenties. It was an inquiry about her appearing in a future edition of the Ziegfeld Follies. She read it over and over again.

The world of the theatre and the world of politics can but wonder what would have occurred if she had thrown the cable into the wastebasket. But in those times, one did not throw cables signed "Ziegfeld" into the wastebasket.

Florenz Ziegfeld and Josephine burned up the Atlantic cable with their messages back and forth. She had never been so thrilled in her life. But she finally told him that she could not accept his offer, as she was in the middle of one of the many editions of her own Folies.

Then, later, during Josephine's greatest period, Ziegfeld was having his worst. The 1929 crash had wiped him out, and there were intimations that Billie Burke, with her outrageous spending habits, had finished what the stock market had not been able to do.

Josephine was devastated when she realized that she would not be seen in New York City and that she would not be presented by Ziegfeld. She was even more devastated when in 1932 she heard of Ziegfeld's death.

Some years passed, and one day she received another cable. The words "Ziegfeld Follies" jumped out from the cable. It was signed "John Murray Anderson." She did not know who John Murray Anderson was.

She wondered for a moment how there could be a Follies without Ziegfeld. Then she realized that the Folies Bergère had existed long before Derval and Varna, and would exist long after they were gone, and that the same would apply to the Ziegfeld Follies. Unhappily, it did not.

The Folies Bergère endured primarily because it had been in the same house for many years. It was a famous theatre. Only the Folies had ever appeared there. There was a Ziegfeld theatre, but other shows appeared there also, so it was not the same.

Again the cables and letters flew across the Atlantic. It was to be the Ziegfeld Follies of 1936, in which Josephine was to co-star with Fanny Brice and a young comedian named Bob Hope.

She had heard of Fanny Brice, of course. She had never heard of Bob Hope.

This was what Josephine had been waiting for. It was New York again. It was America, where the "real" theatre was.

To examine carefully what occurred then, and later, one must remember Josephine's unsophisticated period in 1925 and 1926, when she first went to France. For in 1935, she was still unsophisticated about the theatre in New York City, and I feel that that is where all the problems started. One cannot deny the facts or varnish them over. The shows in the Casino de Paris and the Folies Bergère were in many respects far superior to any New York shows, including Ziegfeld at his best. But they were designed for different audiences in a different country.

Josephine expected too much. She expected more from her producers than they could—or cared to—give her. She expected that in New York she would be provided with much more in the way of "production" than she had been at her debut in the Casino a few years earlier.

She really did not realize then that what she and Varna had accomplished was the "ultimate." It could not be duplicated, let alone surpassed!

There, quite simply, was the problem. Josephine never really knew how great she or her own revues were. She still looked upon New York City—and Ziegfeld—as heaven.

It was hell. The "great" Ziegfeld and the revue that carried his name were one of the greatest disappointments in her life. So was her encounter with his wife, Billie Burke.

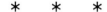

One must comprehend what Josephine was now beginning to experience in order to understand fully the uncontrolled outbursts that were to come from her in later years.

From 1935 on, she tried to keep to herself her feelings about the abuses, the slights, the insults, the abrogated contracts. But they smoldered inside her for years. When they finally exploded, it was like the bomb over Hiroshima. And Americans in particular could not understand. But regrettably, it could not be explained. Nor would anyone care to listen.

It all started on the *Normandie*. Josephine had made two prior trips to America and had met Ziegfeld on one of them. She had always hated the sea—and for good reason. That she occupied the Suite Grand Luxe made not the slightest difference. She was violently ill from the moment the *Normandie* hit the breakwater at Le Havre.

At Le Havre she embarked, the real star. It was Vuitton luggage, and suitcases, and hatboxes, and jewel cases, and it was dogs and a cat, and a private maid. Why not? She was a star.

The *Normandie* was the pride of France and the pride of its designers. It was art deco from its upper mast to its keel. It was *haut monde*. It was class. It was sophistication. It was something.

It was Josephine Baker.

One must remember all this when analyzing what happened on the second night out.

* * *

Billie Burke was a great star, there is no doubt. More important, she was an established MGM star, and that, perhaps, made her even greater. "Billie Burke," said Josephine, "was no lady."

Billie Burke was a passenger on that voyage on the *Normandie*. She would have known that Josephine was on the ship. She must have known also that Josephine was on her way to New York City to appear in a revue bearing her husband's name. She could not have known otherwise; it was actually Billie Burke who presented that revue. "Mrs. Florenz Ziegfeld presents the Ziegfeld Follies of 1936," the program stated.

Josephine and Billie Burke had never met.

"The first time Ziegfeld saw me," Josephine said later, "he thought I was sensational. He had remembered me from *In Bamville,* and had seen me shortly after I became a great hit in the Folies Bergère. When I saw him in New York City that time, I spent a great deal of time with him. Maybe Billie Burke thought I was having an affair with him. Believe me, I certainly was not. If I were, I wouldn't have minded saying so. I never knew if she was jealous of me, or because I was a colored woman. Not many people can get to me. Really get inside of me. I've got a pretty tough hide, but she sure did get to me. I'll never forget it."

Perhaps they should have gone first to Billie Burke. But one can understand their natural inclination toward Josephine. The incident began when the purser of the *Normandie* telephoned Josephine in her suite and informed her that he was making table arrangements for that evening. Josephine knew that Billie Burke was aboard, and she wanted to meet her. She asked to sit at a small, inconspicuous table, and requested the purser to invite Miss Burke to join her.

She had not wanted to go to the dining room: she was still feeling seasick. But she managed to get up. She felt she must pay her respects to the wife of Ziegfeld. After all, she *was* Mrs. Florenz Ziegfeld.

Josephine dressed in a silk chiffon gown by Erté. It was her favorite color—pale lemon—and had a million tiny pleats. She wore her emeralds. And when she walked down that long staircase into the *grande salle à manger,* it must have been something.

The whole room, led by the captain, rose and applauded.

Unfortunately, the purser had not been able to reach Miss Burke to extend Josephine's invitation. He assumed she would automatically accept.

Within a few minutes, the great American movie star, the wife of New York City's greatest producer, walked down the same steps, smiling graciously. The whole dining salon, including Josephine, rose to applaud her. She must have loved the admiring glances, for she could hold her own in the jewelry department. It was her taste for expensive jewelry, they said, that had helped to bankrupt Ziegfeld.

The steward started leading her to Josephine's table. The entire room sat down and watched her. Josephine remained standing.

The steward stopped at the table and pulled out a chair.

I very rarely heard Josephine use the word "nigger." She sang it in songs, but I do not believe I heard her use the term in conversation more than a half dozen times. In relating this incident to me, however, she said:

"Billie Burke just glared at me for a moment. I knew then she was a real nigger-hater."

Billie Burke gave Josephine Baker an icy stare, brushed past the steward, past the captain's table, and marched out of the dining salon. The passengers were stunned.

Josephine took the blow with dignity. She finished her solitary dinner, then rose to leave the dining hall. The entire room rose with her, watching her in silence as she walked toward the great staircase. At the foot of the stairs, however, she suddenly turned and flashed the famous Baker smile on them. They burst into cheers.

* * *

Josephine arrived in New York. She was not met.

If the Billie Burke snub on the *Normandie* was the little flame that lit the fires inside Josephine that were to smolder there for years, the next incident added fuel to those fires.

Josephine left the French Line dock alone. She needed three cabs to help her carry the nearly one hundred pieces of luggage she had brought with her. Even then, most of them were left on the dock for the transfer lines to haul in.

She made for the Waldorf Astoria Hotel. When she emerged from the cab, she marched straight to the desk. She was dressed in an outfit by Balenciaga. There could not have been a more chic woman in all of New York City.

"Hello, I'm Josephine Baker."

The desk clerk could only stare. Finally he said, "But, Miss Baker, we have no reservation for you."

Blow number two.

What Josephine did not know at the time was that when Ziegfeld's managers attempted to arrange a suite for her at the Waldorf, they were told there were no accommodations. They were told the same at the Hotel Plaza, and they were told the same at the Essex House.

The managers knew what the problem was—as would have any black living in America at that time. *But Josephine did not understand.*

She telephoned the Ziegfeld offices from the lobby of the Waldorf. In the meantime, the bell captain had brought in all of her luggage.

For the second time in a few days she swept grandly and quietly out of a problem. Years later she would not do so.

She accepted what they found for her: a small private hotel in the upper Sixties.

* * *

When Josephine had been engaged, she had been promised co-star billing. When she arrived at the Ziegfeld theater, she saw on the marquee:

FANNY BRICE
in
ZIEGFELD FOLLIES OF 1936
with
BOB HOPE & JOSEPHINE BAKER

Slightly different. It was truly an abrogated contract. And by the heirs of Ziegfeld, no less. Perhaps that is why in later years she never hesitated to violate a contract after she signed it, if she thought it would be to her advantage.

Josephine made many mistakes. But, on examination, were they really mistakes? She wanted so much to please everyone. She thought that, since it was a Ziegfeld show, it naturally had to be better than anything she had ever been in, even though Ziegfeld was now gone.

She also thought that everyone in a show of this stature would be pleasant. She expected "a big happy family, like in France." She was doomed to disappointment. When she presented her thoughts and ideas, they were rejected.

Her next blow came at the door of Fanny Brice's dressing room. Josephine had never met her. She knew she was a great American star. "What I didn't know," she said later, "was that Fanny Brice was also a bitch."

When Fanny was told of Josephine's desire to meet her, she snapped, "Tell the kid I'll see her later. I'm busy now."

Josephine had come five thousand miles to be told she would be seen later.

Then, as she crossed the stage, she asked the stage manager where Bob Hope's dressing room was. He happened to be on stage rehearsing at the time. She sat in the front row watching and smiling.

Bob Hope ignored her during the entire dismal run. On his first rehearsal break, when the crew and stagehands walked down to the first row to greet her, he didn't take the four steps down. He stood on the stage and merely said, "Hi, how you doin'?" If it was an unintentional slight, it was still rude. She made no comment.

In 1973, in Los Angeles, California, Josephine Baker made a triumphant appearance at the Ahmanson Theatre of the Music Center. On her final night, two thousand people were turned away, and they waited outside for her to emerge from the theatre. We had to drive my car onto the loading dock and put her into it so we could get her through the crowds. By chance, on that same night, Frank Sinatra and Bob Hope were appearing in a special benefit at the Pavilion Theatre, which was next door to the Ahmanson. Less than a stone's throw.

Josephine wrote Bob Hope a note, which I personally carried over to the Pavilion.

> Dear Bob: Hasn't it been a long time? Would love to see you. Can I sneak over there or can you come over? From your tired old friend from the Ziegfeld days,
>
> Josephine Baker

Bob Hope never sent word, nor did he come over. Maybe he saw the cheering mobs backstage waiting for Josephine. For the Sinatra and Hope show, the theatre had been only half full.

* * *

Another mistake that Josephine made was again unintentional—indeed, on reflection, how could it be called a mistake? Under the impression that she was to provide her own wardrobe for the Follies, she came loaded for bear. There were gowns by Erté, Balenciaga, Dior. There were silks and prints and furs and jewels. It was all, of course, Josephine Baker "stuff."

Now comes another incident in the life of Josephine Baker which is a little difficult to figure out. But that was Josephine—and her life.

"You know," Josephine said, "I adored Vincente and George [Minnelli and Balanchine]. They were the only ones who were pleasant to me. They helped me keep my sanity."

During her last appearances in the United States, and also in her last appearances in the Bobino in Paris, she spoke glowingly of Minnelli, Balanchine, Brice, and Hope. If one listens to that recording made at the Bobino, they will hear her: "*Addio senza Rancore*"—"Farewell without Bitterness."

One day, as Josephine sat in the theatre, someone approached her with some costume sketches.

It will probably never be known whether these sketches were the work of Minnelli or someone else. It is difficult to believe that Minnelli would have created such poor material for Josephine. I am sure he must have adored her.

She was stunned by what they showed her. They were vulgar and unattractive, and could not begin to compare with her own wardrobe. One costume in particular can still be seen in old photos. It is a copy of the banana costume—only it consists of what seems to be carrots sticking out. Definitely third-rate.

She could not make them understand that her banana days were over. She did not have the same muscle in America. She acquiesced. She cooperated. She made a terrible mistake.

She was put into a sketch—in her "banana" costume—in which she sang a song called "Island in the West Indies." It is regrettable that Josephine compromised herself. The Ziegfeld staff convinced her that they were right and she was wrong.

In desperation, her French maid brought Josephine's own wardrobe to the theatre to show them. Unbelievably, the Follies designers asserted that their costume ideas were superior to Josephine's wardrobe. They "pooh-poohed my Paris gowns." And she never forgot Fanny Brice's remark: "If you want to wear that, go to Minsky's."

The Ziegfeld Follies of 1936 was a disastrous show. Josephine, in her *real* American debut, was even more of a disaster. She had compromised herself. "I'm surprised they didn't make me tap-dance; they made me do everything else."

She was dismissed by the dean of American critics, Brooks Atkinson, who called her "a squeak in the dark." The arrow was not lost when he let it loose. It hit home.

* * *

Josephine returned to France, greatly disillusioned. Her dream of being a real American star would never become reality. Not until long afterward did she begin to realize that she was already a great star, that stars could be made in other places besides America.

As Josephine thought about her experiences in America—the scenes with Billie Burke and at the Waldorf, Fanny Brice's comments—their significance began to come home to her. She wondered why the blacks in America stayed there. Why didn't they leave?

But how could they? How many openings were there for black stars in Europe? She also thought, My God, if they did this to me, what must they do to other colored people who are *really* nobodies . . . if anybody can be a nobody?

She began to think about this more and more, and her thoughts fanned her fires. Years later, when the blaze began to rage, not everyone could understand why. It is regrettable that Josephine did not take the time to explain it to them. She could have. She did not.

I wanted her to. She brushed me off. By then it was too late; she felt she didn't have time to explain.

She wanted to right all the wrongs in a day. But not even Josephine Baker could do that.

Chapter 11

"... You know, I zipped and turned, and I swooped up and down.... I had that little Farman plane do everything but stand on its nose. I was looking out over the side of the cockpit, and I could see all the little farmers way below looking up at me. Then I didn't care; I just made a big pass over the Versailles Palace. I made the engines roar, and I could see them running out. They had just finished the restoration work on the Salle des Glaces ... and I thought, Boy, would they be mad if I crashed this thing into their Hall of Mirrors ..."

* * *

At Christmastime in 1933, Josephine Baker took her first airplane flight. She loved it.

"I wasn't a bit afraid. It was like I was just floating up there in the sky. Richard Tauber, the famous singer, was on that little plane too. We were going to Copenhagen, where I was going to do some concerts. We sat next to each other—it was his first flight too—and we kept marveling about how advanced science was. I said to him that it probably wouldn't be long before we would be flying to New York and places overseas. He said it could never happen because you could only build a plane so big. If you built them too big, they would be too heavy and would not be able to get off the ground. Neither one of us ever dreamed that not too much later we would be traveling in those huge planes back and forth across the world."

The Associated Press carried the story that Josephine Baker and Richard Tauber had just landed at Copenhagen Airport. The article stated:

> Two world-famous artists, Richard Tauber and Josephine Baker, arrived in the same aeroplane at Copenhagen, to give *individual* recitals, however.

"When I read that story the next day, I laughed. Did they think Tauber and I would be in the same show?"

The important thing was that now she was becoming recognized as a "world-famous artist." But no papers in the United States carried the story. It is doubtful that even the editors knew who Josephine Baker was.

"Traveling by air was very expensive in those days. I was with The Sixteen Baker Boys—they were my own jazz band, and boy, could they blow! I even offered to buy their tickets on the plane so they could have the same thrill that I had, but they were afraid. They ended up going by train. I wasn't afraid of anything in those days—and I guess I'm still not afraid of anything."

Soon after her return from "that dismal failure," as she referred to her Ziegfeld Follies debacle, Josephine became restless and bored. She needed to throw herself into something.

There were three things she immediately threw herself into: the first was aviation; the second, motion pictures; and the third, houses.

Of the three, she had the greatest success with her flying experiences. She had little luck with her motion-picture career. And her third passion—houses and homes and their decor—would lead ultimately to her downfall and to her bankruptcy.

"When I got back from New York, I was so bored I just didn't know what to do. Then one day I was reading in the paper about a school that had opened up and was going to be giving flying lessons. I thought, Gee, that sounds like a lot of fun.

"Now, you have to remember that by then I was a pretty big star, and when I went into a show, a lot was riding on me. In those days they didn't have insurance on stars like they do now; and if something happened and I couldn't make it to a performance, they just closed for the night.

"I remember one time that Varna saw one of my hot boyfriends bringing me to the theatre on a motorcycle. I loved it when he revved up that engine, and he would screech to a halt in front of the stage door. Varna would go white.

" 'Josephine,' he would say, 'what will happen to me if you break a leg with this kind of foolishness?'

" 'You'll become even richer than you are now, Henri,' I would tell him, ' 'cause all Paris will come to see Josephine do the Charleston with a cast on her leg.'

"Poor Henri could only shake his head. I didn't care, though. I was still crazy. I guess I didn't really start growing up until after the war. You know, it really was bad for them, because with Josephine Baker, there just was no understudy—after all, how could there be? I was not playing any parts—I was playing *me*.

"But that day I got on the phone to those people who were running that flying school, and I asked them about lessons. They wanted to know if the lessons were for my son or my husband. I laughed. At the time I didn't have any husband, and I certainly did not have a son, and so I said, 'But of course not, Monsieur, the lessons are for me.' He was dumfounded. He didn't say anything for a long time. Of course, he did not know who he was talking to yet. So he said, '*Pardon, Mademoiselle, est-ce qu'un homme? Est-ce q'une femme?*' [Are you a man? Are you a woman?] You know, I dropped the phone, laughing. I just couldn't stop for a long time. That, of course, was what the French had been saying about me for a long time, and he still didn't know who I was.

"Finally I just said, 'Monsieur, this is Josephine!'

" 'Ah, Josephine! *Merde alors!*'

"Well, I fell down again on the floor, and this time I thought I would never get up. That man was so funny. It turned out he was some big executive with the Farman Company, and they wanted people to learn how to fly so they would be able to sell more planes.

"When he recovered, he offered to teach me himself, and said if I would let them take a picture of me in their plane I could have the lessons for nothing. I jumped at the chance. Later Henri [Varna] said I was a fool. If I had held out, they probably would have given me a million francs for the endorsement of the plane. But I didn't care.

"I was the first woman they had ever taught to fly. It was something. They had a field out behind the Versailles Palace. I would jump into my car and go racing over there and spend the entire afternoon flying. Boy, did I love that! How I wish I had kept it up; maybe I could still have been doing it. 'Cause that was the only time I felt really free, when I was up there alone in that plane.

"Nowadays when the pilots of Air France know I'm on the plane, and if they are old enough, they remember about my flying scandals. They would invite me up in the cockpit of those big new planes. Well, when I learned, it was only a little stick between your legs, and that plane would do anything. Now you have to be a genius.

"When I did my first solo flight, I did everything. I zipped and turned, and I swooped up and down. I had that little Farman plane do everything but stand on its nose. I was looking out over the side of the cockpit, and I could see all the little farmers way below looking up at me. Then I didn't care; I just made a big pass over the Versailles Palace. I made the engines roar, and I could see them running out. They had just finished the restoration work on the Salle des Glaces, and I thought, Boy, would they be mad if I crashed this thing into their Hall of Mirrors.

"As long as they were looking I decided I'd give them a good one. I went in for one long nose dive, and they all ran for cover. They thought for sure I would land in one of old Louis' [Louis XIV] fountains, or even

Josephine, about 1942. Believed to be in a uniform of the Ladies' Auxiliary of the French Air Force. It was not long afterward that she stopped wearing the uniform, as she became heavily involved in the underground and did not want to attract attention to herself.

Profondément touchée de la marque de sympathie que vous m'avez témoignée à l'occasion de la remise de ma Légion d'Honneur, je vous exprime ici mes très sincères remerciements et vous prie d'accepter mes amicales pensées.

(Right) The Music Room, Château des Milandes. It was here that Mama, Margaret, Elmo and the author sat, when Josephine and Benny rolled up the carpet and did "Bake That Chicken Pie," a long way from the Memphis Theater, where she first performed it publicly.

(Below) The Château des Milandes, Castlenaud-Fayrac, Dordogne, France. A view from the Park. It sits on 600 acres. Josephine completely restored the Château, which was to be her home of International Brotherhood, an experiment that cost her both her fortune and her health.

(Below right) Josephine's bedroom in the Château, and the famous bed of Marie Antoinette. Whenever she was at the Château most of her business was done in this bedroom. It was here that the constant wrangles with her accountants took place. The Virgins on either side of the bed were a gift from the President of Mexico.

The dining room of Château des Milandes. On the table is a Chantilly lace cloth. The sterling candelabra had been a gift from the Czar to the Varna family prior to the revolution. Varna gave them to Josephine as a housewarming gift. They (among other things) were snatched from the table during her battle with creditors. There were two more matching tables and 24 more chairs for really large dinner parties.

Le Grand Salon. At Christmastime great logs burned 24 hours a day in the massive fireplace. In the Vitrine on the far right were the Faberge music boxes and the really rare jade. All were lost during the rampage of creditors through the house. "When they were dragging me through the salon during the eviction, I looked down and some thief had dropped one of my beautiful Faberge Easter eggs. It was smashed in a thousand pieces. Those thugs didn't even know its value, and do you know, about a year later, I was walking down the street in Paris, and I looked into an antique shop, and I saw my beautiful little music box that played 'J'ai Deux Amours.' . . . Talk about sadness . . . no one should ever go through what I have in my life."

(At left) Jo and Joe—Jo and Josephine—in happier times with some of the Rainbow Children at Milandes. Josephine is holding Marianne, then the only daughter. In the background is a portion of the great Château.

LES MILANDES

JE VOUS ENVOIE MES VŒUX LES PLUS SINCERES POUR CETTE NOUVELLE ANNEE, AINSI QUE CEUX DE MES ENFANTS.

L.A. Sentinel

(At left) Late 1950s. The "pony tail" period gave way to the "Oriental" look. The headdresses now began covering the rapidly receding hairline. In this outfit, the chiffon cape matched the scenery and was attached to it. At the end of the number, it was flown out and became a part of the set itself.

(Below) During the bad period just after the loss of all properties. Her costumes had now been put together from many others she had previously used. Here the foxes were put on an older white velvet. However, even during the extremely bad period, they were still quite spectacular.

(At right) About 1959, in Paris at the Olympia Music Hall. The show was "Paris Mon Amour." She closed the show to return to America. This was just prior to the arrest in Canada. This same revue was reopened in the early 1960s, again very successfully.

(Below) Josephine ". . . during what I called my pink period . . ." Pink foxes, pink satin, pink tulle gown, pink gloves, etc. Josephine designed this outfit herself. While of course striking, it was no match for some of those designed by professionals.

Muchin-Havana

(At left) Josephine at the beginning of her famous "pony tail" period. This photograph was made during a Cuban engagement. This look was soon to evolve into the "Oriental" period.

(Below) The late 1950s. Experimenting with the lips, she gave up the hot red, but only temporarily. Here she was outlining the pale shades then in vogue. It was soon back to the hot red slashed mouth. "In the twenties I thought I might have mine (her lips) tattooed red — but they told me it would hurt, so I changed my mind." A good story, true or not.

"Don't you think I look a lot like Rosalind Russell?" One of her favorite films was *Auntie Mame*. She had badly wanted to do the French version on the stage, but it did not happen. This photo, made in Italy, shows her with a large microphone, which she hated. "Why, my face is so little, you can't see me." She preferred the slender mikes that she covered with her jeweled casings.

in his house. I came out of it, though. It was crazy, sure, but as I said, I was *still* crazy. I didn't really grow up until after the war, and if I think about it, maybe I haven't grown up yet."

Josephine's love affair with airplanes and flying never diminished. She always looked forward to a journey by air. It bothered her not at all to finish a performance at 11 P.M., arrive at an airport at midnight, and be on an overseas flight to some distant country by one in the morning.

* * *

Shifting her attention from her first love, the legitimate theatre, Josephine began to make a try for "one really big picture."

She had flirted with the medium a little in the twenties and in the early thirties. "But you know," she said, "I just couldn't get into films. I would go and see one film after another. And I studied those stars and would try to figure out how I could do something better than they could. Then when talkies came in, I started all over again trying to do the same thing.

"I still had my big cheetah, and I would even take him to the movies with me. At first it caused a sensation, but then they got used to it. He would just jump into a seat beside me. If he fell asleep, I knew the picture was no good, and we would leave. He liked those jungle pictures best, and when those drums started going he would put his big paws on the back of the seat in front of him and just stare straight ahead. He loved those films."

The cheetah's theatre-going career came to an abrupt end when Josephine decided that if he liked films so much, he would surely love the theatre and even the opera. She took him to a performance of *Aida* at the famous Paris Opéra, thinking he might "feel at home in that scenario." But apparently he hated *Aida;* he jumped into the pit and mauled the conductor, thus bringing the performance to a sudden halt. Thereafter no theatre would allow Josephine to bring him inside.

"Oh, it was terrible. He really cried for a long time. Then I thought that maybe he needed a wife, and I called the zoo, and we found one for him. He was crazy about her, and they had all kinds of babies, and after that he never wanted to come home with me anymore. So I just left him there, and I would go see him every once in a while. He always remembered me, too. He just loved showing me his little family.

"But you know, movies were never for me, I decided. One time I went, and I'll bet I saw Mae Murray and *The Merry Widow* twenty-five times. I tried to imitate her in one of my films. That was a silly move; it wasn't Josephine, and it wasn't Mae Murray. The director thought I was acting crazy.

"I liked *Zou Zou;* I thought I looked good in that picture. But you know, my voice was so funny. I would say the words in the right way, but when they came out they would sound different.

"I had made *Tam Tam,* and I didn't like that, and *La Sirène des Tropiques.* Then, when I made *Zou Zou,* they advertised that 'Baker Talks.' They got that from MGM and Garbo—'Garbo Talks.' Boy, did I talk, and some newspaper took the dialogue the way I said it and twisted it just a little, and made it sound like I was saying obscene things.

"I just couldn't make it in the cinema, no matter how hard I tried. They gave me the best directors, too.

"The best thing I ever got out of films was meeting Jean Gabin. I liked him very much, and still do. He would come to my club in the Montmartre, and we would dance. He was the best dancer I ever worked with. He could take my body and make it do anything. Yes, that was the best thing I ever got out of films.

"When they do my life story, they won't have to worry too much about putting anything in there about films, 'cause that was the one place where Josephine fell flat. But that's all right, isn't it? Everybody has a place. Some stars are Broadway stars, and some are film stars, and some are recording stars. I happen to be a stage star. I'm at my best on a stage or in a night club. So there is nothing wrong with my never making it in films."

* * *

Although Josephine had failed in Hollywood, France, of course, welcomed her with open arms, and she went immediately into a new revue at the Casino de Paris. Varna and Josephine had been dickering a little; her terms were getting stiffer. Varna had thought to "show her," as she said, that he did not need her, and he had engaged Cecile Sorel for one of the revues. Josephine couldn't have cared less.

It was the same many years later when Darryl Zanuck decided he was going to teach Marilyn Monroe a lesson by engaging Sheree North as "competition." That didn't work either. But had Zanuck and Fox Studios put the time and effort into Sheree North that they did into Monroe, she undoubtedly would have become something. Sidney Skolsky once wrote that the worst thing that ever happened to North was that Monroe came back.

Stiff terms or no, Varna engaged her again for the Casino de Paris. And on and on it went during the 1930s.

"One of my favorite shows at that time was when I did *La Creole.* That was the Offenbach operetta. It was beautiful, and the critics raved about me. I was another person. That person I could relate to on the stage as I could not relate to characters in films. I don't know why. It just seems to be that way."

Now Josephine threw herself with wild abandon into several new projects. She joined the Red Cross Aid Program for the Poor and spent hours on end working for them. She threw herself into the Offenbach operetta, and she threw herself into her first *real* marriage. It might be mentioned that she did it in that order.

She also opened a second Chez Josephine. "It was so much better than the first one," she said. "It had a floor that was made of glass. Not clear glass, mind you, but sort of foggy, like it was Lalique or something. And it had about ten glass steps going down to it, and I had them put colored lights underneath the solid glass steps and under the glass dance floor. We could make it red or green or amber, and change slowly from one color to another just like in a theatre. You know, I think I must have invented that idea, if you can call it an invention.

"Then, when I would dance, and the orchestra would play certain songs, I had the electricians cued, and they would do certain lighting effects when I danced certain songs.

"When we would do 'Dengoza,' Jean and I, it would start as a pale lavender and go through reds and blues. And when we got to the hot part, the chorus—it was like a tango—it would go all red.

"I used to work all day rehearsing or doing a picture or something or maybe flying a little, then I would go and do my revue at night; and believe it or not, I would dance till two or three in the morning and be up before eight the next day and do it all over again. Sometimes I wonder why I didn't just drop."

Then Josephine would just stare at the ceiling or at the canopy over her bed, and you knew that she was reliving those moments. When she told of the "glass floor" she had "invented," you couldn't help but believe her.

"I even showed the waiters in France how to pour champagne. I learned that up in Harlem, and I learned it good. If you take up the bottle real fast and act as if you are going to pour another drink, when you get to the host you tilt the bottle up only part way and quickly put the towel around it and act like it's empty. Then the host is of course embarrassed and orders again.

"When you get good at it—and I really trained them—at least a third of a bottle of champagne would go back to the kitchen. Then they would be filled up again with house champagne, and we had a machine that recorked them so that when the waiter brought them out again, it looked like it had just come out of an ice chest. That's another little trick I taught those French night-club operators. Nobody ever got a fair shake in a French night club, and they still don't. But it is no different anywhere else in the world, is it?"

* * *

In the late thirties, Josephine made her first tour to Latin America. She played Buenos Aires, Rio de Janeiro, and Bogota, and ended up in Mexico City.

There is little doubt that Spain, Latin America, and particularly Mexico, adored and loved Josephine. When she died, *Hola,* the Spanish picture magazine, devoted sixteen pages to her funeral alone.

If the Latin American tour could be termed a success, one wonders how to describe her reception in Mexico City. They had never seen anyone or anything like Josephine. She sang to them in *their* language, and she sang from the heart.

Then she did something that had never been done before: she gave a benefit performance in the Grand Plaza de Toros. There were eighty thousand seats in the bullring, of which she reserved ten thousand for the rich—at 100 pesos per seat, an unheard of sum which they nevertheless paid gladly. The remaining seventy thousand seats she gave to the poor of Mexico. For many it was their first and last theatrical adventure until Cantinflas emulated her gesture years later.

Josephine donated the proceeds of the concert to the Mexican Red Cross. And at the end of the concert she fought a baby bull. As the victor, she hopped on his back and rode him out of the bullring. Some exit! The Mexicans went wild.

They gave her the bull, which she sent to a ranch in Morelos, with instructions for its care and money for its keep. She never failed to pay El Toro a visit when in Mexico. Happily, when he died some twenty years later, it was because of love and obesity. To my knowledge, she had never attended a bullfight.

* * *

On her return to Paris, Josephine threw herself into yet another project: her new townhouse. She conferred with Frank Lloyd Wright during his visit to Paris. He accompanied her when she bought a "shell," as she called it, an old house which had been gutted. The inside was then reconstructed to her specifications. It turned out to be some house. However, she never talked about it much. Perhaps houses were too painful a subject for her.

I do, however, remember her once describing her bath—a solid block of onyx. It took a hundred gallons of water to warm it up; then it was drained, and another hundred gallons were added to it for her bath. What a job for the personal maid!

The dining salon seated thirty for sit-down dinners. The house also had a "summer and winter kitchen"; I was never able to figure out what that meant. The entrance hall was five stories high and ran through the house from top to bottom. The house also had one of the few private elevators in Paris at the time. Josephine was spending money!

But that elevator was to cause her a great deal of grief in the years ahead.

While the house was being built, the boots of Germany were marching across Poland. It was not long before those same boots marched up the

Champs Elysées, where Josephine had once walked Sheik the panther and Ethel the chimpanzee. They finally marched to the Arc de Triomphe.

Then Hitler himself arrived. He danced his jig in front of the Eiffel Tower. He demanded the Elysées Palace for his Paris home and received it. Other high Nazis demanded or took what they wanted.

Hermann Goering took Josephine's townhouse, primarily because of its elevator. He hated steps.

* * *

"One day the strangest thing happened to me in that house—like it had happened to me before outside the theatre in East St. Louis. Something just kept telling me to go upstairs.

"The maids lived on the fifth or sixth floor—I don't remember which—and so did the butler and his wife. I got along real well with those maids. They did their job, and they did it well. Because I had showed them how. For you know, I can still wash and iron and clean, and even cook.

"But that day I went up there, and I hadn't been up there for a long time. Now, it was on that floor that I had stored all my costumes from all those years. It was almost fifteen years of costumes, I guess, from all my shows. The banana costume in all its different versions, and all my beautiful gowns, and my hats and headdresses. In my contracts I always stipulated that the wardrobe belonged to me, and later I would change, or add something, or take something off, and use the same ones in my clubs and appearances around the world.

"I opened those closet doors, and I can tell you there must have been five hundred different costumes from everything I had done. Also, there were the gowns I didn't wear much anymore. Those things Erté did for me, and poor Poiret, and other beautiful gowns.

"I don't know why I did all that. I just started going through them. Then I came to the huge closet for my furs, I think you call it cedar—yes, like a cedar chest. [In her later years, Josephine thought so much in the French language that she forgot little words and expressions in English that come naturally to Americans.]

"And I want to tell you I had *some* furs, too. I had sables, and floor-length chinchillas, and foxes. I had beaver coats and shawls and wraps. And in there also were the fur trimmings from my costumes. All I had to do was take a black chiffon gown out of my closet, and if I didn't think it was right for that night, I would call my personal maid and tell her to go up to the fur vault and bring down a big black fox. Then she would tack it on the bottom of a gown, and it would become important almost instantly.

"But I just kept moseying around up there, not really knowing why. Now, in the back of the fur vault was another room, but nobody except my private maid and the butler knew about it. You moved back a panel by pushing a button, and there was a steel door, and that was the vault I used for my jewels and my really good things.

"It was a heavy steel door, just like a safe. It had a combination and keys. Something told me to go down to my room and get the keys, and I did. I pushed the button, and the panel moved back, and I worked the combination and opened the door with my keys. I hadn't been up there for a long time, and I looked around, and everything seemed to be in order. It was all there, it seemed.

"I had a Vuitton trunk that had little drawers lined with maroon velvet. It was a huge jewel case. It was designed so that it could fit into a stateroom on a ship or in a compartment on a train, and I took the keys and opened that, and everything there was okay too.

"And I thought, Now, what in the world is bothering me? So I started looking around real good. I checked all the silver plate I had, and the gold plate—and you know that I had plenty, because for fifteen years I had been buying it myself, and people had been giving it to me.

"I checked my beautiful Sèvres porcelains, and they were okay. I had a dinner and crystal service by Sèvres for two hundred people, Yes, *two hundred people!* And can you imagine, as a little girl we used to eat on the ironing board.

"I also had two or three sets of silver flat diningware by Tiffany. It was even in trunks. There was every imaginable kind of piece, for in those days people ate differently. There were three or four different kinds of soup spoons, and even two or three different kinds of dessert spoons, and you can't imagine what else in those trunks.

"I even opened some drawers and found a collection of silver-and-gold lighters and cigarette holders that were worth a fortune—and I didn't even smoke.

"And as I was doing this, I was saying to myself, 'My God, Josephine, *you are worth a fortune!* You had better watch this stuff more carefully.' Then I said it to myself again, and this time it hit me: it wasn't me talking; it was somebody else. 'My God, Josephine, you are worth a fortune, you had better watch this stuff more carefully.'

"Of course, then it did hit me. It was that *voice,* warning me that the war was coming and that I might have to be leaving Paris.

"You know, too, it warned me when I bought the Milandes. That time I ignored it. What a shame. Ignoring that voice cost me the Milandes and my fortune, and almost my life. And because I ignored it, that voice has never again come to warn me.

"That very day I called my butler and my personal maid. I told them what we must do. They could not believe me. They thought I was crazy or something.

"We packed everything I had. All my beautiful wardrobe. We packed the silver, and the porcelains, and the best furs, and the little things like the cigarette boxes and holders. I packed all the china in great boxes and crates, and in less than a week that room was empty. I had friends all over France and in England and in Switzerland. I sent some here and there and everywhere.

"Then the next morning I made a reservation on the train to Switzerland. I didn't want to be seen carrying any boxes that had to go through customs, for I didn't want anybody to know that I was moving my things out of France. It would not have been good. I covered my arms with my diamond bracelets, and they went up one arm and down the other, and around my waist, and I did the same to my maid. Then, when we left for the station, we put on heavy coats and suits, and when we went through customs they examined only our little bags.

"The next day I went to the bank and deposited all my jewelry there in private vaults, and so when the end of the war came I still had everything. They got only my house, which they had destroyed. Many people lost their entire fortunes.

"Unfortunately, because I didn't pay any attention to that little voice, I eventually lost it all, anyway. But at least the Germans didn't get it. I would never have believed, of course, that the *French* would.

"The only thing I lost were my paintings and sketches. Picasso had given me so much. And I had enough Klees to cover a wall. But that was lost in the fire that destroyed the house—or, I don't know, maybe Goering had it all sent to Germany. To this day I have never found them."

* * *

Hermann Goering spent more time in the green onyx bath than Josephine had. When she returned after the war, years later, she found the house gutted. She walked away from it and never returned.

Josephine Baker hated the Germans. She tried to think of what she could do for France—for *her* country; in 1937 she had become a French citizen.

Chapter 12

"While our boys were over there stopping bullets, Jose-Phony Baker *was living it up, making oodles of dough in Paris, wining and dining the Nazis and Mussolini's bigwig generals. Now she's over here trying the same thing with her pinko stories and trying to make a comeback and take our American dollars back to France to support her commie causes."*

* * *

This was journalism at its worst, by one of the most popular commentators on world events of the time. It was Walter Winchell speaking on the radio.

It is true, of course, that Josephine was in Paris during the war, entertaining Nazi and Italian generals. But there was a reason. Much later, those close to Josephine, including myself, were furious with her for never coming forward to defend herself against these scurrilous attacks. She would only brush them off, saying, "Why, they're so outrageous that I would not even acknowledge them, let alone try to defend myself against them. The man is obviously mad."

Unfortunately, millions of Americans did not think that Walter Winchell was mad. They believed him.

Arthur Garfield Hayes was one of the most prestigious attorneys in the United States. At the time, he too was outraged by the remarks. He insisted that Josephine return to the United States immediately, emphatically deny all the remarks and charges, and institute a major lawsuit for damages against Walter Winchell and the newspapers that carried his column.

She did not think it worth the effort. She was now beginning to be deeply involved in "*l'affaire Milandes,*" as she called it.

"Everybody knows it's not the truth." Unfortunately, "everybody" did *not* know.

* * *

"There's a lot to talk about, when we write my record of the war years. I keep telling you and everybody that my life should be done in three parts. But you and nobody else seem to want to think about that. Listen here. First my life in the theatre. Then my life as a humanitarian. God, Stephen, even you know that President Tito has made the statement that I am one of the world's greatest humanitarians, and it is true. And what about the other things I am doing? Before I forget, you must go to Zsa Zsa again and talk about that school in Yugoslavia. And then I want you to come there with her, and we will be there together. President Tito has given me this fabulous little island for my school, and as I have told you, Zsa Zsa is the only person in America who really wants to help me."

Josephine was talking to me on the telephone from New York City. I was in Peoria, Illinois, visiting my mother and father, both Yugoslavs. Suddenly, Josephine insisted on saying something to my parents.

"*Kaka ste vi,* Mr. Papich?"

"*Dobro, dobro.*"

She was incredible—even beginning, at her age, to learn smatterings of the Croatian language. They talked of Yugoslavia for a time, and my father told me that he grew up not far from the very island that Tito had given her.

"Now," Josephine continued, "that is the humanitarian part, and you know there are thousands of other stories, too. When they wanted to cut the ribbon, opening the bridge across the Bosporus, they called me and Danny Kaye. So there is a great book there, too.

"Now, about the war years. Let us proceed very slowly. That will be the last chapter we will do for the book. Because, you see, I must proceed slowly, and when the time is just right I will go to the proper people and see that we get the necessary permissions to reveal the whole story. But we must be very careful, as always. There is a great deal I know, and I must not under any circumstances reveal anything without proper authority. In addition to the microfilm tapes that you already know about, there is another incident which will astound the world. Perhaps someday the Americans will really know what Josephine did for them. Why do you think that President Kennedy and the attorney general [Robert Kennedy] made arrangements for me to be allowed immediately into the country when the immigration officials forbade it? Because, you see, they know about me and what I was able to accomplish.

"The real story has not been written as yet. Those books about the war stories that are now being published are kid stuff. Believe me. Why do you think they [the Germans] wanted to kill me? I was important, and I was doing important things, and they knew it."

Unfortunately, I was never told the "big stuff," as she called it. I heard only what she called the "kid stuff." Undeniably, she knew a great many people. And too little has been written about her compatriots.

* * *

100,000 FRANCS REWARD

> Following the decree establishing the death penalty for all those who associate with, or in any manner or way function with, the anti-German group calling themselves the Maquis, or any who hide English soldiers, or members of the so-called Maquis, the German High Command announces that it will pay a 100,000 francs reward to any person or persons providing names and addresses of those engaged in this criminal activity.
>
> The German High Command will also pay the sum of 100,000 francs to any person or persons providing information as to the whereabouts of any of the following persons who are known to be collaborators with the so-called Resistance Movement.

There followed a list of about three hundred persons. Under the Bs was included, "Baker, Josephine."

It is interesting to note that no one came forward to collect any rewards.

* * *

Josephine Baker was a Maquisard—a member of the Maquis. It was a name that became famous in Europe.

The Maquis was a group of elitists dedicated to the overthrow of the Germans. They were the leaders of the Resistance. Over a period of time they quietly infiltrated every segment of the French population. They knew most of what was happening everywhere.

In the early 1940s, when the Germans entered France, Josephine was a member of the Red Cross Nurses Corps. She was not immediately a suspect.

There was a certain apprehension on her part for her husband, who was Jewish. If she was suspected at all by the Germans, it was because of Jean Leon.

Jean Leon falls into that strange nether world of people about whom Josephine spoke so little. He falls into the world of Sister, and Mama, and Papa, and Nephew. The one thing we know for sure is that she thought him to be a very wealthy man. She was doomed to disappointment. It was almost a copy of *l'affaire Pepe*.

However, in his defense, he did make an attempt to support her. He suggested that she give up her career and retire. He suggested children and a home in the country. But it was all wrong, and she knew it from the beginning. Only the intervention of the war prevented her from leaving him long before. Eventually, after the war, her marriage to Jean Leon was dissolved by the French courts.

Because he was a Jew, Jean Leon was responsible for bringing Josephine to the attention of the Gestapo almost at once.

"You know, Stephen, when they started to make all those statements in America that I was a Jew-hater, and that I told the colored people in Harlem to burn their houses down because they had Jewish landlords, I couldn't believe what I was hearing. Nobody, particularly Winchell, bothered to even say that I was once married to a Jew."

Josephine seems never to have been frightened by the Gestapo. Perhaps she did not realize their real danger. Even if she had, though, it probably would have made no difference in the decisions she was to make later.

But it was the manner in which the Gestapo acted that concerned Josephine. "They were rough. You must believe me. When they first came, half the servants left in the night. They were frightened to be in the employ of anyone on whom the Gestapo even called.

"They came late one night and pounded on the door till I thought it would break down. I looked out the window, and I saw a German soldier pounding on the door with the butt of his rifle. I can tell you, that is a frightening situation. They came in the night, always. Many times I have thought about those poor, unfortunate people they took in the quiet of the night and who never returned. I thought about that when I visited the concentration camps after the war. I became ill then, and couldn't bear to go on with the inspection. It was too horrible.

"That night they wanted to know about 'the Jew who is your husband.' "

At the time, Jean Leon was out of the country on business. According to Josephine, she was immediately in contact with him, warning him not to return. Apparently he did not. It was the only mention she ever made of him.

"Why talk about poor Jean Leon? He was such a little part of my life. It was a *mistake* from the beginning. Like it was a *mistake* with Jo [Bouillon] too. They all wanted to control me. You know that was impossible. It just couldn't be done. You know, it was so silly, Jean wanting me to give up my career for him. How would we have eaten? People don't think about those things when they are in love. Fortunately, I do."

Josephine knew that the going-over she received from the Gestapo was probably a mild version of what others in less important positions were receiving. Her mind was working. And when she received the first call, she was ready.

The Resistance were just laying their foundations, and they laid them well. They knew that Josephine traveled in the upper strata of rarefied air—Paris high society. They knew also that that society was the hangout of the important Nazis and Italians. They needed someone who traveled in those circles.

"I can tell you, there were very few people of importance that I did not know. I doubt if there were any. And my friends were in every business that meant anything in France, and in other places in the world. Eventually I began to know things before the real big shots got to know them.

* * *

To show how well the Resistance had infiltrated their own camp as well as the Germans', it was Josephine's personal maid who made the first overtures. She had been planted there to get the line on Josephine's thinking. Her reports were, of course, favorable. How she got her information and how she made the necessary contact will never be known. Even the French were wary of one another.

After working her way into Josephine's employ, the maid slowly started feeling out Josephine concerning her attitude toward the Resistance. She left newspaper articles around the house for Josephine to see. Finally, one day, she broached the subject: "Wouldn't it be a wonderful thing for France if everyone could work in the Resistance? Of course, a person in a maid's position could do little. It would take a more important person."

Josephine went for the bait—carefully at first, for she could not be sure that the maid was not in the employ of the Nazis. Such was the temperament of the time. One could not even trust his own family, let alone his servants.

However, as this employer-employee relationship ripened, a feeling of trust developed between the two women. The Resistance decided on their first move.

* * *

The director of the Resistance was also a captain in the Army of France. Josephine never revealed his name; however, he might have been Jacques Abtey, who later wrote a book on his war experiences. This officer, whatever his identity, was something of a dilettante. He dressed immaculately—always in uniform. He had an affected, foppish, almost effeminate air. He was at all times beautifully groomed and perfumed. He was known to associate with a number of young Frenchmen who for all outward appearances were his "lovers." Particularly after the occupation, he was constantly seen with one or two of these "companions." He would imbibe too much, carouse too much, and sometimes have to be carried out of the various clubs and restaurants where he partied.

This officer soon came to be greatly disliked by the French, who felt that a captain in the Army of France should be doing something—anything but what he was doing. If he was an embarrassment to the French at first, he soon became a disgrace. For in his little groups the more handsome Nazi officers began to appear frequently. Many Frenchmen were outraged.

Very few people knew that this officer was one of the most dangerous men in all of France. He was a true Maquisard, a master of his murderous and stealthy art. He knew his business well.

* * *

Christine Granville. Chris Grand. Christopher Grandville. The Countess Grandville. These were all names adopted by a young woman who very soon was to brush lives with Josephine Baker.

The woman's real name was Crystina Gizencka. When Josephine met her, she was going by the name Jacqueline Armand. She had an impressive background: she was indeed a countess, and a master linguist. She was also, incredible as it seems, a master spy for British Intelligence in Egypt, Turkey, and other Middle Eastern countries.

The beautiful young "Countess Grandville" was also a Maquisard—as a matter of fact, the most dangerous of them all. She had been approached to join the cause in Cairo, and had parachuted into France in 1941. A master saboteur, an expert in dynamite, she was soon to take part in "Operation Montagnard."

"I have killed many men," she said. "It does not bother me. And I always carry my sudden-death capsule, but I can tell you, I would never use it."

In 1973 Josephine and I were in Detroit, where she was giving an interview to a reporter from the Detroit *Free Press*. I almost fell out of my chair when she casually started talking about her war activities.

"Oh, yes, I always had my 'pillules.' I even put one into my mouth on a couple of occasions, when I thought the end had come, 'cause you know they would never get an ounce of information out of Josephine. Fortunately I never had to use it. They said it would kill almost instantly. Others, unfortunately, had to use it. I did not."

Like Josephine, Christine Granville never had to either. Even though she was involved in some incredible activities during the war, the Gestapo was not responsible for putting an end to this remarkable woman. Years later, in London, she was murdered in her bed by a jealous lover.

It seems unbelievable that someone has never written at length about Christine Granville. Indeed, very little has ever been published about any of the other Maquisards. And, unfortunately for the world, very little has ever been published about Josephine Baker and her wartime activities. But before we continue, one more character must enter our scenario.

Michel Trotobus was a member of the Maquis, and a master of espionage and sabotage. In his wake he left a trail of destroyed locomotive works, bridges, buildings, and munitions dumps, as well as a baffled Gestapo.

Michel Trotobus did not last out the war: he went down in the fire of twenty Gestapo machine guns as he pumped grenades into the munitions dump at Lyon. His last one hit home, and he, the Gestapo, and the dump went to the next plane in a funeral pyre that would have been the envy of the greatest Balinese maharaja. The fire burned for thirty days. The supplies had been crucial to resist the coming Allied invasion.

So now, in the early 1940s, the lives of these four people—Josephine Baker, Christine Granville, Michel Trotobus, and the mysterious Resistance director—were thrown together.

* * *

Josephine says that she was as cool as she could be as she drank her coffee in the outdoor café on the Champs Elysées.

She had taken the bait from her maid, and had been asked to wait in the café for an important visitor. A half hour passed. The important vistor never arrived.

Josephine stood up to leave when a clumsy waiter bumped into her and drenched her with hot coffee. From the entire room, captains and waiters came rushing to her aid. She was hustled into the kitchen to be cleaned up. Surrounded by people with cleaning fluid who were muttering a thousand apologies, she was suddenly pushed back into a little room. The door was closed.

Instantly a panel was removed from the back wall, and she was led down bank after bank of rough stone steps. They were illuminated with the smallest bulbs imaginable.

Then she was hit with the stench of the Paris sewers. Down one tunnel they went, and into another; and finally they emerged before a small door. Three knocks, and it flew open.

Josephine Baker found herself in the headquarters of the Resistance. Sitting at a table, surrounded by his usual group of handsome men, was the smiling director.

No one could have been more amazed than Josephine. She soon discovered that the "dilettante" of the Paris café society and his friends were some of the most dangerous men in all of Europe. With them sat Michel Trotobus and the girl of a thousand aliases—Christine Granville.

Josephine Baker was about to be initiated into the ranks of the greatest underground fighting force ever assembled in any war.

It seems incredible that this portion of her career has been glossed over by writers of the times. But she herself spoke of it so little. It is my belief that the need for secrecy was so impressed on her during this period that even in her later years this lesson still remained with her, and she was reluctant to talk.

Long afterward, when Josephine asked me to start putting details of her life down for her, I did a little research. I discovered that Michel Trotobus, Captain Abtey, and even Christine Granville had indeed existed.

Little was written about them, but everything told me by Josephine seemed to be corroborated by the few things I could find.

* * *

That night Josephine Baker, hidden away in the sewers of Paris, took the oath of the Maquisard. Her contributions to France during the war are a matter of record: she was awarded that country's highest military honors.

Josephine told me that after ten nights of training down in the sewers, she could shoot out a candle at twenty yards. I believed her. Knowing her as I did, I wouldn't have been surprised if she could have done it at fifty yards. She learned other tricks, too. Before most Americans had ever heard of karate, she was something of an expert in it. She never lost her skill at it, either, judging from the fight she put up after her arrest years later in Canada, when it took four police officers to subdue her. "What asses, the Canadian police!" she said after that incident. "I could have escaped ten times over if I'd wanted to."

She was required to take a memory-training course not unlike those about which much has been written today, where associations are made to jog the memory. She could read a document, grasp its contents, and deliver the message three months later to the person for whom it was intended.

Then she made a move that delighted her fellow Maquis: she suggested she report her maid to the Gestapo. Bravo.

Two weeks later, Josephine was ready to spring her surprise on the Gestapo, her maid having safely made off in the night "with some of my best jewelry."

They had a surprise for her too. She was informed that she had twenty-four hours to vacate her home for a high-ranking Nazi officer. It would be required, she was told, for Hermann Goering and his staff.

"I don't know if they believed me when I told them about the maid," she said, smiling. "But I believed them when they took my house."

Josephine left the house the following morning, never to return. Her best possessions were by now hidden all over the continent, her jewels safe in vaults in Swiss banks. However, the only piece of furniture she ever recovered was the bed that had belonged to Marie Antoinette. Years later, she moved it to the Milandes. It was, unfortunately, a bed that two women lost their heads over—one figuratively, one literally.

The German acquisition of her house solved the problem of how to explain her departure on her first mission.

Now she threw herself into her work. She moved through the occupation society of France like a whirlwind.

It was easy for her. She was an actress, and a first-rate one at that. She quickly made friends with Nazis, with Italians, with collaborators.

It was the Italians from whom she received her most important secret information.

Years earlier, when she had played Parma, a young man sat in the audience enraptured with *la Divina*. He was one of the street celebrants who had thrown her chauffeur out of her car and had driven it themselves.

Now he was the chief attaché at the Italian Embassy. He had access to top secret documents and, more important, to the codes.

If Josephine ever did anything for the world, it was this: she delivered the original copy of the Italian-German codebook to the Resistance.

She tells it as though it were a simple matter. Perhaps it was for her. "It wasn't difficult. He was sympathetic. Besides, he was wild about me."

I had thought that this incident would, in the telling, resemble a good (or even a bad) Hollywood movie scene, complete with bullets, secret missions, clandestine meetings, and so on. I thought of it as in the Mata Hari tradition. But apparently it was not. Incredibly, the attaché just handed the codebook to her one evening, and she dropped it into her purse. The only thing "exciting" about it all was that the book was later reduced to microfilm.

One evening the Resistance director and his "gay" entourage arrived at the Chez Josephine. Soon afterward Josephine came over to his table, took out a cigarette, and asked for a light. He handed her a cigarette case with a lighter built into the top, and received one from Josephine in return; in it was the microfilmed code.

If the Germans in his party had been smart, they would have known that Josephine did not smoke. Also, a "fop," as the director was supposed to have been, would certainly have risen to the occasion to light a lady's cigarette.

Perhaps, though, one of the Germans in the party did catch on—unfortunately for him and his companions. For the next morning, in a tiny third-floor flat on the rue de Danzig, five handsome young German officers were found lying in pools of blood, their throats slit. It was the end "of a wild homosexual party that had taken place between French and German officers." The article did not appear on the pages of the Nazi-controlled daily papers. The French did read of the massacre in the then quietly circulating underground papers.

Josephine left immediately to go "on tour." However, the implications of the situation were not lost on the German High Command. Word was sent down for a careful scrutiny of Josephine Baker. The directive landed on the desk of Hermann Goering. That he was sitting at a Louis Seize desk that belonged to Josephine, and that he was sitting in her own home as he read the directive, makes our story even more interesting.

Goering, who had long suspected Josephine, made an initial report to the Command in Berlin, and a terse report was soon received: Arrest, imprison and convict her. "Convict" was the key word: it meant the firing squad. But Goering was too smart for that. He knew that the execution of such an important and popular figure would create an uproar. He decided to bide his time.

Josephine Baker then left on a very much publicized "theatrical tour." It might be added that no impresario in his right mind would have booked her.

She went first to London, then to Pau in the south of France, then back to London, Rio de Janeiro, Mexico City, Havana, Rio de Janeiro again, Havana again, and Marseilles, in the south of France. Few people seemed to notice that the only city in which she performed on this incredible "tour" was Rio de Janeiro, and that happened to be a benefit.

The only part of her wartime activity that smacks of Hollywood was the fact that two of the most wanted Maquisards—Christine Granville and Michel Trotobus—traveled with her as agent and personal maid.

They traveled well disguised, as was necessary. The closest she ever came to divulging information about the journey was a simple answer to my question about what the hell she had been doing: "Just running some errands for De Gaulle," she said.

They must have been *some* errands, and she must have accomplished them well, for De Gaulle himself later signed the documents that made it possible for her to receive the Legion of Honor and the Rosette of the Resistance. Also, she was in his party when he marched triumphantly up the Champs Elysées during the reoccupation.

Josephine ended this strange tour without her "maid" and without her "agent." Upon her return to France, Josephine immediately joined the Marseilles Opera and opened in a new company of *La Creole*. After her opening-night performance, an old Marseilles farmer was waiting backstage to offer his greetings. As he kissed both her cheeks he whispered, "*Cette fois c'est la bonne*." "This time they mean business."

Josephine recognized the voice of Michel Trotobus. It was, Josephine said later, the only line that ever frightened her.

The Maquis had their information right—but it was not in time.

As Josephine left the stage early, a staff car of the Gestapo pulled in front of her. At eight the next morning, she was told, she would accompany them to Paris, where she was to be the "guest" of Hermann Goering. And, "in the event she might need something during the night," she would find two officers of the Gestapo outside her door.

Josephine was playing big games, and she was playing them with the big boys.

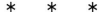

Josephine's hour was up. She knew it, and the Maquis knew it.

The expected was happening, and it was being done cleverly: Hermann Goering was simply inviting Josephine Baker to dinner. That the newspapers carried the story of the invitation even before it was extended says something for the intelligence and the public relations flair of the Germans.

Josephine was allowed to change clothes in a suite at the George V. When she asked for a floor maid to help her dress, the guards permitted it without any suspicion. It was a huge mistake for the Gestapo. Unknown to them, the maid was a member of the Resistance, and she and Josephine held a hurried conversation in Spanish in the presence of the guards, who fortunately did not speak the language. It all smacks of a scene from the television show *Mission Impossible*.

Few people know of this incident, in which Josephine Baker was invited to her own home for dinner—in reality, for her execution—by one of the highest officer in the German Army. Even years later, it is regrettable that few people in America knew—or cared to know—who Josephine Baker was. There, undoubtedly, lies the reason that the story has never been told. As Josephine said: "If I told it, they would disbelieve." They probably would have. They might even have snickered.

As she entered her own home, Goering offered her sherry in her own living room. They chitchatted for a while. He remarked on the comfort of her house. It must have been a bizarre conversation.

But Josephine was not without a sense of drama herself; and if she was going out, she decided, she would go out in style.

"I had been hearing all those stories about the German officers in High Command. I could tell now that they were true. His [Goering's] eyes were glazed. Everyone had been saying that he was hooked on narcotics. I don't know much about narcotics, but I have been around the theatre long enough, and have seen enough people hooked on drugs, to know that Goering was a prime example. Even while we were at the table, he kept taking a small vial out of his pocket. He would put it up to his nose and take a long sniff out of it. I guess it was cocaine.

"I heard too that by this time he was also on heroin. And I had to believe that too. His eyes would close part way, then roll back in his head. Then he would sort of shake his head and start talking about nothing in particular. He was talking about what a marvelous star I was, though I don't believe he ever saw me perform. Also, he kept scratching himself—a sure sign of a heroin user. Boy, those guys were dangerous. And imagine, if you can, that he was one of the top generals in the German Army. My God, they must have all been mad—insane—even Hitler. They had to be to do what they were doing."

When Goering had taken over her house, she had packed her entire wardrobe and was preparing to transport it out of the country; however, the Germans had allowed her to take only three cases. Unfortunately, the three she chose had been packed with old wardrobe from the late teens, the twenties, and the thirties.

The night of her "dinner engagement" with Goering, Josephine wore an old gown of lime green chiffon with dyed lime egrets, designed by Poiret. By this time, the fabulous designer had died in abject poverty, having been reduced from the greatest couturier of Paris to "nobody" in what seemed like overnight. His fortune was gone. It seemed to appeal to Josephine's sense of the theatre of the bizarre when she chose to wear this very pre-WWI-style Poiret gown. But underneath, she was all business.

Josephine and Goering entered the dining room, Josephine taking a seat to the right of the Nazi general. Below the salt, so to speak, were the witnesses to the execution—high-ranking officers of the party and the army. She had been warned in her room at the George V that the fish course would contain cyanide. She later maintained that she was not frightened. Perhaps not.

She did know that in the powder room off the main foyer was a little-used laundry chute that emptied into the ironing room in the subbasement. It was a drop of two floors.

Just as the soup was being cleared, she rose to excuse herself for a moment. It was her intention to make it to the powder room and drop down the laundry chute. At the bottom, she hoped, having informed the maid in the George V of her escape plans, she would fall into the arms of her Maquisard friends.

The officers at the table rose, and a servant pulled back Josephine's chair. With cool deliberation, Goering reached for his revolver, clicked the safety catch and, with a slight smile on his face, pointed the weapon directly at her. She immediately sat back down.

For some reason, for a woman who could "snuff out a candle at twenty yards," Josephine resolutely refused to carry a gun. "If I had had a gun that night, I would have got him first."

While the cyanide-laced fish course was being served, the Germans sitting at the table smiled. Josephine ate all the fish; later she always wondered why she didn't collapse on the spot. Complaining of a slight dizziness, she asked to be excused. Her "hosts" granted the request. It was the Germans' second mistake.

She remembers only making it to the powder room; somehow she managed to throw open the laundry-chute doors and then plunge headfirst into it. Two men at the bottom broke her fall. Luckily for her, the maid had succeeded in conveying her plan to the Maquis.

In an underground clinic, her stomach was pumped and she was administered to. She did not recover complete consciousness for a month.

Shortly afterward, the world's newspapers carried the story that Josephine Baker had died in Marrakech, Morocco. They had jumped the gun. For over a year she hovered on the brink; then slowly she recovered.

It was the end of one of the most intriguing—and most unknown—of all war stories. It was also the end of her career as an agent for the underground.

It was then that she sent her famous cable to Mistinguett in Paris:

> DARLING. PLEASE KEEP THE STAGE HOT FOR ME UNTIL I GET BACK.
> LOVE. JOSEPHINE.

Chapter 13

"I don't know what was happening to the people. I think they were all going mad. They wrote and said the craziest things about me. That I had a harem of men in my house in Morocco. They wrote that King Farouk had me arrested. They said that I had sold my war citations 'cause I was broke. . . . Why, they even said that I was dead, and hundreds of newspapers around the world carried my obituary."

* * *

After rescuing her, Josephine's fellow Maquis members spirited her out of France. She left Marseilles late in the night on a troop ship bound for Casablanca. She immediately entered a hospital, and for the next two years she was in and out constantly.

"Talk about being sick! When I first went to France when I was a kid, I thought that there could never be anything like being seasick to make you feel really bad. I didn't have any idea then what being really sick was. Now I can tell you that I was *really* sick. I cannot remember the number of operations I had. I believe it was either three or four. It seemed there was one every few months.

"I didn't do much of anything, actually. When I wasn't in the hospital, I was at home. I did have a nice house, but I was hardly in it. One thing I know is that I didn't have much money. I was able to get a cable through to the bank in Switzerland where I had my jewels. The bankers there knew they were in their vaults, and they advanced me a considerable amount of money which I used to live on when I was there. The French government gave me a small allowance and paid my hospital bills and for all my operations. But as for being extravagant, that is certainly not the case. I was so ill that I could not even keep up with the war as it progressed. It was over long before I actually thought it would be.

"As the war started turning and as the Allies began to take it for granted that our side was going to win, the people just sort of let go.

"I don't know what was happening to the people. I think they were all going mad. They wrote and said the craziest things about me. That I had a harem of men in my house in Morocco. They wrote that King Farouk had me arrested. They said that I had sold my war citations 'cause I was broke. . . . Why, they even said that I was dead, and hundreds of newspapers around the world carried my obituary.

"The article about my death even appeared in a Moroccan paper. I think I was over in Rabat or in Marrakech visiting with some friends, and a friend of theirs did not know I was even in town. They came running to tell their friend that Josephine Baker was dead. Then I walked out of my bedroom when I heard all the shouting. I sat down and read my own obituary. That was a good laugh. I got on the phone to the UPI or the AP, or one of the wire services to the newspapers, to report to them that I really wasn't dead. They didn't believe me.

" 'Well, believe me or not,' I told them, 'if you want to print the news right you had better do a retraction.'

"Then they wanted me to come into their offices to present myself to them, and 'prove' that I was alive, and that I *was* Josephine Baker. Imagine asking me to do that, and imagine their not sending someone out to see me. I guess they thought it was another hoax, as there had been so many during the war.

"Finally one of the senior editors got on the phone, and I started screaming at him on the phone. When I finished, he said:

" 'Madame Baker, I have never met you, but I have heard a great deal about you, and the woman who is screaming at me on the phone right now sounds just like the Josephine Baker I heard so much about—so you *must* be Josephine Baker.'

"Then I really laughed, and we talked for a while, and he was convinced that I was Josephine. He got a great scoop too. When he reported the story it made news all over again, and all the other newspapers who had run my obituary had to retract it. Then the people didn't know if I was dead or alive.

"But that's how it was getting near the end of the war, and even after the end of it. It was only a lot later that they were writing about what I had been able to do, entertaining and all, when I was well enough to do it. I remember one time in Marrakech it was raining cats and dogs, and I was doing shows on the back of a truck. It had been raining for days, and that mud was a foot deep, but those guys just stood there in that rain and that mud listening to me. And you know, not too many of them, even the colored ones, knew who I was. But I did it."

* * *

Josephine threw herself into an incredible round of troop entertaining. It was then that she noticed something that threw more fuel on the flames that were smoldering within her.

When the American stars arrived to entertain the troops in Morocco, it was the white soldiers who took the seats in front. The blacks stood at the back. And when the entertainers moved out into the crowds after their shows to say a few words to the crowds, they never quite made it to the blacks in the rear.

Josephine changed all that. When she entertained, she insisted that blacks have equal rights with whites for the few seats available; and when her performances were over, she headed right to the black troops and spent additional hours with them. She wrote to as many of their parents as she could, and years later, when I traveled in the United States with her, black mothers and fathers would brings letters backstage to show her. They were letters that she had written to them about their sons thirty years before. Sometimes there were tears when Josephine learned of a soldier who never returned.

Years later, in Las Vegas, Nevada, Josephine insisted on and tried this same seating formula. It was another huge mistake, and I calculated that over the years it cost her at least a million dollars.

* * *

"Well, I did my share for the war and for my country, and for a lot of other countries too. Not only in my security activities, but in my entertainment activities as well. And I can tell you that many was the time I got up feeling violently ill but still went out to perform so as not to disappoint a group of men who had been waiting for a show.

"Then, when all that Winchell and all that commie stuff began circulating in America, I didn't even try to defend myself against the accusations because I knew they were so ridiculous. I thought that the newspapers and all the others who knew what I really had done would defend me. I was wrong. People forget very easily. Not one newspaper came to my defense. Instead, they started making up stories of their own. I guess it sells newspapers, so what difference did it make what happened to Josephine Baker?

"I can't say I did a lot in the war, for there were many who did much more than me, but I pulled my share of it, and you know I didn't receive my decorations because I was sitting home resting and eating candy.

"Then almost overnight, it seemed, the war was over. We couldn't believe it. I wanted to get back to France as soon as possible. I was going to fly, but at the last minute I decided I didn't want to. I was in Corsica,

I think, and there was a big night club there, and none of those people had ever seen me work. So I decided to do a show for them. That night I got excited all over again. I felt good again. I sang and danced like I had never done before. Now I really wanted to get back 'home' and go to work. I knew it was going to be a lot of work, and it was—and I felt, Well, let's get started now.

"Again, I returned to France on a ship—I can't remember the name. It was a freighter, a Liberty ship, and this time I wasn't sick at all. I guess the water was calm. The weather was beautiful, and there were only a few passengers, and they stayed by themselves, and I had plenty of time to start thinking about what I was going to do in the future.

"I would have to visit my house, but even then I had heard that it had been destroyed. You know, I didn't regret it much. I still had the lease on the Milandes, and I thought, Maybe I'll buy that place. I thought about how before the Germans came I had sent all my things away to safety, and I would have to worry about getting them all back now. And, of course, it would take time.

"Then I was thinking about myself and what was going to happen to me. I wasn't getting any younger. I thought if only I could marry the right guy, one I really loved, then I would settle down. Maybe even retire from the theatre. After all, I had had twenty good years, and was still a famous star. I thought it would have been wonderful to have some children. But now, I knew that would be impossible. After all those operations I had had in Morocco, I knew that was a dream.

"I envied those men and women who had children. Of course many had been lost in the war, but how happy it would be for those that returned. I wouldn't be able to share in any of that. I didn't have a husband, and I didn't have any children to come home to. I was really alone.

"But then, I remember it was evening and the sun had set quickly, and I had been in that chair daydreaming about my life for a long time—about the past, and about what would be happening to me in the future. And that is when and where it all came to me about the children.

"I was sitting in a deck chair on the back of that ship when I thought first about an adopted child, at first a little girl. Then I thought about a boy. But what kind, where? Then I began to think about a lot of little children, and slowly the plan came to me. And I began to think of children being brought up in a totally different environment.

"I thought, Now that the war is over, maybe people will have some sense. Maybe we can all work together and prevent wars like the one we had just come through. But you cannot prevent this sort of thing unless you have harmony and peace within yourself. I knew that then. That's what I thought, at least. Little did I realize that I was in for a rude awakening. If anything, people were even worse.

"Then I said that someone has to start somewhere and in some little way. After all, experiments are made in many fields—in medicine, on the kind of weather we have, on new inventions, and all that. Why not an experiment in brotherhood? And then all at once it hit me that I should be the one to do it. After all, I was still young enough—and I could afford it.

"I thought about it a great deal the rest of that voyage, and by the time I got off the boat in France I knew what I was going to do. And I would do it at the Milandes. It would be my own experiment in brotherhood, and I would use a unique formula. I decided to adopt as many children as I could, and to segregate them from the environments that they were in; and not only would I teach them, but I would bring in people to teach them all sorts of things I did not know. As they grew up with each other in close harmony, not knowing anything about what life was really like in the outside world, as they grew up they could go out as emissaries of peace and brotherhood themselves, and pretty soon their children, and even *their* children, could spread the word of brotherhood. I figured that if someone didn't start all this no one ever would, and I decided then it would be me.

"I would get children from every race, every creed, every religion. They would be every color of the rainbow. Then it hit me all at once. They would be the Rainbow Children of Josephine Baker."

We were in Los Angeles at the Hilton Hotel the first time she told me this story. She was in bed, where it seemed that most of her stories came from. At this point in the story, Robert Wood happened to walk in. In previous years she had always guarded what she said in front of others; now it seemed not to matter to her.

She told Robert and me some hair-raising stories of the children. They seemed hard to believe; I had first met them as little babies, and she never failed when writing to send me their love. Now it seemed different. She began to tell us of some of the little scrapes they had gotten into.

I assured her that they were little skirmishes that every parent in the world has to suffer at some time. But as she continued, I knew that her problems were different. They were very serious indeed. There was dissension in the ranks of the brotherhood, dissension between the leader and the future emissaries. It was never healed; if anything, at the time of her death it had widened.

In another chapter I will deal at length with Josephine's brotherhood ideal, and with her children. I will reveal her feelings as she poured them out to us that day. Perhaps it is well for the Rainbow Children of Josephine Baker to know what their mother thought of them in her last days.

* * *

After the war Josephine seemed to get a new lease on life. A new fire burned within her.

She visited her gutted house, then walked away and checked into a small hotel.

"A lot of people wrote that I was broke and that I was around town begging for money, and using my friends. The stories horrified me. It couldn't have been further from the truth. Then I had plenty of money. I was one of few who had most of my possessions, and I still had my jewels too. Those stories were just untrue.

"For a while, I was doing a few benefit shows. It was to raise funds for the benefit of France, and I did it gladly. I was all over France, and particularly Paris.

"I was doing one of those benefits one day, and that is where I first met Jo [Bouillon].

"Also about that time they had just let the people out of Buchenwald, and I was asked to go as a witness. A witness, mind you! I was a *terrible* witness. I could hardly go into the place. I felt I could hear the screams of those children calling for their mamas and their daddies, and of wives calling for their husbands, and all that, and it was terrible. I could not stay there. I felt I would go mad if I did. And I must tell you, it was terrible, and it remained with me all my life, though I was only there a short time."

Slowly Josephine gathered together her possessions. For years they had been hidden away in barns, and in the ground, and in attics, and in any place that someone could hide something for her.

"You know, I didn't miss a single thing. Everything was intact. I had gone to Switzerland to get my jewels, and they were all intact. I paid the advances they made to me.

"I had everything sent to a big warehouse outside of Paris, and slowly I started going through everything. Again, I never realized I had so much. I was able to meet with my accountants and get my business straight. Believe it or not, I had some investments in the United States, and they were now worth a lot of money. So in all, I was still a millionairess. You can hardly call that being poor.

"At the end of the forties, I went back to the Folies Bergère. But I was afraid. I was not young anymore—at least, not like I was when I had my great sensations there. I thought about it a great deal before I did it, and then when I decided, I just threw myself into it. I worked and worked, like I always did for a revue.

"And it paid off. And I shouldn't have been worried, 'cause I was a sensation still—not *again*, but *still*. The French, and all the others who came from other countries, adored me; and I had never received such press notices in my entire career.

"In 1947 or 1948 I had gone back to America again to see if I could get anything going. I did all right, I guess you could say, but nothing like I thought I should be doing. I played in New York City, and I believe I went to Boston and Philadelphia. But I just wasn't satisfied. I felt maybe if I had another revue in France, it would be better for me in America. That's how I decided to do the Folies Bergère again.

"Also during that time I decided to marry Jo. He had been asking me for a long time—he was mad about me, and finally I guess he sort of wore me out."

Again, who can separate fact from fiction? Josephine is gone, and Jo Bouillon is left with his bitter memories, and the worry of twelve of the famous Rainbow Children on his shoulders, so there is little doubt that his version of the story would not be without some bias.

It is my opinion that she married him so that her future adopted children would have a father. She once let the cat out of the bag, so to speak, when she mentioned that she had previously tried adopting a child, but, being a single woman, even *she* had experienced difficulties. "It was easy for the married couples. But they just didn't like the idea of an unmarried woman having a child. I guess they were right."

From the very beginning of her marriage to Jo Bouillon, there were problems.

"When that wedding gown didn't arrive in time, I figured we were going to have problems. And then, we never really did have a honeymoon. I ate some red-hot soup the French make. They called it a wedding soup. It's supposed to 'get you going' on your wedding night. Well, it made me violently ill. Ever since then, I haven't been able to eat anything spicy or heavily seasoned; and I guess I can blame it all on my operations."

It was indeed not a propitious start for the marriage. It began and ended with storm clouds overhead.

I knew Jo Bouillon only a short while. The last time I saw him was in the early 1960s in the Milandes. By then, if not before, she was treating him like a servant. It was a sad turn of affairs. He was a brilliant musician and orchestrator, an extremely talented man with marvelous taste. It is very possible that he was also something of a businessman. Unfortunately, he was never able to exert any authority over Josephine.

Jo was responsible for some of the major renewal projects in the Château des Milandes. He was also responsible for the selection of such items as the fine china and the linens that were used in the Château and in the restaurants. He had a sensitive good taste, as one could tell from observing the estate and the properties.

In the end, there were bitter accusations and counteraccusations. She blamed him for many of her problems, but it is my belief that his only real connection with those problems was the fact that he allowed himself to be led into them.

Josephine maintained that in the "final hour" Jo abandoned her and the children. It is more likely that he was hounded out, both by the creditors and by Josephine. She made some startling accusations against the man and claimed that he was responsible for the many blackmail attempts that were made against her later.

I have no idea whether her accusations were based on fact. When it came to Josephine's telling me about Jo Bouillon, I was not a sympathetic audience, and she sensed this. I rather liked the man. I only met him on a few occasions, but in those fleeting minutes he would try to tell me his side of the affair. And I must confess that his version certainly sounded plausible.

But I could not be friends with both Bouillon and Josephine. I remained a friend of Josephine. I had no choice. When I was a guest at the Milandes, I stayed as far away from Jo as possible, for I knew that it annoyed Josephine to see him talking either to me or to her accountants and other business associates. It was a path down which I did not want to venture. It was strictly a matter between husband and wife. Frankly, I still believe she married him in order to give her children a father. But their problems went back farther than that.

* * *

The final separation came in the early 1960s, after about thirteen years of marriage. On March 7, 1961, she wrote me a long letter from the Milandes.

> . . . Jo and I have completely separated since this Taub affair [which will be described later]. He has asked me for a divorce. He has acted very badly towards me, but there is nothing I can do. He told me to not go to America because of Winchell and Taub. I did against his will, and lost on all sides.
>
> So he is taking advantage of the whole situation. He saw Taub last summer in the South and as usual Taub told him a lot of lies, but *he believed him.*
>
> Well, dear Steve, nothing to do now but forget Jo. . . .
>
> I don't know, Steve, if I will do *The Merry Widow,* because now that Jo and I are separated I have the whole responsibility of the Village on my shoulders. So I cannot leave the Village so easily.
>
> . . . That is why I ask you about the film affair.

So it was the end of the marriage. Josephine later told me that after that they saw each other only a few times, and each time it ended in a violent argument. She said that she could take no more of it, and had decided never to see him again.

It is my feeling that their real problem was the Château des Milandes.

Chapter 14

"What is this lovely château, Father?"

"It is the Château des Milandes, Madame."

* * *

The Château des Milandes lies nestled on the bank of the River Dordogne. It was, and I am sure still is, incredibly beautiful. It also has a long and interesting history. It was the home of the lords of Castelnaud-Fayrac, in whose veins ran the blood of the kings of France. Perhaps its greatest moment was when Louis XIV, the Sun King—*le Roi Soleil,* God's gift to France—spent the night there. The villagers tell the story yet today.

It must have been a brilliant sight. Even then, the château was old. Louis was journeying to the south of France, and, having stopped in Sarlat for the famous paté of Perigord, he decided to spend the night. The Lord of Castelnaud-Fayrac made his home available to him.

It was the village's first great moment in history; I guess its second was when Josephine rumbled up in a Bugatti Royale.

The outriders had galloped on ahead of the royal coaches, their trumpets sounding on that beautiful summer day. Accompanying Louis were Madame de Maintenon, not yet the queen, and the mistress, Louise de La Vallière.

Louis was known for his remarkable control over his kidneys. His staff and mistresses dreaded traveling in the coach with him, for they dared not call for a halt to answer nature's demand.

Obviously, it had been a difficult journey for Louise de La Vallière. For when the coach came to a halt, she immediately leaped out; and things being as they were in those days, she merely lifted her skirts near the front door and relieved herself.

Centuries later, Josephine pointed to the ground and said to me, "This is the spot where Louise made peepee." I pictured it in my mind.

King Louis himself "loved the little house." Indeed, it was a *little* house to Louis, who was still building the Versailles. He wandered all around, and at the bottom of the hill he and Louise came upon the little Château Clair de Lune. This was, of course, long before the song of that name was written, and I often wondered whether the composers knew that the château even existed.

Little Louise, the playful imp, was mad about it, and in a gesture that must have endeared Louis to the Lord of Castelnaud-Fayrac for the rest of his life, he made a present of the Château Clair de Lune to Louise de La Vallière. She was ecstatic.

It is sad that she never saw it again, for not much later, she fell out of favor with Louis, who suspected that she was involved with Madame de Brinvilliers, the famous poisoner. He ordered this beautiful and vivacious girl to the Convent of the Sisters of the Holy Cross, where she spent her few remaining years in the drudgery of prayers and scrubbing.

When the king left the following morning, he promised the lord of the château a gift of one of the Versailles palace mirrors. He did not forget his promise; sometime thereafter, a beautiful Tremeau mirror was delivered to the château, where it hung for more than three hundred years—until the creditors of Josephine Baker demanded and received it along with her other possessions to satisfy her debts.

In one of her own great moments of generosity, Josephine gave the Clair de Lune to two of her friends. They had known her from the moment of her arrival in France, and she loved them both dearly. On the day she signed the deed, she wrote: "Now may you live here long and happily."

It was a very romantic story, and a very romantic gesture on the part of Josephine. She loved the Clair de Lune.

The French are not particularly given to exaggerating stories, and these friends were very much down-to-earth civil employees. But when I first visited there, they told me that on every night of the full moon they saw standing on the banks of the River Dordogne, looking wistfully at the Clair de Lune, the ghost of Louise de La Vallière, smiling at them and gazing at her château.

Then they told me with great emotion and sincerity that after Josephine had been put out of the property, Louise de La Vallière came only one time more—this time not smiling her wistful smile. This time she was crying. After that, the ghost of Louise left and never returned. Thereafter they looked for her on the banks of the Dordogne every full moon . . . in vain.

* * *

So that was the first time that the Château des Milandes touched history; centuries later it was to do so again. But this time the people of the world would see photographs of Josephine Baker huddling near the back door of the "little house" where Louis XIV, the Sun King, had spent the night. She sat there in the cold, shielding her little kitten from the rain.

It was this château that helped bring Josephine Baker to her ruin. However, if she had it to live over again, I am sure she would have done it in the same manner.

* * *

It was the early 1930s, and Josephine and Pepe d'Albertini were driving through the south of France. She was trying to get over her one great love affair and needed to "get out, to run away, to get some air someplace."

They stopped by the banks of the River Dordogne and watched it winding through the province of Dordogne on its journey westward. She looked around her, and it seemed that all she saw were little castles and châteaus on every hill and bank. Far off in the distance, one château particularly caught her eye, and it seemed to be making an appeal to her. "It was as if it were calling to me to come over to see it. Like it needed help from me. Do you believe that anyone can fall in love with a house? After all, it is only a pile of stones and mortar and wood and all. But I fell in love with it. It seemed to want me to help it."

They stopped in the little village of Sarlat. They ate some of the famous paté of that area, drank a little wine, and then continued their journey.

"A friend of mine had lent me his Bugatti Royale. You know, that was the big one—the important one. Bugatti only made them for people he liked. It was fast and it was fabulous. It would really go, and you know I liked speed. A few years later I had a big Renault myself, and when I used to get it on the road I would hit 110 miles an hour with it. Yes, I mean in *those* days. Many's the time I could hit well over a hundred. And I loved it, too."

Then it seemed that all of a sudden, when they rounded a curve and drove up a small grade, there in front of her was the château she had seen from far below in the valley. It was the château that had seemed to be calling to her.

"What is this lovely château, Father?" she said to a priest who was walking slowly through the neglected park. He removed his hat and smiled at her as she leaned against the Bugatti.

"It is the Château des Milandes, Madame."

She ran all around the empty, neglected place. It had been built in the twelfth century, and during its existence it had probably been in this condition before. It undoubtedly had had a history of neglect, and a history, too, of being in an appalling state of disrepair.

A small portion of the château was habitable. She inquired about the owners, and in no time at all she had made arrangements to lease the property, for use on little weekends and trips into the country. No doubt the owners were delighted.

Then, after the war, when her Paris town house was in ruins and she had already formed in her mind her venture into brotherhood, she went there again. This time she moved even more quickly.

By this time, Josephine was a very rich woman. She was worth, by her accountant's figures, about $1,600,000. She often repeated to me in later years: "Oh, my God, oh, my God, Stephen, if you only knew! Then I could have paid cash for it. Why did I accept those mortgages? I could have bought it for *peanuts,* and I had so much money."

Probably one of the reasons that Josephine bought the property was her sense of the theatre, the dramatic, and the romantic. She loved the stories of King Louis and Louise de La Vallière. And when she first led me through her little palace, she would imagine where the king would have walked, and talked, and maybe danced in the salon. She even imagined that he had slept in her room, and he very likely did, for it was the loveliest suite in the château.

And, I must confess, in the first years, and during my first visits to the Milandes, it was an experience that one could never forget.

* * *

Josephine told me that she was elated when President Kennedy was elected. She wrote me on December 5, 1960, from the Milandes:

> . . . Thank God for Kennedy. I sent a long telegram of hearty congratulations. I was so happy that I could hardly wait for the final results.
>
> I sent congratulation telegrams to the American Embassy and all the consulates. . . .

In the next paragraph, incidentally, she said:

> . . . What's new for a possibility of a film on my life story?

Even then, she was beginning to feel the pinch. She felt the film could bring in the badly needed money.

When President Kennedy was elected, Josephine sent him a photograph of another beautiful château that belonged to a neighbor. She particularly requested that he make sure that Mrs. Kennedy received it. It was the famous Château de Rastignac. For years it has carried the inscription: "*Le Château de Rastignac, ayant servi de modele poul la Maison Blanche à Washington.*" (The Château de Rastignac, which served as the model for the White House in Washington, D.C.) It is very likely that it did; when one looks at a photograph of it, there is a remarkable resemblance. If it were not that it stands on a bluff and is surrounded by a huge park, at first glance one would wonder what the White House was doing there.

"Every time I pass Rastignac it makes me happy. I think of America. Of course, in the bad days, when the stories were flying, I thought a little

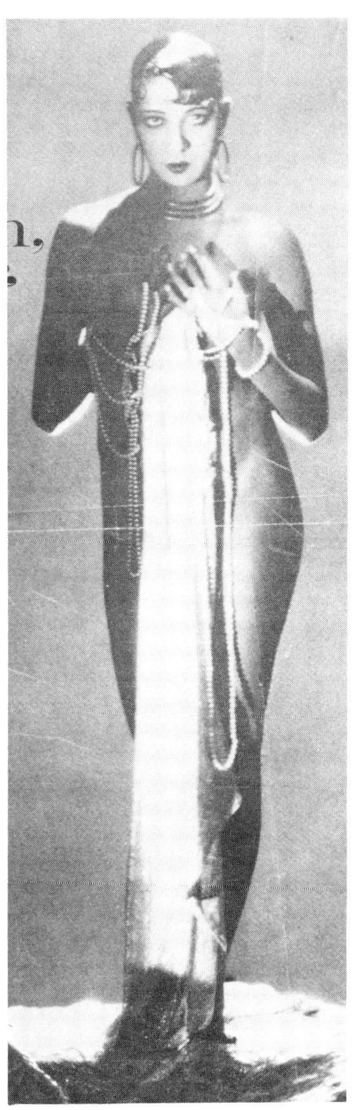

On the left, Josephine about 1926. On the right, as she was during the last American tour in 1973. If anything, her figure seems a little more trim. The 1926 photo indicates a seriousness not present in most Josephine Baker pictures.

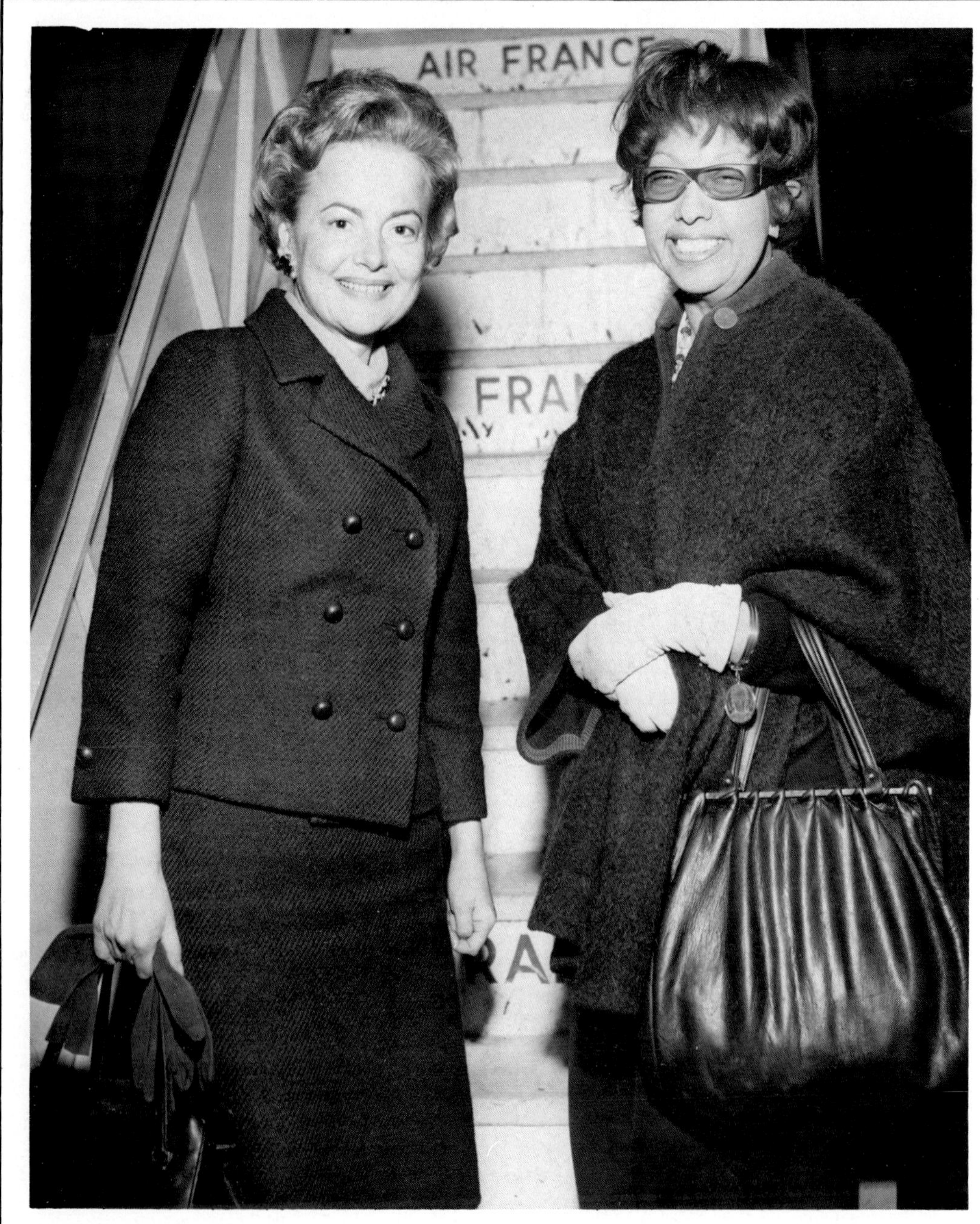

Air France

FOR IMMEDIATE RELEASE

KENNEDY INTERNATIONAL AIRPORT . . . *Stars of two Continents: (l to r) Olivia De Havilland of the films and Josephine Baker of the musicals and Europe's elegant night clubs, shown about to board an Air France intercontinental jet for Paris to spend the Easter holidays with their children.*

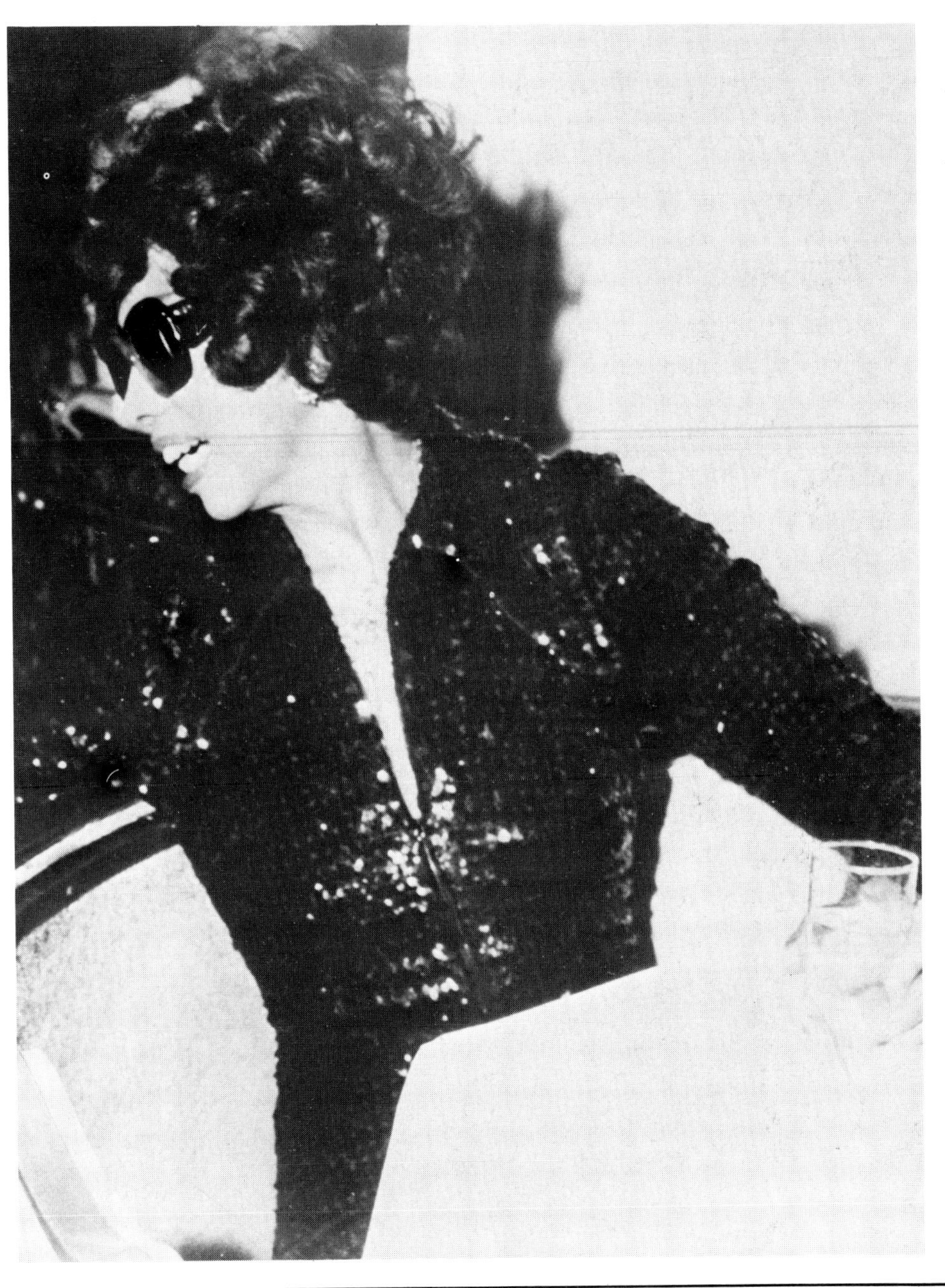

Birthday party at the Hotel Plaza in New York City. She is probably seventy. By now the sunglasses are an ever-present feature. Her weight is almost the same as fifty years ago. "You know, I don't believe I varied more than five or six pounds in all those years."

Paris-Match

Paris-Mat

L.A. Music Center Archives

Josephine as a Southern belle. Taken during a performance at the Ahmanson Theater, Los Angeles, in 1973. The train was twelve feet long and weighed over fifty pounds. The song was the theme from *Love Story,* and the rose was eventually passed all over the theater, bringing everyone a little happiness.

Paris-Match

Paris-Match

Paris-Match

Paris-Match

Josephine Baker in her last professional photograph, on stage at the Bobino Music Hall. She is probably seventy-two years old. It is opening night of the "Josephine" revue. She died two days later.

differently, but I still think of Washington, and the White House, and the Château de Rastignac. Don't you feel the same way when we pass it?"

I certainly did.

But in addition to the Château de Rastignac, Josephine was in really great company. She was not far from the famous villages of Beynac et Cazenac. And her neighbors and their châteaus were indeed really something.

There was Brantome, built in the eleventh century. There was the magnificent Château de Losse, built up high on the banks of the river, and there were the Château de Fenelon and the incredibly beautiful Montfort, which was built at the same time as the Versailles.

Also near Josephine's château was the famous Lascaux Cave, with its prehistoric paintings. She visited there very frequently, and when the guide would leave out some important detail in describing the cave paintings to her visitors, she would interrupt him to point out certain things that he was omitting. It thrilled her that thousands upon thousands of years ago people were living in "her" neighborhood.

So, then, Josephine was in good company. She was in rich company. And the money that supported the wonderful castles and châteaus of her neighbors had been in those families for years. Further, they knew how to husband each franc, each sou, so that it would last from generation to generation, so they and their châteaus and their castles could survive during the bad times. This was a French trait that, sad to say, did not rub off on Josephine.

The Château des Milandes—really a village—sat in the midst of over six hundred acres. Through the very center of the property and a stone's throw from the château itself ran the River Dordogne. From every window Josephine had a view that went for miles and miles, and she loved the early morning, when she would gaze out her window at the low fogs which would envelop her property before the sun would rise and dissipate it.

It did indeed have more than fifty rooms; I was in every one. From the attic rooms to the basements, and even to chambers deep down under the château that Josephine thought had been dungeons at one time. Very likely they had.

"That day, when the papers had been finished and stamped and marked with ribbons, and all those things the French are so famous for when it comes to legal documents, and those papers had been handed to me, I felt I was on top of the world. That I had made it. And I guess I had. You know, I was the first one to say it. Nobody gets credit for it but me, and it is true of course.

"It really was 'from shanty to château'!

"I had made it. I don't mind complimenting myself. And I did it all alone. Sure, I had a lot of help and guidance from others in my career, but when I walked out on those stages I was the one who had to deliver; I did it then, and I am still doing it now. And I did it the hard way, and I did take rocky paths. And I did fight hard, and I swallowed my pride, and I did take insults. But I still did it. That is what I have tried to instill in my people whenever I am in America. Some of them listen, I guess, but the others just go along in their own little way. They don't realize that if they fight hard enough and think hard enough they can have the same thing I had.

"I dreamed of my castle for years and years, from the time I was a little girl, and I promised Mama that I was going to have a great big house 'over in St. Louis.' Well, it wasn't in St. Louis, but I can tell you that no one in St. Louis has one like mine. I was determined to have the best, and I got it.

"I didn't rush headlong into it. I was concerned that it should be restored to something of its original feeling. And I believe that I accomplished that. I spent thousands of dollars concealing the wiring and the pipes for the plumbing in the walls. Then I had old masons who knew the style of what I wanted, and they would repair the walls that were torn up, and you couldn't tell the difference when they were through!

"First I fixed up the inside. And I must say Jo was wonderful then. He threw himself into it. He helped me with the furniture and the china and the linens and the carpets—he helped me with everything.

"And you know, before I knew it, it was finished. And it was fabulous."

Indeed it was.

Josephine poured thousands upon thousands of dollars into the château itself. Later she was to pour millions into the balance of the property, her "village."

If she particularly liked you, she would personally take you on a tour and explain everything to you. It took an entire day, and she always finished the first part in the dining hall. Then you would have lunch, and continue on until cocktail time. It was exhausting, and must have been murderous during times when the château was being renovated and refurnished.

"Now, look here closely over the fireplace. You will see the coat of arms of the lords of Castelnaud-Fayrac. These chairs are originals of those Louis himself designed for the Salle des Glaces in the Versailles. Three people had to pass on each piece of furniture before it could be placed there, and while these are perfect, they were not approved for some very minor detail. If you examine them, you can wonder what the originals that were approved were like."

The grand salon of the Château des Milandes was magnificent. It was a little overpowering when you were in it alone, but when it was filled with people, you delighted in it. The floors were a beautiful parquet, laid by hand, and the fireplace was enormous. At Christmastime huge trees would be brought in and thrown onto the fire, and they would burn night and day. There were the finest Oriental carpets on the floors, and the tops of the various tables were covered with her finest pieces and mementos.

"Here is my little collection of Sèvres music boxes. Wait—I'll wind them up and they can play and sing for you."

She wound up one, and it played "*J'ai deux amours*." She would sing along with it, and when it got to the end and started repeating itself, she would do the same, perhaps two or three times, and then she would laugh and carefully put it away. As it ran down, she would let her own voice run down with it, until she was singing a low baritone. Then, when it stopped, she would too, and the laughter would start all over again.

"And here is my pride and joy. It is the only thing that came with the château when I purchased it." It was the beautiful mirror that Louis XIV had sent as a gift to the lord of the castle a long time ago. It rose from the floor to the ceiling.

The music room was the same size as the salon. It contained mirrors, and huge candelabra, and marble-topped *bombé* chests, and more Oriental rugs. There was a collection of art deco figurines that must have been priceless, and a collection of jade equally so.

"Look here at the piano. Isn't that beautiful? Imagine the months and months that it took some artist to paint those scenes and designs."

Then we would be ushered into the dining room. It could seat sixty people for formal sit-down dinners. It also had a huge fireplace, as did the grand salon, and at Christmastime it also burned huge logs night and day.

"For really big parties, I can put on the dog when I want to. Then I send up to the storerooms in the attic and bring down the matching chairs, and up there we also have two more tables that match this one. Then we can make a great U-shaped table out of the three, and it is really something. Now, Stephen, look at these candelabra. When the family of Henri [Varna] was visiting in Russia before the Revolution, the czar and the czarina gave them these candlesticks as a gift; and he eventually inherited them. When I came here, he wanted to give me something really dear to him, and he gave me those for my dining salon. Feel them. It takes a giant to lift them up, and they look so light."

Josephine could serve as many as two hundred for a buffet, and use matching silver and china. And she did so on countless occasions. But her sit-down dinners for about a dozen people were the best. Then she would sit at the head of the table, and the stories would come out one after another.

One time Edith Piaf came to spend the weekend. And then the stories rolled on and on without stopping. When Piaf told one, it reminded Josephine of another, and then Piaf would be reminded of another, and so it went for hours.

In the château were countless rooms. There were over a dozen bedrooms, many of them suites with their own sitting rooms, dressing rooms and baths. There were dens and libraries and morning rooms and breakfast rooms, and two little dining rooms. Then, in the attic, there were storage rooms, and food-keeping rooms with hams hanging and cheeses laid out on wooden racks, and an ingenious sort of chimney that drew in the outside air and eventually expelled it through the roof. There were laundry rooms and ironing rooms and linen rooms.

On and on it went. Finally the tour reached Josephine's bedroom. By the standards of the other rooms in the château, it bordered on the severe. It was rather small—she liked it that way—but there were huge windows that would let in the morning sun. By this time Josephine had become a Catholic. On her little writing desk was a large crucifix, and a photograph of her mother. Over her bed was a smaller crucifix, and on either side were two paintings of the Virgin on plaster; one was the Virgin of Guadalupe. They had been given to her by the President of Mexico long ago.

There were a chaise, the usual carpets on the floor, and two tiny reading lamps with tulip shades. Commanding the entire room was the famous bed of Marie Antoinette. Its canopy rose almost nine feet high, and the spread was a striped silk. It was in this bed that Josephine did most of her thinking.

"I just love this little bed of mine. When I am in it, I can really think. Sometimes I rest here looking out of first one window and then the other, and I try to get my thoughts together like I used to. It seems it doesn't come as easy to me as it did, though. When I was younger, I could think it all out very quickly and understand it, too. Now it is a little different. I guess maybe I'm getting old.

"One of these days I'm going to get just too tired. Then I'm going to come up here and lay down to get some rest, and that is where they will find me, I guess. With an old towel wrapped around my head, and a heavy old bathrobe wrapped around what will be left of me. Then probably the undertaker will take one look at me and say, 'Is that Josephine Baker?' "

She thought it was an hysterical joke, and sometimes she would elaborate on it even more. She did not die in her bed or in her château; both were long since gone. She died on a stage, really—and that, I believe, she would have liked even better.

* * *

If the inside of the château was magnificent, its grounds and park were equal to it; so, when Josephine finished with the château itself, she started on the grounds. She came on building after building—for, as mentioned before, the Milandes was really a village—and wondered what she could do with them.

It occurred to her that if the Milandes was to be her experiment in brotherhood, if it was really to become a "village of the world," then there would need to be accommodations for the visitors and the pilgrims who visited there. With this in mind, she embarked on the great venture that eventually bankrupted her.

The carriage houses and the stables became hotels, and the gardeners' cottages became "model farms"; she restored the tiny church and had the ancient cemetery tidied up. She built a dock into the river; she took an old guest house and converted it into a bar and night club; she built fifty little African huts to house the young people who would come. There were outdoor restaurants, and a place for the young people to dance. There was a huge Olympic-size swimming pool with dressing rooms, and another restaurant adjoining it. There was a museum that housed all of her wardrobe, her artifacts, her archives.

It was an entire city, and it was operated on an almost socialistic basis. The farms provided the fruits and vegetables and dairy products that were used by the entire village. There were homes for the maids, butlers, and cooks who did not work in the château but who worked in the other hotels and restaurants. All in all, everything that everyone needed was provided for.

Josephine wanted desperately to have a gambling casino, and I did considerable work toward this end. Eventually four friends of mine who were familiar with gambling operations, having worked in Las Vegas and Reno, went to the Milandes to study the situation. Everything they reported back to me was perfect, except for one thing: no one would come. Not because they would not want to, but because they could not. The Milandes, they explained, was totally isolated. It was too far to drive for a weekend or an evening; the railroad transportation was not good; there was no air transportation; and there certainly were not enough people living within a hundred-mile radius to support a substantial casino. Their report also stated that they doubted very much that the village could exist even as a little tourist attraction.

It was at this time that I began to be concerned for Josephine. Of course, now was not the time to speak to her about retrenching or cutting back, or to warn her about her "dream."

Now she was deeply into the children, her "village du monde"—what I referred to as her venture into futility. It was now that she entered into the great venture of her life—her venture into brotherhood.

Chapter 15

". . . My opinion is that I was blessed to have been chosen by God to be exactly the one bestowed with such a responsibility.

I will never have given enough of myself to please God, and have done my duty, in giving a 'world symbol of brotherhood' as true and as beautiful as that of my children.

Because my children have proved that there were no more continents,

No more obstacles,

No more problems which could prevent understanding and respect between humans,

No more excuses that color and religious differences prevent unity . . ."

* * *

Josephine now embarked on the one really great adventure in her life that was not theatrical. She sailed into that part of her life that dealt with humanity, with the brotherhood of man. But she was out of her milieu. She was in "deep water" that she could not understand, psychologically speaking. She wanted to prove something to the world. She would not succeed.

She resolutely refused to believe that her great dream of "brotherhood for the world" could not be realized. She gave everything that she could to her cause. Along with material possessions—her money, her jewels, her other properties—she poured herself into it. It drained her. It sapped the strength from her. In the end, it killed her.

I saw years ago that the venture was doomed. I never once suggested it to her. My only suggestion to her was that she should husband her resources and her strength.

She lavished both on her dreams. More important, she lavished her love.

* * *

So, in the early 1950s, Josephine Baker "retired from the theatre." She then descended on the Milandes, surrounded by her staff; Margaret and Elmo; her mother, whom she had brought to France; and her first children.

"*Mon village . . . le village du monde . . . la capitale du monde de la fraternité.*" ("My village, the village of the world, the capital of the world of brotherhood.") The Milandes was to be her little "New Harmony," a utopian society in the United States founded in 1821. What Josephine did not know about New Harmony was that it had been generously financed; it had also failed. And while Josephine was a very wealthy woman by standards of the time, her wealth was no match for her ambitions. In order to have a plan, one must also have the ingredients.

Much has been written about the adopted children of Josephine Baker—her Rainbow Children. She chose them carefully. They were truly of every race, creed, and religion.

* * *

"Stephen—oh, my God, Stephen," she said, laughing hysterically. "What am I going to do with my little babies? Will you just come up and see what they have done now? And Jannine has left them only for a moment. They have dumped the baby oil on the linoleum floor, and they are skating around on it like it was an ice-skating rink—and the ones who can't stand up are using their little behinds for skates."

There were times when they gave her great pleasure. There is no doubt that on some days they were amusing. They were like kittens and puppies—cuddly and full of love. They were wonderful—until they started scratching the furniture or biting the legs of the piano. It was then that Josephine could not cope.

"When Jo and I sit down to dinner, the napkin rings read: Akio (Korea); Jari (Finland); Jean-Claude (France); Jeannot (Japan); Luis (Colombia); Moise (Israel); Brahim (Algiers); Mara (Venezuela); Koffi (Ivory Coast); Marianne (France); Noel (France).

"All my life I have maintained that the people of the world can learn to live together in peace if they are not brought up in prejudice. This is why I traveled all over the world to adopt my eleven youngsters."

The above was quoted by Joan Cook of *The New York Times* in the early 1960s, in an exclusive interview with Josephine concerning her "international family." Josephine finished the rather long interview, which the *Times* carried prominently in its theatrical section, with this statement:

"[When I come again] I'm bringing the children. . . . I'll rent a house in the country—so they can get to know American youngsters. That would be all right, don't you think?"

"That would be all right, don't you think?" By this time Josephine was wondering about the entire venture. She was beginning to doubt herself.

I had written only a few weeks before, but now it seemed that I had to report to her almost weekly. On April 13, 1961, Josephine wrote me again from the Milandes:

> . . . Just a word to say that I haven't heard from you in such a long time that I am wondering if you are ill. Please write—have you found someone to make a loan of $50,000 with interest, paying back the sum by $2,000 a month, with interest?
>
> Please write me. Love to all of you. The children are well.

In her own hand she signed her name, and added, "The children are well, so are all of us."

It is pointless to go into the details of why her plan did not work; the most important reason, as the above letter indicates, was lack of funds. For by now the money was running out of her bank accounts like wine from a broken bottle. Even if she had had all the money in the world behind her, it is doubtful whether the experiment would have worked.

Perhaps things would have been different if Josephine had spent her entire time with the children. But she was not able to, for she felt that she had to stay on top of the near pandemonium that reigned at the Milandes. There were always laborers, carpenters, plumbers, electricians, and every kind of mechanic and builder, as well as their assistants and the people responsible for running the little city she was building. Their work was far beyond her understanding, yet she still tried to supervise and direct them all.

Further, she would not delegate responsibility. She would be in a meeting discussing, perhaps, the building of a swimming pool, then would abruptly leave to see how her "little club" was being built, and forget to return. Then the swimming pool people would be invited to stay over as her guests to continue the discussion the following day. But then other problems would arise to draw her away, causing a delay of another four or five days, during which time the businesses of the swimming pool people would have to run by themselves.

Understandably, they became annoyed—but Josephine could not understand why. What was more, when she received huge bills for their time, she would be outraged. But she would pay. She had to.

Later, the time would come when she could not pay.

* * *

Of course, there were always the children.

The children of Josephine Baker were the most pampered, looked after, educated, played with and cared for children of any in the entire world. They were also the most spoiled. They were totally undisciplined. The only one who could control them was Josephine—but she was never there. She was building a swimming pool, or decorating a hotel, or helping make wine, or even trying to show an old peasant farmer's wife how to make butter. Of course, the farmer's wife had been doing it for forty years, but still Josephine had to show her how.

None of the servants, tutors, or employees could make the children behave. When one child received a bowl of hot oatmeal in the face from another, Josephine, on hearing about it, would howl with delight. She did not discipline them; and again, she delegated no authority. She did not know how. Eventually, when some poor, unsuspecting visitor would get a karate punch in the back from one of the children, even the servants and tutors would laugh—because that's what Josephine did. And, of course, Josephine was paying the bills. She never thought to let the tutors, servants and governesses in on her brotherhood theme. Perhaps if they had known what her plan was, they would have acted differently.

She brought tutors from the country where each child was born. They usually fled in a few weeks.

One day while she and I were going over some accounts in her bedroom, the door flew open, and an enraged young man from Israel charged in. He had been there only a week or two, and I felt he really knew what he was doing. He was one of few who understood Josephine's plan.

He had young Moise by the hand, with the intention of lecturing him in front of his mother for some misdeed. I thought to myself, Well, here is one who will stand up to her and knows what he is doing.

Little Moise had three times run away from his Hebrew lessons; each time he was found alone, playing about the pool. The Israeli tutor wanted to discipline him but felt that a confrontation involving himself, Moise and Josephine would be good.

When the child saw his mother in bed, he began crying and ran to her. She put him under the covers with her.

"Now, what is the matter here, Monsieur? Tell me all about this."

The tutor, I felt, told his story very well. It was really only a matter of a little discipline.

"But, sir," she responded, "you obviously don't understand children. Don't you see, there is something down by the pool that is more important to him than his Hebrew lesson. So you must go to the pool with him and discover what that is. Then, as his tutor, you will see that that desire is fulfilled first, then the Hebrew lesson will come easily for him."

The tutor explained that Moise was interested in nothing more than a little swim.

"It's obvious that you don't understand me at all," Josephine said, "and you are supposed to be an educated man. Do as I say, and you will see that it will work. Obviously the child has other interests too, and you must discover what they are. Now leave me, because I am busy, and report to me in a week."

The tutor never reported back; instead, he left the Milandes after breakfast the next morning, commenting to me before his departure: "Mr. Papich, I think that woman is mad. Don't you?"

Josephine did not miss him for a month. She saw the children so little that she did not even know their tutor had left weeks before.

* * *

Then on and on went the building, and the tearing down, and the building up again. And everything was meticulously done so as to preserve the nature and the quality of the originals. Then came the upholsterers and the drapery makers and the rug merchants, followed by the linen people, the china makers, the purveyors of silverware, and sellers of this and that, from soap to towels to foodstuffs—everything it takes to run a little village.

There was also during this time a great influx of people to run the village. Soon there was more "help" than tourists or customers.

"Never mind," Josephine said. "When they see what I have done, and when they know what my idea is, the walls will be bulging."

For Josephine's sake, I really hoped that one day I would see the walls bulging. I never did. Neither did she.

Thus it continued. And during this period I would come and I would go, and each time it would seem that there was even more madness. I had arranged a $50,000 loan for her; it was but a drop in her ocean of debts.

Up to a certain point, Josephine paid in cash for everything as she ordered it. Then, before she knew it—even before her accountants knew it—she ran out of money. What happened next is an old story: the purveyors of everything from a napkin to a bar of soap, and all the contractors, started extending her credit.

On and on it went. She would order without written bids, and the costs would soar. The accountants and I, when I was there, begged her not to order without at least some sort of written purchase order. But by the time we had explained to her what a purchase order was and impressed its necessity on her, it was too late. By that time, there were various types of mortgages, liens and orders hanging over the property like great rain clouds. Still, she did not understand.

Then one day, miraculously, it was finished. Why it had not killed her by then I do not know, for she had given it everything.

And she had done it for her children. She had done it to "prove to the world" that her theme of the brotherhood of man could be made to work.

The world, as it would turn out, could not have been less interested.

* * *

Now, when the opportunity came, when her building was finished and she could devote her time to putting her children into this marvelous environment she had created for them, she was not able to, for she was broke and had to "come out of retirement" to earn the money to keep the machinery of brotherhood going.

Perhaps if she had had that time to devote all her attention to the children, and if she could have put them through their paces—for in those days they did behave in her presence, and I believe they did love her—her plan might have worked. Or, if she had been able to delegate responsibility, to give someone else her ideas to project to others her enthusiam about brotherhood, they might have carried on for her. She did not know how, and she did not have the time.

Josephine begged me constantly to help her raise funds for her cause. In America, she appealed to her important contemporaries in the theatre, many of whom became enthusiastic and promised to help. The help never came.

Finally I asked her to take some time off, if only a week, and write me of her plan in detail. To give me her thoughts on brotherhood, on her ideal, so I could better convey these thoughts to others and maybe infuse them with some of her own enthusiasm. The situation was not yet desperate. I thought I might just be able to help her.

There had been one close brush with bankruptcy, and she had been bailed out to some extent. Brigitte Bardot had gone on French network television in her behalf to appeal for funds; and while it was not, as Josephine said, "a colossal success," it did help. Old friends came through for her, sending sometimes a dollar, sometimes more. But the debts were so massive by now that it made only a dent.

By this time also, what was happening was that she was soliciting funds from "the world," so to speak, for a cause that she herself was neglecting outrageously. But she did not understand this.

For without the children to prove the point, there could be no cause. They were the catalyst that was supposed to make the plan work. And by now she had so neglected the children that it was almost hopeless. It was like pots and pans without a cook, a hospital without a doctor, a car without a driver. What good was the Château des Milandes, her village of the world, her village of brotherhood and peace, if she would not devote the time to seeing that her children received the necessary instruction and guidance to make it all work?

I discussed all this with her at great length. She agreed to closet herself away and divulge to me all her plans, her ideals, her thoughts, her goals—everything that she thought about her ideals of brotherhood.

Then on September 18, 1964, I received a special-delivery letter from the Milandes. It was really a little treatise.

Josephine had telephoned me to say it was on the way. "I've written it in French, Stephen," she had said, "and it's exactly what I feel. I want you to take it to the Alliance Française and have it translated. You know, I have been here for so long, I seem to think better in French, so that is what I have done."

When the letter arrived, it was nine pages of single-spaced typing. I read it over and over to see if I was getting its proper meaning. It was then that I started to worry very much for Josephine.

I will not quote the entire letter; I will only extract those paragraphs that I believe typify her feelings. Her "treatise" began:

The Ideal of Brotherhood in the Milandes
as Seen by Josephine Baker (1964)

I am still very healthy for the present. I believe I can earn enough money to guarantee my children's complete lives and our household, and to pay the personnel that we need.

I believe also that we are blessed from heaven to be helped so much by the countries of the world which came to our aid, countries very far away, because our distress was enormous, and at one time I felt very, very discouraged.

In spite of this state of mind, I forced myself to keep my courage, my hope and my dignity for my children, for the ideal they represent and for all who believe in us.

I know that there are some who think I undertook too large a responsibility.

My opinion is that I was blessed to have been chosen by God to be exactly the one bestowed with such a responsibility.

I will never have given enough of myself to please God, and have done my duty, in giving a "world symbol of brotherhood" as true and as beautiful as that of my children.

Because my children have proved that there were no more continents,
No more obstacles,
No more problems which could prevent understanding and respect between humans,
No more excuses that color and religious differences prevent unity.

Isn't it true that God is the Father of us all, and we know that it is possible to live together respecting equality, beliefs and human rights?

I have brushed aside, in my life, all bad spirits which could harm this success.

However, I have tried to push tolerance to the extreme in order to better understand the human being.

Of course, I have deep wounds in all the little doors of my heart, but my conscience, my morale and my conviction have not been damaged.

One cannot receive anything without giving something.

I take this opportunity to thank all those, all over the world, who have been so close to me during the last days of this illness. [*Author's note:* Josephine was referring to her first warning of heart trouble, which was to plague her until her death.] It was a fight for my life, because of the panic of my little heart, because, as they say: "You can reason with your head, but not with your heart."

I am not complaining.

On the contrary, I have a kind of gratefulness to God for having made me suffer morally, physically and spiritually for the ideal that the Milandes represents.

Equality, my ideal, my children, are my reason for living.

I have had the happiness of staying with my fellow men a little longer to verify that my struggle, my conviction and man's right were not in vain.

More than ever, I am convinced that unity, understanding, love, and brotherhood are our only salvation.

I wanted the Milandes to be known and respected as a world village.

Destiny wanted me to find this little hamlet which is, without a doubt, a little earthly paradise for those in search of peace for their soul.

I didn't look for it specially.

I found it naturally, and I held on to it fiercely, for it is my resting place.

It is here that my children can pursue their brotherly education in peace, without being influenced by bad spirits, for this is very important for the ideal which they represent.

It must not be thought that I am trying to make little gods of them, but only normal beings—just, honest toward themselves and toward others, guided by purity and the conscience of sensible men.

I know that we are ahead of our time.

That is why there has been so much confusion about me and about others who think as we do.

An enormous number of people did not want to believe, but many people believed.

It is thanks to all this confidence in the world that I found "Help" at the desired moment.

It is thanks also to this unity of all social classes which I brought together by the spirit of the heart during my long years of traveling and of perseverance for our ideal that the Milandes will remain, for always, our world village.

The children prove that all this is possible. Time will do the rest.

I thank all those little children who sent us dried flower petals in their letters and who opened their piggy banks so that the "children of the world" wouldn't lose their home.

This type of letter, incidentally, came in by the thousands; children, it seemed, understood her plan better than adults. It was amazing what the children would write and would send to share with their "brothers and sisters" far away. Many of the letters contained dried flowers, blades of grass, the "little hairs from a child's kitten," along with a few pennies, or sous, or pesos, or whatever. Josephine would be so touched that tears would come to her eyes.

Sadly, though, the "brothers and sisters" in the Milandes did not seem to care. In her interview with *The New York Times,* Josephine had stated, "The children sleep in a dormitory, take their differences for granted, and bicker amiably among themselves. . . ." She must have made the statement through clenched teeth. For now she was trapped. She had been spreading the word: She had prepared a place for the practice of the concept of brotherhood. But at home, the ranks were even then deserting the battle. She knew it too.

One day I went up to the nursery, and Marianne, then the only daughter, was there alone. She was about seven or eight at the time. I showed her a few of the letters and told her about what the other children in the world were doing to help them. One of the letters, from a little girl in the American Midwest, contained a charming photograph of the girl holding a baby duck. The child had also enclosed one of the duck's feathers, writing that she could not send the duck, but that she felt that the children could know all about the little duck by just seeing the feather. It was marvelous thinking that adults could well emulate.

I told Marianne that the little girl lived near where I had lived as a child. She just stared sullenly at me, hardly looking at the photo or the other letters. Then she noticed on the back of the photograph a dime that the little girl had taped on. All of a sudden she snatched the photograph from me, tore it into several pieces to get at the dime, then ran out of the room.

I decided to tell Josephine the story. When I finished, she stared ahead for a long time. Finally she said, "What is it you say in America?—I think I have bitten off more than I can chew. But what can I do now? It is already in my mouth." I thought so too, but I did not answer. It is too bad that the children for the great experiment in brotherhood could not have been more thoroughly screened. But, of course, that would have defeated the purpose of the experiment.

> I warmly thank [the "treatise" continued] all the teachers who took up collections from their students of all ages.
>
> I thank Brigitte Bardot for her big heart and her unselfish generosity.
>
> This is the first time in the history of the world that a small private hamlet lost in the arms of mother nature has found so much world help for such an appeal.
>
> I thank Mrs. De Gaulle, who is a mother, for the sum which she sent us, as well as all other members of the government, and as well as the entire French population in all social, artistic, political, literary, scientific, medical, etc., classes.
>
> I thank also all the international personalities, of all social classes, for their moral, affectionate and financial support, as well as the artists, impresarios, theatre directors, industrialists, and businessmen, in France

and elsewhere, for the benefit parties and for the means which they found to bring in gifts.

They all united so that the Milandes would not be lost.

I think of President Felix Houphouët-Boigny, sponsor of my little Koffi, age six and a half, born in Abidjan (Ivory Coast), from the same Baoule tribe of his sponsor, who came to the rescue of his little godchild, of his brothers and sister, and also of the ideal that the Milandes represents.

I thank Mr. Liege, director of the Grand Hotel of Abidjan, who, with the agreement of President Houphouët-Boigny, organized, on June 26, 1964, a benefit party which brought in, to the profit of the Milandes, an enormous sum.

I immediately told Koffi, his brothers and his sisters, who were eating lunch, that the African and European population had entirely answered our appeal.

The smile of contentment on the face of this child was beautiful to see, and his little brothers and sister were proud of him, and I was proud of humanity.

This statement, and the following few, are what Josephine would have *liked* to have occurred, not what actually *did* occur. But, as she said, she was now trapped by her own creation, and she had to continue, for "it is already in my mouth."

The telephone rang at the same time to inform me that Japan had made the same appeal, with as wonderful a result.

This good news was the continuation of the celebration of the children.

I'm so glad that I had the foresight at the beginning of the life of my little ones to explain to them their origins, their colors, their religions, their countries, and so on.

Today, my children are proud that the whole world come to our aid.

They are equally proud to belong to the family of the world, because isn't it during times of trouble and danger that the family should unite?

You see, if I hadn't prepared them in advance, they would have received a shock which could have been disastrous to them for their entire lives.

The other day, my little Moise, who is nine, came to me to talk about battles he saw on television between whites and blacks in the streets of the U.S.A.

This is a disgraceful situation for the century in which we live, even though we pretend to have made enormous progress since the Middle Ages.

These problems were the cause, for twelve years, until the nomination to power of our dear President Kennedy, for the refusal of my right of entry and work in the U.S.A., because I took my responsibility to heart.

I opened the battle without respite, knowing what I was doing,

The personal price I would have to pay,

Taking on my shoulders a responsibility that few others, at that time, could take, because of reprisals, persecution, and cold war against them.

I went to the front ranks of the battle with the most courageous.

I paid for this audacity in many ways.

I gave myself without thinking.

Yes, I was among those great surgeons who cut to the quick a problem *against racism.*

Many fell on the battlefield, exiled, tortured morally and physically.

I am glad that it was not all in vain.

That I was among those who opened the eyes of those who were asleep for too long, and who now follow the revolution without detour and without the slightest yielding.

Today, we declare that the death of the abscess will not stop until the body is completely purified.

Unfortunately, this revolution will be more and more bloody.

But there, also, it is too late. As I have said for years, *an elephant does not know his force as long as he is not mortally wounded.*

That is why you must always avoid hate and vengeance.

My heart bleeds to see brothers of the same human race tear each other apart, when all this could have been avoided long ago:

By recognizing human rights since the abolition of slavery,

By nullifying the existing laws which support these horrible injustices, without forgetting the first North Americans, the Indians.

I am sad to say that once the bull sees blood (this is the time to say it) *he sees red.*

Time was lost, because we could have been on the road to unity if President Kennedy had not been assassinated.

Because he was in agreement with all in the world who supported human rights.

Unfortunately, the whole world will experience the eruption of this volcano, asleep for a long time, and progress will stop for a moment, because we cannot remain indifferent to this big revolution which will become with time . . . EVOLUTION.

I am sure that the abscess of South Africa will perish, followed by other abscesses, small and large, which infect our world body.

Let us all unite in the same burst of heart and justice for the rights of man, before it's too late.

Neither our guns, nor our cannons, nor our bombs, whatever they may be;

Neither our words of pacification, our promises, our malices, our hatreds, nor our physical forces, nor our jealousies, nor our finances, nor our publication forces, whatever they may be, will be able to stop the march of time and of human justice.

But we can avoid catastrophes, shedding of blood, by wisdom, and *this wisdom is simply brotherhood, respect, unity and the rights of man.*

My little Moise, as my other children, were not surprised at what they saw on television, since they were aware of world conflicts between the peoples for which their mother has been fighting her whole life.

But they were very shocked that the so-called adults could fight and kill each other for reasons of color, religion—racial or social—reasons which most children of today, in most countries, assume are completely natural and represent no problem.

They told me that they understood very well why I went to get them in their countries of origin, making them live together here under the motto "Worldly Brotherhood."

You see, there is already an enormous progress visible, because other children of their age, four to twelve years, not living in a country with these troubles, would never have understood.

Therefore, the education that I give them is the right one for the future of the peace of the world.

That is why I have said for years, and I repeat it today more strongly than ever, we must *change the system of education and instruction* in the homes and schools, in all countries where there are racial problems of color, religion or social problems.

Facts are facts, and they must be faced in order to be conquered, to achieve a better future for the world.

Mothers, heads of state, teaching and *law* are responsible for the success of this ideal.

And, at the same time, their presence will serve as a symbol and encouragement for all those who are fighting for exactly this ideal.

It is curious that, without wishing it, and without looking for it specifically, this example is taking place exactly in Dordogne, the cradle of prehistory, because it is here that is found the Cro-Magnon and the past of the first men.

We think of the Milandes as an immense barge which almost went down.

It is the desire to reach a balance such as the Milandes, home for children, of the ideal they represent, and refuge for human beings of the world, to find peace.

The Milandes must remain a center of "World Brotherhood" and become a "Cultural Center."

The Milandes must become populated.

It must have buildings, hotels, houses-restaurants-stores-villas-museums-amusements-tennis-heliports-gas stations-campsites-concourses-theatres-swimming pools. . . .

It must have the most extraordinary artistic attractions so that the people enjoy themselves and are happy to live there.

I would like to have a special school built in the Milandes so that all who wish to know themselves and to learn brotherhood may come there.

For, unfortunately, history shows us that brotherhood must be learned, when it should be natural.

There must be more motels at reasonable prices for the students.

I would like them to come from everywhere to give lectures, exchange ideas, have debates and speak freely without fear of giving their opinion.

The festivals of the Milandes must continue in a different form every year.

Finally, everything must be done to create a complete village of brotherhood, to meditate in the beauty of nature, to live with her and not against her.

The directors and the personnel must be chosen with care in order to safeguard our religion of brotherhood.

I would like for my children to work here in order to earn their living, as must all honest people, followed by a committee which will not be ordinary parents, but special, to keep our home, our ideal, pure, because it is *well-behaved youth* that represents our future.

I think that I owe you this explantation, because we are all the parents of my little ones, mine who are yours, and yours who are mine, given that God is the Father of all of us.

Therefore, the distress of the Milandes is yours, and we will not stop fighting together until this is all found and realized.

The Milandes is our home of calm.

The resting place for those who need tranquility and appeasement.

The Milandes is the earthly paradise.

It is for all this that I persist.

Not only for my children.

Not for myself as long as I'm on this earth, but for the crowd that has such a need for a little respite to continue the battle for PEACE.

This is my desire—my ideal.

Your sister
Josephine Baker

This, then, is what Josephine wanted. I read it over many times. Finally I decided it would be best not to show it to the people who I thought would be helpful to her cause. I especially did not like the idea that she was attempting to raise money for the cause, however valid it was, knowing all the while that there was dissension in the ranks.

I showed the letter to a few businessmen in an effort to seek their advice and aid. They called it "Marxist thinking," "Communist thinking," "rabble-rousing by some crazy woman no one has ever heard of." They particularly resented the idea that they would be responsible for raising vast sums of money to "bail her out," and let her "travel around the world with her troupe of kids" at someone else's expense. "If she wants all those things," one of them said, "let her raise the money herself."

I do not know how many people have copies of what I call the "Famous Baker Treatise on Brotherhood." I know she mailed out many of them herself. But I did not use it in my effort to support her cause. Maybe it was a mistake; maybe if I had, she would have obtained the needed support.

The only reason I did not throw myself into it wholeheartedly was that I knew that unless she completely changed her way of thinking, and could see her way to spend every moment with the children, they would let her down. Only she could guide them.

She did not have—or could not find—that time. When the cruel period came years later, the children did not help her. Still, she fought for her cause. But now her banners were muddied; they had fallen many times. Eventually she was not able to extricate them from the mud at all.

Briefly, it was Josephine's idea that if a group of infants from all races, all creeds, and all religions were brought together, away from the influence of a normal environment and knowing nothing of cultural and racial biases, they could grow together in a spirit of love and friendship. It was her vision, then, that these children, brought up on this hearty diet of love and friendship, could then go forth and teach the doctrine of brotherhood to the world.

They would have been a remarkable group of leaders and teachers.

How could she now reveal to the world that her experiment had been a failure? She could not and would not. There was only one escape—and that was death. And eventually she escaped.

How could she tell the world that one of her children had stood in her bedroom screaming, "You are nothing but a slut, a whore—yes, you are a prostitute who dropped her clothes to show the world her body"?

After relating this incident to me, Josephine said: "Bad blood, Stephen, is just bad blood, and there is nothing, I have found out, that can be done about it."

It was the closest she ever came to admitting her failure to me; she never, to my knowledge, expressed this sentiment to another person. Perhaps, if Josephine were alive today, she would not forgive me for revealing her secret. But when she revealed it to me, it ceased to be a secret. She began to reveal the stories to me—stories she dragged up from her torn and shattered insides. It was these experiences with her children, too, that helped to kill her; she suffered her first heart attack after the encounter with her daughter.

She simply could not control them, but she would not admit it to herself, let alone to the world. For she had always preached humanity and brotherhood, and she had desperately crusaded against man's inhumanity to man.

Imagine how she must have felt when the police of the principality of Monaco were given orders not to arrest Josephine Baker's children for their infractions of the law. They were to be delivered to the Palace, and then Josephine was to be notified.

They pillaged her fabulous archives. They pawned what they could, and sold or gave away the rest to the American tourists in front of the casino.

"Hey, you! You wanna buy something? My mother is Josephine Baker, and here is an award given her by the President of Abidjan. You want it? Fifty francs."

They stole money from her purse, and stole from neighbors as well. And where they borrowed, Josephine paid back. In the end, they were just kids, with all the problems of kids—one deeply into narcotics, one a thief.

In their defense, not all were cut from the same cloth. But Josephine did not take them individually. They were a group, a fraternity. In the end, they were nothing.

The funeral of Josephine Baker, I am afraid, as far as her children are concerned, could be likened to a Hollywood film. It was *Imitation of Life* over and over again. Sometimes the colors of the actors were right, and sometimes they were wrong, but it was still *Imitation of Life*.

If it appears that I am being harsh on Josephine's children, that is too bad. It is as she told it to Robert Wood and me not very long ago, as she lay in her bed in a suite in the Beverly Hilton Hotel. I have tried only to set the record straight. And if someday the Rainbow Children of Josephine Baker read this little remembrance, perhaps it is good for them to know what their mother thought of them in the late evening of her life.

* * *

Josephine, deciding that perhaps the Milandes could be made into some sort of tourist attraction, proceeded to embark on a plan of financing and refinancing, of first mortgages, and second, and third. It was a plan that the most knowledgeable accountants would not have been able to fathom. Unfortunately, most of these transactions she made alone, without the advice of any of her friends, employees, or business associates. She would mysteriously disappear for a few days, then reappear with a purseful of money. The extent of these secret dealings first became clear when Jo Bouillon suggested that they mortgage the property to relieve the financial pressures, only to find that it had long since been done.

To complicate matters further, Josephine could not understand what was happening to the children. She blamed the servants and Jo for their fights, for their temperament, for their inability to cope with one another. When the birthday of one would come, or a national holiday that had to be celebrated, there were nothing but sullen faces in the presence of Mama. It is tragic that she did not bring in someone experienced in the psychological problems of children.

Josephine decided that the Milandes should be put on a paying basis. Now it would be even better. People the world over would come. They could stay at the inn or the hotel. Dine in her restaurants. Relax in the country. Swim in the pool. Be entertained in the club. And, most important, they could watch and see "brotherhood" in action. They could be an actual part of the capital of the world of brotherhood.

That did not work either; it proved to be only another disaster. She started by inviting people from the entire world to witness her dream in action. They arrived in droves. But none of them paid: they all assumed they were her guests. Some even sued her for the air fare, and collected.

Then, when the few regular tourists did start arriving, they never got to see either Josephine or her children. She now built a huge fence around the château, over which could be seen only the towers and turrets. It was an impenetrable fortress. The tourists left angry.

It might be that she did not want to expose the children—or that she could not. For they were beginning to exhibit some less than exemplary behavior, and she feared that the stories might get out.

Inside, protected by the centuries-old walls, the lessons continued. She kept playing the game, and the money kept pouring out. But none of these grand efforts rubbed off on the children.

She was devastated. Worse, the financial noose started to tighten. Again she mustered her strength. Incredibly, if only temporarily, she threw the noose from around her neck and started battling anew. Work—yes, she would return to the theatre. Hard work was good for her, and she could earn whatever she needed for her ideal of brotherhood.

Chapter 16

"And here we are, Monsieur. Yes, here we are. You told me then it would bankrupt me. But then you laughed . . . today you are not laughing."

"Today, Madame, I am not laughing. Today we are facing truth."

"Today, Monsieur, we are facing him again—Old Man Trouble."

* * *

Then one day she was broke. Josephine Baker, who had retired just a few years earlier, now had to make a comeback. And where best to make that comeback but in the United States, where the money was good and where a dollar at that time meant three times as much when converted to francs? She headed for New York City.

On the way, she had to make a stop that must have been a bitter pill to swallow: she paid a visit to the offices of the Paris moneylenders—pawnbrokers to the rich. In less than half an hour, she had given up a major portion of one of the world's most important private jewelry collections. Not long afterward, the balance of that collection went the same way. The dealers and brokers in diamonds and emeralds and pearls fought with one another for the jewels; they were well aware of the value of the collection. Its quality was so high that on countless occasions the finest houses would borrow certain specimens from it to use as a "barometer" against which to compare other jewels. Josephine knew quality herself, and she could call it—this one was "one river," this one "three river," and so on, in the language of the diamond experts. I never understood.

Josephine was thus reduced to the company of many others whose intentions are high and honorable. "Of course, I'll be back for them in a few months, for I'm going to America." But she never returned to redeem her collection, and eventually it was broken up; so great was its total value that no single buyer could be found.

And what was probably her most heartbreaking experience was the night when she returned to pawn her knight in shining armor, astride his prancing charger with his shining red eye. It must have been with trembling hands that she unpinned it from her Chanel suit and threw it down on the jeweler's velvet to be evaluated with the rest. She never came back for it or the other jewels she pawned that night. They too were broken up and sold, little jewel by little jewel, where they brought their greatest value.

"My God, Stephen, why is God punishing me like this?"

I didn't know.

* * *

But this story of the agony that Josephine was going through cannot be told in a few pages.

"That, Stephen, was the beginning of the most awful period of my life. I tried to think my way out a thousand times, and at every point I reached a dead end. I could not escape. All my friends, and certainly you, Stephen, who have stuck by me through thick and thin, tried to help, but I could not be helped. It was not meant to be, and that is all there is to it. When one cannot and will not help himself, then others cannot help him either."

The details of "my real agony on the cross, if one can have an agony," did not come out all at once. I myself was a witness to the first part of this agony.

* * *

It was one of those beautiful summer days in the south of France. It was so peaceful that we could hear the birds chirping. For some reason, I remember in the stillness of her bedroom I could hear a tractor in the fields. It was a quiet drone, getting louder as it neared, and then fainter as it moved away, plowing the fields.

She was in bed, and she loved the light streaming through the windows. It was the period when I was beginning to know her well. I was allowed to see her wearing her old terrycloth robe, with a towel around her head. She looked almost frumpy. Now, too, she was never without her dark glasses.

Her accountant of many years was also present, to do some "business" with Josephine.

"Maybe between the two of us, Monsieur Papich," he had said earlier, "we can change her way of thinking. I am really going to be firm with her when we go in. You will see." He was as firm as a pudding.

On her bed he piled his books and records, meticulously kept over the years. Then suddenly he burst out at her. It seemed he had reached the end of his patience. I was amazed, for he was a mild sort. By this time she was making verbal deals for purchases and contracting work without putting anything in writing—neither of which she had ever done before—and it was driving him mad.

"That is the sum of it, Madame. Can I put it to you more clearly? This is absolute madness. The millions that you are spending here. . . . The well is dry, Josephine. How can I tell you?"

She did not say a word. She just stared stonily at the pile of books and records. I was glad for him; he was finally telling her what he had obviously been thinking for years.

"Madame, please bear with me one last time. This hotel will be the straw that breaks the camel's back. I have calculated that if the hotel is full seven days a week, fifty-two weeks a year, it will still lose thousands of francs. And in the winter season, who comes to Dordogne? It is empty!"

Everything he was saying was true. He was telling it better than I could. I regretted that it was all in French and I was probably missing a great deal.

"I beg of you, Madame. You must stop this now or you will be bankrupt. I have money for only one more week of operation, and then it is over."

His anger now seemed to be spent; he did not know what else to say. He looked at me and shrugged his shoulders. But somehow he managed to muster a little more energy, and he let fly at her again. He moved around to the head of the bed, where he could be closer to her. Josephine had been gazing off into space, but now she looked up at him. I got the feeling that she was at last letting the truth penetrate.

"Madame, do you realize I cannot sleep at night? Do you realize that? I cannot sleep at night! And why?" Now he had gained control again, and he continued his attack. "Because I am worrying about you and your finances, Madame. You refuse to worry about them, so I must do the worrying for you."

I had never seen him so agitated before. Now he spoke slowly, and made every word count. I could see it was hitting home.

"Today and tonight, Madame, I worry no more. Tonight when I have my supper and go to bed, I will sleep, because at this moment I hand over the worry and the trouble to you, Josephine. I wash my hands of it." He made a washing gesture with his hands in front of her. "*Voilà . . . voilà!*"

Up to this point I had not said a word. I was now about to get a lesson in the old Josephine Baker black magic, as I often called it. She used it frequently on stage, but she could also use it off stage when she wanted to.

She looked up at both of us. I sensed that she was not too well that day.

I was about to be taken, as was her accountant, like a piece of putty and molded into whatever Josephine desired.

"Ah, gentlemen, I am rude. Sit down, won't you? Stephen, pour me some chocolate, please. Take a cup for yourself. . . . Both of you have some, and bring up your chairs. I'm just not feeling well today."

I poured us all some chocolate, and we sat down with her. Now the room became as silent as a tomb, the only sound being the occasional rustling of the curtains in the breeze. She looked away from us and once again began staring off into space.

"Why don't you have a cigarette? You will feel better. Do you know what I was thinking about while you were talking to me?"

Of course, the accountant knew Josephine well; he realized that he was trapped, and that a story was coming. Now he was sorry for what he had said to her. I could tell also that he really adored her.

"You know, I was thinking about the time you came to my dressing room at the Folies . . . it was way, way back. I can't even remember. You know, time is still my enemy. It was just before I ran away to Sweden with the king, and you were furious with me, that time when you came in with your papers and books. I remember it so well. You were young then. So was I."

Then slowly she took us back; it was is if we were watching a flashback in a great motion picture. She returned to a night long ago, and she had not forgotten a single detail.

"You knocked at my door, and you were so apologetic. I remember that you were glad to get my account because you were going to get married and you needed the money. I got the dogs or the cats or whatever off a chair so you could sit down, and you told me that you had finished all my books. You were so pleased with yourself. You were so pleased that you had to come to see me immediately, and you thought I might be annoyed . . ."

I could tell that the man was in his own seventh heaven. He was polishing his glasses, and his cigarette was burning down and dropping ashes on his vest. But he was all ears—and for a story that he probably had heard countless times before.

". . . Then I asked you to give me the verdict. I didn't say it too well, and you didn't understand that I wanted to know what my real financial position was. Then you understood, and I started singing and laughing. I was singing . . . 'My fate is in your hands, yes, my fate is in your hands.' And how you laughed, because that was from a song that I had been using. Do you remember, Monsieur, '*Comme il banque*' [later recorded in English, "Feelin' Like a Million"]? Of course you do!"

He was nodding vigorously, and I could see the moisture in his eyes.

"And you stood up so tall and straight and so formally, and I knew then that you had accounted for every penny, every sou, and that you even had a receipt for it. Ah, Monsieur, if everyone had treated me as honestly as you have, we would not be here today.

"And you had said that that very day you had finished the job, and you told me how much I was worth, and it was enormous—over a million—in dollars, too. And I'll never forget when you said, '*Alors,* Mademoiselle, what a fortune!'

"And I couldn't believe it either. I grabbed a pencil and a paper and figured francs to dollars, for then I figured it that way. Now I am old and so used to francs. I make dollars go into francs, but what's the difference? It is all the same. You have it, or you do not.

"You grinned from ear to ear. You seemed to be happier for me than I was for myself. It was wonderful to be a millionaire and so young.

"Then I remember going on that drive with Pepe. And you remember him well, Monsieur. For I feel you did not approve. But that is the way it was."

He frowned a little at this but said nothing. The story was too good. He wanted to relive it all too, to escape even momentarily from the problems pressing them both.

"We drove all over in that Bugatti. And it was a Royale, too. I don't think there were over a dozen, and it had been lent to me. That crazy Pepe was driving, I remember, and we were speeding down those roads like mad. I was singing at the top of my voice."

Then she started to sing, and it was exactly like the record she eventually made in both French and English: " 'I'm feeling like a million . . . da da da de do . . .' " She put in her own little jargon where she had forgotten the words.

"And then we came here. Yes, right to the Milandes, where we all are now. And I have told you that this house called to me to help it, and I tried. I am still trying. And I asked an old priest coming out of the little church what château it was, and he told me it was the Château des Milandes."

"And here we are, Monsieur. Yes, here we are. You told me then it would bankrupt me. But then you laughed . . . today you are not laughing."

I looked at this kindly, wonderful old gentleman. The tears now filled his eyes. I could tell that he hated to say what he had to say.

"Today, Madame, I am not laughing. Today we are facing the truth."

"Today, Monsieur," she responded, "we are facing him again—Old Man Trouble."

During this entire dialogue I had not said a word. There was now a long pause as they studied each other silently.

"Well, Monsieur," she said at last, "I must go to work. Yes, I must go to work again."

"It is true, Madame. Yes, it is true. But in the meantime we are being pressed by creditor after creditor. And what I said earlier is not true, Madame. *I will not sleep tonight, either.*" He said it carefully and deliberately, as if to let her know that he would still worry for her as he had in the past. "Sleep will not come to me . . . because I am worried. Yes . . . I am now really worried."

"I know, and I thank you."

She sat up in bed, and he kissed both her cheeks. She watched him fondly as he picked up all his papers and books.

When he had gone, she asked me to excuse her. As I went out the door she reached for the telephone.

Two days later, a pleasant, friendly-looking little businessman came to the château. He stayed closeted with Josephine a long time. I was sitting in front of the château reading some of her old correspondence when she emerged to see the man to his car. She was saying, "So then, Monsieur, thank you very much for your trouble and for your kindness to me. I will see you very soon."

He then walked over and shook my hand. We chatted briefly, and he was soon back in his car and off down the road.

Years later his path and mine were to cross again. He had been Josephine's agent—or, to be more precise, her pawnbroker. He had not seen Josephine for some time. After hearing Josephine's story and his own, I found it easy to piece it all together, and there were no discrepancies.

The man represented several wealthy people who lent their money on good security. He dealt almost exclusively in jewels. He was from Russia originally and had come to France just before the Revolution. His family had gone to Buenos Aires, Argentina, and at the time of our second meeting he had just returned from there. We began to talk about that beautiful country. Then his wife came up, and he introduced her. We sat in the lobby of the Hotel de Castiglione in Paris and had an aperitif, and they told me the story.

He and his wife had loved Josephine and had been fans of hers for many years. When Josephine had telephoned him, he had come immediately and agreed to secure substantial amounts of money for her. In return, she pledged a portion of her jewelry collection as security.

Then, late one night, Josephine came to their office again. They were delighted to see her.

"I have all your jewels, Madame," the broker said. "I can deliver them to you tomorrow."

"I have not come for my jewels, Monsieur. . . . I have come for more money."

The agent was stunned. "But, Madame, when you telephoned I thought it was to redeem them. I have gone the limit on your collection. I could not extract a cent more from my sources."

They remembered that she was dressed beautifully. His wife described her as wearing a Chanel suit and a beautiful fur hat. "You would never think, Monsieur," she told me, "that she needed a centime."

Josephine informed them that she needed $50,000 immediately, and from her purse she took the balance of her jewelry and put it on the black velvet cloth on his desk.

The agent had had no idea that her collection was so vast. He studied the jewels carefully, then told her he would call at her hotel the following day with the necessary draft.

"But they must be redeemed in six months," he told her. "My sources will wait no longer. There can be no extensions. In six months, if not redeemed, they will be sold. I must caution you, Madame."

She said she understood.

Then the broker's eyes fell on another beautiful piece pinned to her suit. He and his wife had laughed at the little bracelets and the choker of Ethel the chimpanzee, which she had turned over to them earlier. All her jewels were incredible, but he was especially intrigued with this piece.

"Do you like it, Monsieur?" Josephine asked him.

"It is a magnificent piece."

She unclipped from her suit the knight in shining armor with his arm held high, sword in hand, the ruby eye of the horse flashing in the light.

"What would it bring, Monsieur?"

He studied it very carefully, turning it around in his hands. He told her it might bring as much as $20,000.

Josephine was silent a long while. Maybe her thousand violins were playing for her again—now, perhaps, for the last time.

"Take it, Monsieur," she finally said. "And add the money to what you bring me tomorrow."

Then she quickly left their office. They never saw her again, for she never redeemed her jewels. Now they were all gone. . . .

The broker stared at his Cinzano for a long time, and finally spoke:

"That day when she telephoned me, I thought it was to redeem the jewels she had already pledged. I was happy for her, too. She was different, the little black lady. But she turned out to be like all the others: she never redeemed them. When the time came, I extended it six more months. It was difficult, but I did it. But then that time passed too, and the owners then passed them out to be sold. The style was a little old-fashioned by that time, and, after all, who then could use jewels for monkeys?

"And no one liked wearing those great pieces, or those belts of diamonds and emeralds. So they were broken up, and the jewels themselves were removed and sold bit by bit. And they ended up in every shop in Paris.

Very likely, anyone you pass in the street could be wearing them. From the shopgirls to the rich—and even the whores."

* * *

So Josephine knew too: "The whores of the streets of Paris are wearing my jewels," she once said to me. It is probably true. Somewhere now, no doubt, on the rue de Vignon, leans a lady of the night against some damp wall, and on her chest flashes a shining ruby that was once the eye of a prancing charger. It was one of the many prices Josephine had to pay.

* * *

"Ah, Madame," the jewelry broker's wife had said to Josephine the night she pawned what was left of her jewels. "You are going to America? How wonderful to be going home."

"Home?" Josephine had responded. "Where is that Madame? I have looked for it a long time."

It is true: Josephine made a home for others, but I do not really believe she ever had one herself. True, she owned the Milandes; she paid the bills; she ran the establishment and directed the servants. But I still do not believe she regarded it as a home. If Josephine had a home at all, it was the theatre. And perhaps it was the theatre that was making her pay the price she was paying. She had deserted it, and the theatre was quite some time in forgiving her. Perhaps it didn't forgive her completely until her final years.

Now she was in New York City, being interviewed by the press. She described the Château des Milandes in great detail, and the reporters ate it up. She did not boast; she did not have to. She told them about every room, all fifty of them. She described the furniture in detail, and the hotel, the restaurants, the clubs, and so on.

"Why do you want such a fabulous palace, Josie?" a reporter asked.

"I don't want it for me, sir; I want it for my children. I give them the best I can, and you see I can afford the best. But isn't it wonderful? When they are little, I am taking care of them, and when I am old and worn out, they will take care of me."

As it happened, she never had to call on the children for any aid.

The tour was extremely successful. Her notion was to play the old movie palaces. She played the Strand in New York, the Paramount in Los Angeles, and the Golden Gate in San Francisco. It was one of the most exhausting tours any star could make: two weeks in each city, five shows a day, and six on weekends. Josephine thrived on it. After the performance, it was out for dinner, usually for soul food; and her car would wind around through the deserted black neighborhoods as she looked for some little all-night restaurant where she could get grits, peas, greens, and chitlins. The owners never failed to be astounded when she walked in. They could not do enough for her. Even if it was three in the morning and the restaurants were empty, word would get out, and people would actually hop out of bed and come in to see her. She loved these moments.

And so it was in New York City after an evening's performance. "Children, I am starving. Let's go and get some good food somewhere." The wife of Roger Rico, the singer, had heard a great deal about the Stork Club, the famous playground of society, of New York millionaires. "Okay," said Josephine. "We won't get any chitlins, but we'll get something."

She did get something, too.

Chapter 17

". . . Far as I know, Sherman's only got it in for one race—that's the drunken brawling Irishmen. But, as to niggers, well, you know he caters only to the finest people, and it wouldn't do him any good to let all the niggers in there.

"But I remember Sherman was real nice to a nigger boy named Nappy who my father took in when he was only three. When Sherman opened the club, he took Nappy with him. . . ."

* * *

Josephine Baker is *really* fabulous . . . the word was made for her. . . . If you want to describe something really great, just call it a Josephine Baker . . . (1939)

* * *

Josephine Baker, the Stemmers hear, is destitute on the French Riviera and isn't permitted to work because she is married to a Jew. One of these days those Nazi mugs will get it, and I'll be the first to shake Josie's hand for all the efforts she is giving . . . (1941)

* * *

Josephine Baker fans report that she is again the toast of Paree, where a new type of lighting makes her decades younger. (1949)

* * *

Josephine Baker was signed by Monte Prosser five minutes before the Waldorf phoned it wanted her for one of their very smart rooms where Negroes would be served—which her contract stipulates. (1951)

* * *

. . . I am appalled at the agony and embarrassment caused Josephine Baker and her friends at the Stork Club. But I am equally appalled at the efforts to involve me in an incident in which I had no part.

Walter Winchell
(Before 1952)

* * *

Josephine Baker . . .
is always looking around for trouble when she goes out to eat.
"is in the picket line at the Stork Club (about Baker) where there were three Communists marching."
. . . is pro-Mussolini . . .
. . . is anti-Semitic . . .
. . . is a troublemaker, and there never was any problem in the Stork Club.
. . . is noisy and objectionable . . .
. . . hates colored people as much as she hates Jews . . .
. . . is a very dangerous woman . . .
. . . is on the D.D. [drop dead] list, and she should have been there long ago . . .
. . . is being boycotted for her commie connections by the important impresarios and managers, and she should be . . .
. . . is responsible for a colored man in Harlem on a sound truck telling Negroes to patronize only black shops . . . some idea for brotherhood. Yes, indeedy . . .
is in the United States, and this country is too small to hold the both of us . . .

Walter Winchell
(After 1952)

* * *

Walter Winchell was a very powerful journalist. He was known in the 1950s for the huge efforts he was making on behalf of civil rights. He was loved by blacks and respected by whites, and he never hesitated to reveal an injustice of any sort in his campaign against racial discrimination. In his newspaper column and on his radio show, he fought for the cause of blacks, minorities, and Jews alike. He never failed to take a stand, and it was always a stand for the minority. He was eminently fair.

But Walter Winchell was also justly famous for character assassination. And there is little doubt that Winchell, for reasons known only to himself, directed toward Josephine Baker a campaign of the most vituperative character assassination that one could conceive of.

Whatever was left of any career for Josephine Baker was shattered by Walter Winchell.

* * *

In the early 1950s, the famous Stork Club in New York was the watering spot of the city. Sherman Billingsley was the owner and operator. The ashtrays, the lighters, and the rest of the stuff he handed out to celebrities were much prized—and they all sported the stork logo. Not a day went by that one did not see a photograph of some celebrity sitting in a banquette with a stork on the ashtray. Everyone knew it was the "Stork."

To determine what sort of man Sherman Billingsley was, one need only read a quote by his brother:

> . . . Far as I know, Sherman's only got it in for one race—that's the drunken brawling Irishmen. But, as to niggers, well, you know he caters only to the finest people, and it wouldn't do him any good to let all the niggers in there.
>
> But I remember Sherman was real nice to a nigger boy named Nappy who my father took in when he was only three. When Sherman opened the club, he took Nappy with him . . .

The Stork Club was very expensive, very exclusive and very anti-black. The famous velvet rope was not let down for any black. How Josephine made it inside the first time, on that day in 1950, I still do not understand.

I have never met a captain, a waiter, or a maître d' who has not told the story in a different fashion. It was really very simple. And it happened very quietly and very quickly.

Josephine was seated; water was brought to the table, and a round of drinks. Everyone ordered dinner, and that was that. Across the room at his usual table sat Walter Winchell. Perhaps if he had not been there, no notice of the incident would ever have been taken. But he was there, and he witnessed the entire affair.

After Josephine and her party had ordered, the captain came to the table and told Josephine that she could not be served. It was against the policies of the club, he said, and he requested that she leave.

Naturally, everyone was offended. Josephine was the first up, and on the way out, she stopped by Winchell's table to ask him if he had seen what happened. Winchell only shook his head up and down like a robot while she talked. The whole story spilled out of her, and it ended with the statement that this was the kind of thing she was fighting, and she was proud of the stand that he took in matters such as this.

She ended up on 125th Street, happy that Winchell had seen the incident. She told her friends, "Wait'll you hear what Winchell says tomorrow."

Wait indeed—for the next day, and for many years thereafter. It is the classic story of the poison pen. Thereafter, Winchell always referred to Josephine as "Jose-Phony." He commenced to manufacture the most outrageous stories, not a single one of which was true. He accused her in his column of being pro-communist, pro-Fascist, anti-American, anti-Semitic, and, of all things, anti-Negro! He demanded in the newspapers and on the radio that Senator McCarthy investigate her, and McCarthy did just that. When the senator reported to Winchell that he found no basis on which to make any charges, it infuriated Winchell even more. Everyone knows the tenor of the man McCarthy, and for him to have come to Josephine's defense seems incredible. Very little of the senator's report was printed.

Then Winchell demanded that the F.B.I. investigate Josephine, and they later did. They also investigated me—and they continued to do so years later.

Ten years after the Stork Club incident, in a letter dated December 5, 1960, Josephine wrote to me:

> Although Walter Winchell has been a real devil on this earth, I am sorry for him and shall pray for him with all my heart. . . .

* * *

In the early 1960s, I was presenting Katherine Dunham in her New Revue at the Huntington Hartford Theatre in Hollywood. On opening night, I looked out the stage door after the appearance and saw Mitzi Gaynor, Betty Grable, and the Ambassador from Morocco, as well as the usual hundreds of Katherine Dunham fans. I went out to say hello to Mitzi, and I spotted Walter Winchell standing way in the back.

I suddenly felt sorry for him. At one time the crowds would have made way for him, but now everyone ignored him. I cleared a path and told him that Miss Dunham had asked me to bring him in. He seemed very pleased that he should be noticed or even remembered.

Inside the theatre, he spoke very flatteringly of her performance and of the company itself. In his column the next day, he wrote of her in quite glowing terms.

After paying his respects to Miss Dunham, Winchell motioned me over into a corner to speak with him, as he wanted some details of a number she had just choreographed. It was "The Diamond Thief," probably one of her most outstanding.

Then he looked at me for a long time, and said, "Didn't you use to be with Josephine Baker?"

I replied that indeed I had been with her on many occasions. He gave me another long look, then slowly shook his head.

"You know," he said, "that never, never should have happened."

A few days later, I telephoned Josephine to tell her about this incident. Of course, by then it was too late. He would never have made any retractions, but by then no one read his column anyway. It would have meant nothing.

* * *

On her last trip to the United States, Josephine and I talked about Winchell at some length. There is little doubt that his attacks had made a tremendous impact on her career.

"After that," she said, "there was nothing left for me in America. What little there was left, he ruined for me. I cannot understand why. Why, oh, why did he take off on me like that? He had always written such wonderful things about me.

"You see, if that had not happened when it did, I would then have had what I am having now; and my problems would never have come about. Walter Winchell is totally responsible for the most disastrous twenty years of my life. But isn't it remarkable how I have outlived them all? They are all gone—imagine that. Even the Stork Club is gone, and Billingsley, and Winchell, and all those people—and Josephine is still going on. Well, what do you think of that? I can't make it out.

"When he started his campaign against me, the others picked it up too. Imagine, even the people in the government. How in the world can those things ever happen? They read his column and believed what he was saying—without investigating, mind you—and then moved to keep me out of the country—which they did, too.

"But isn't it even more incredible? Look at this Nixon situation. How in the world can those things ever happen? It is because they are afraid. They are frightened. It is like the Revolution in Russia. They were afraid, and the communists are still afraid. Mark my words, one of these days those people in Russia will rise up like they did before, and that will be the end of communism for them.

"You cannot keep a people on such tight rein for any lengthy period of time. And if you do not believe it, look at the black situation. Once, in Harlem, when there was no heat, somebody said, 'Never mind, it is a cold, cold, long winter, but the summer is going to be very hot.' Well, it didn't happen in New York. It happened in Los Angeles, and I believe it was August—and it did get hot [referring to the Watts riots].

"Well, I am getting old and tired. I wonder if there will be anyone who has the courage to stand up and say the things I did. If there is, I would like to meet them. After that Winchell business, I couldn't open my mouth anyplace in the world that they didn't twist my words and make them say what they wanted me and those words to say. How could I defend myself? Because the first thing that would happen is that my words would appear in print, and Winchell and the others would start all over on me."

In the end, just prior to his death, Walter Winchell publicly apologized to Josephine Baker at a small club in Juin le Pain, in the south of France. It was his very actions that had contributed to her being reduced to performing in such a place. When he held out his hand, she refused to take it.

No one has ever been able to figure out the reason for Winchell's violent attacks on Josephine. Josephine might have understood if anyone had bothered to explain it to her.

* * *

"The United States is a barbarous land where persecutions are more shocking than before World War II, with lynchings, condemnations without trial, and electrocutions the order of the day.

"I feel only compassion for those obliged to live on American soil, because it is not a free country."

While I and the rest of America were reading these words—supposedly statements made by Josephine Baker—which had been transmitted over all the wire services, Josephine was in the south of France at the Château des Milandes, performing at the opening of her newest club, the Lou Tornoli. It was New Year's Eve. The club was beautiful; it had cost her $100,000. It seated nearly four hundred, but that night there were only about fifty people there—all invited. It was more madness on her part.

I telephoned Josephine immediately and read her the articles. She was shocked. She emphatically denied having made the statements, and I believed her. She told me that she had been doing a radio interview show with Eva Perón, wife of the Argentine dictator, and when asked about conditions in America, Josephine had stated that they were difficult. It was true, she had said, that she could not register in certain hotels, that in the South she must use a separate toilet and drinking fountain, and that she was refused service at the Stork Club. She had also said that if such things could happen to her—and she liked to think that she had the weight of an education and a rather fabulous theatrical career behind her—she shuddered at what must be happening to the uneducated, unsophisticated masses, who could not afford, or were fearful of taking advantage of, certain legal protections they were entitled to.

What she had said was absolute truth. However, she was speaking to *La Critica,* for radio and newspapers—and they were the official mouthpieces of the Perón regime. Her words were not "hot" enough for them; they probed her for more. When it was not forthcoming, they did what they knew how to do quite well: they invented.

Now we all begged Josephine to come to America and defend herself against all these unfair and unfounded accusations with which the American press was having a field day. She thought that since she had stated the truth, it should stand on its own. And she expected the American press to support her. She made calls to Reuters and to the Associated Press in France. In those calls, she reiterated the position she took with me. If these press releases ever reached the United States, they were ignored.

I understood the situation all too clearly. She was caught in the web of the Milandes she had woven. America was thousands of miles away; the creditors were at the front door. Her energies, she felt, must be directed to the front door.

* * *

It was beginning. At first the milkman, the baker, and the butcher tapped lightly on the back door and spoke to the servants. But as the monthly bills mounted up, they became bolder and demanded to see her. When she would not see them, and could not pay, they cut off supplies to the château and to the restaurants, and stopped delivering the linens to the hotels. Times were tough, but they were to get tougher. It was during this period that the second lot of her jewel collection went to the diamond brokers in Paris.

She had a few offers in Paris, some in Copenhagen, and an offer in London. She chose to return to America instead.

Chapter 18

"So, gentlemen, that's the way it is. No seats, no Josephine Baker—take it or leave it."

* * *

"Take it or leave it." Those five words cost Josephine Baker at least a million dollars, and probably more. It was one of the few things she regretted in her life. The time was the early 1950s; the place, the Old Desert Inn in Las Vegas, Nevada.

Seymour Heller, Liberace's manager, loved Josephine. He was greatly respected in Las Vegas, and I had enlisted his aid in an attempt to get Josephine a booking there. He was mulling over an idea I had presented to him about presenting Liberace and Josephine on the same bill. It would have been a tour-de-force for the two greatest "clothes horses" of all time.

Seymour called on the office of one of the most prominent booking managers in Las Vegas, with the intention of pitching him the Baker package. Seymour opened his briefcase and took out a large manilla envelope which he proceeded to set down on the floor next to his chair. It contained information about Josephine Baker—reviews from her smash appearances at Carnegie Hall and in Los Angeles—that I had given him earlier. On the front of the envelope, Seymour's secretary had written with a heavy black pen, "Josephine Baker Material."

The booking manager looked at the envelope, and before Seymour could open his mouth, he said, "Seymour, if you're here to talk about Josephine Baker, forget it. I know you, and I love you, and I'll give you some advice: don't waste your time. There's not a hotel in Vegas that will touch her. Now, let's talk about Liberace."

Seymour said not another word about Josephine. He proceeded to close an incredible deal for his fabulous client—Liberace.

It was the kind of money Josephine should have been earning in Vegas. How sad that she never did. To find the reason, we must return to the Las Vegas of the early 1950s.

* * *

Josephine had been booked into the Old Desert Inn immediately after her engagement at the Strand in New York City. She was to appear in Vegas following her engagement at the Golden Gate in San Francisco.

In spite of all the bad publicity that she was getting from Walter Winchell, the booking managers did not cancel her engagements. It seemed not to have affected them in the least. Booking managers in Las Vegas are interested in only two things: whether an artist can bring customers into the showroom, and whether he or she can deliver when on stage.

In the beginning they were happy with Josephine, because she was delivering. Those were the longest lines I have ever seen. Then they asked her to add a second show on weekends, an unprecedented request. She did even better than that—she added a *third* show *every night*. She had just come from the movie houses, doing a performance after each picture—five a day, and six on weekends. It was nothing to her.

Her original contract called for $25,000 a week, a huge sum in the early 1950s in Las Vegas. They also gave her a $10,000 weekly bonus for the extra shows. And they picked up 100 percent of her expenses—which means exactly what it says. Air fares for the entire party, rooms, wine, liquor, food, miscellaneous expenses, tips, telephones—the works.

The management was happy, and so was Josephine. I could see her coming to Vegas for twenty years, and at that moment I believe they would have entered into such an agreement.

Then came the incident that sent Josephine into one of the greatest rages I have ever seen her in. On reflection, I believe that was when the fires deep within her began to burn furiously. I cannot defend her actions. She was absolutely wrong. The operators were neither right nor wrong; I will say, though, that they were the most cooperative group of gentlemen I have ever encountered in the theatre. I have never seen an artist act in a more vile or despicable fashion. I told her so, and she turned on me. I must confess that I thought she had gone temporarily insane.

Josephine took out on me and the operators of that hotel what she should have taken out on the railroad toughs and rednecks that burned Boxcar Town. What she should have taken out on Billie Burke, on the Waldorf and other hotels for refusing her accommodations, on Walter Winchell and the Stork Club.

In her defense, we must remember that during this period Las Vegas was one of the most segregated cities in the nation. No black could gain admittance to the casinos, clubs, or restaurants. Countless numbers of black stars played there, it is true, but they and their staffs generally were forced to stay on the other side of town. Josephine liked to think that she was responsible for changing all that, and maybe she was. But I wish it had been someone else—and in the end, so did she.

* * *

While Josephine was appearing at the Old Desert Inn, two friends of hers, both of them black, came to visit her from San Francisco. Josephine invited them to the show, and I requested a table for them. The management provided one in the very front row, and then declined to send a check to the table or to Josephine. Her friends enjoyed themselves immensely. It was caviar, filet mignon, and champagne, all on the house.

On stage, Josephine was now in her incredible "pony tail" and "exotic-Oriental" period. She was great, no doubt about it. Her wardrobe was fantastic. It was all pony tails, Oriental headdresses, exotic furs and glistening fabrics.

Then she suggested that at the early shows she wear her own street clothes, which were no less gorgeous. The first shows were advertised as "ladies' shows." She wore the street wear and evening wear of Balmain, Balenciaga, Cardin, Chanel. After the early show, the ladies would get back in line to see the "real costumes" that she displayed in the second and third shows. Most important, while they waited between shows, they hit the tables. I had never seen a happier audience, or a happier management.

Josephine was one of the few great artists of the clubs who attracted the "wine drinkers." In the trade, the wine drinkers meant those who immediately ordered champagne, which was brought out in bottles and magnums.

It was the heavily monied Texas set. And it was caviar-and-wine time. They ordered wine because it was the thing to do; then they had their bourbon on the side. I never saw so much Moët and Chandon go back to the kitchen, where the bottles were thrown into a huge metal box and destroyed, as required by law. It must have been thousands of gallons.

It was her greatest period in the clubs. I do not believe she was ever rivaled. She talked about it for years.

Then, late one night in her suite, her San Francisco friends planted something in Josephine's mind that set off the blaze. They explained that Vegas was a "closed town" and that she, of all people, should "open it up." I listened very quietly; I knew what was coming. They convinced her that she should demand that the management admit, even without reservations, any blacks who came to see her.

I could not believe what Josephine was about to do. Ignoring the fact that it was four in the morning, she grabbed the phone and demanded that the booking agent and managers come to her suite immediately. They routed themselves out of bed and came; Josephine meant business to them.

But she meant other business now, spurred on by her two friends. It would be pointless to reveal their names. There is no doubt that they were using her. Later, when we were arrested in Canada, we tried desperately to contact them. Josephine, who was broke by this time, was counting on them to "rally the black people of America for me, as I did for them in Las Vegas." They promised to come immediately to Canada. They did not. Neither of these "friends" would ever return a phone call. *Addio senza rancore . . .*

They coached and guided her, and she was a willing pupil. It was under their tutelage that she made her outrageous demands.

They told her that they must immediately advertise in the black papers that the room where she worked would be open to all blacks. Also, because the blacks were very poor, and because the hotel was making such huge sums of money from her engagement, all the blacks were to have fifty percent deducted from their checks. Further, they were to be offered the best front-row tables. Josephine informed the management that "her people" had suffered long enough and that now they were to be provided with the best.

I tried to explain to Josephine that, while it was true that the hotel was making a lot of money, so was she. But by now her mind was a blank.

In insisting on the front-row tables, she was probably thinking of her troop-entertaining days years before in Morocco, where she had made the same demands and the generals had acquiesced. But in Morocco she had worked for nothing.

Incredible as it seems, the booking agents of that hotel and the management agreed to every one of her demands. Josephine and her two San Francisco friends had expected a fight, and I think they were disappointed that they did not get it.

On the first night after the publicity department promoted this outrageous scheme in the black section of East Las Vegas, about thirty blacks showed up.

Josephine's conduct that night was revolting. She made comments that were utterly unlike her, such as, "How does it feel to sit in the front row for a change, instead of nigger heaven?" She embarrassed the blacks and the management. For the second show that night, seven or eight blacks were admitted. For the third show, none showed up, leaving the entire front row empty. Josephine was disappointed.

The management of the hotel was keeping its end of the bargain: it had met every one of her demands. It was the most cooperative management an artist could have had.

On the second night, about ten blacks came for the first show. She repeated her performance. None came for the second or third show.

On the third night, no blacks came for any show, and all the front-row table were empty. What distress this must have caused the maître d' cannot be imagined. While lines of people waited outside to be admitted, some twenty of the best tables remained vacant.

Josephine felt trapped; she did not know what to do. Her friends had returned to San Francisco, but when she called them, they continued to advise her to "hold out." Soon, they said, the press would have to pick up on what was happening. Soon the impossible feat that Josephine had accomplished for the blacks in Las Vegas would become known the world over. But it was not to be; the blacks could not have been less interested. None came rallying to the cry, then or later.

Then the management hit upon an idea that should have solved the problem. They came to Josephine and made her a proposition, phrasing it as politely and as persuasively as they could. Perhaps, they said, the blacks in East Las Vegas were concerned about their attire and felt intimidated and out of place in the casino. They suggested that she give a performance in the gymnasium on the east side. At this performance, to be done at her convenience, all blacks would be admitted free, and the hotel would cater the best dinner possible under the circumstances. Further, the hotel would assume all costs for the entire party, and in addition they would pay Josephine $5,000 for the performance.

It was an incredible offer; even Josephine had to agree to it. But she still made ridiculous demands. She insisted on a menu that was totally out of character for a Sunday afternoon. I remember it well—shrimp, lobster, fillets, squab, and dozens of vegetables; and I will never forget her insisting on crème de sorrel soup. For dessert there was to be baked Alaska, and it went on and on. It bordered on insanity.

What was happening in her room was even more disgusting. When some of the less timid blacks called on her at the hotel for a photo or an autograph, she would insist that they stay for breakfast, or luncheon or dinner, or whatever. She would order food from the dining room, deliberately selecting the most expensive things on the menu. Then, before the food arrived, the embarrassed guests would be hustled out of her bedroom to eat in her adjoining living room—alone! Many left even before the food came up.

I cannot imagine how many completely untouched dinners and plates of fine food and drink went back to the kitchen. In the end, even her two dogs rebelled at this glut of food, refusing even to come near the little fillets she would grab off the trays to give to them.

To this day, I will never understand why the hotel management did not just throw her and her entourage out. For some reason, it went through this entire performance without a murmur.

Came the Sunday afternoon of the "gala," as she called it, for her people. The hotel managers had prepared for a thousand people. They had decorated the gymnasium beautifully: tables with pink cloths and napkins, flowers, their best china and silver. The food waited in steaming trays in the locker room. They had done a fine job of promoting the event. Posters, handouts, and even radio invitations were prepared. Now we began to worry that the thousand places would not be enough.

It was a small worry. In the gymnasium that day at her "gala," fewer than a hundred and fifty black people showed up. And one must remember that the star attraction was Josephine Baker, and the food and drink were on the house. Actually, they just did not care, not during this period. Later they did care, and they cared a great, great deal. But now she could not be given to the blacks. It was all in the timing.

It was one of the saddest experiences we ever went through. We were to live through others that were frightening and depressing, but I do not believe she ever went through a sadder—or more enlightening—one. The lesson was not lost on her. Despite all my prior warnings, though, in later years I never once said, "I told you so."

We returned to the hotel, and she barricaded herself in her bedroom and tried to call her friends in San Francisco. She could not get through. So much for those friends.

Then she called Buenos Aires and spoke with a promoter whom she asked to present her there. He agreed immediately. She accepted $2,000 per week, and she was to pay all her own expenses. I was appalled. In Vegas she was getting close to $50,000.

How regrettable that Josephine chose to vent her years of pent-up fury on Las Vegas. When we begged her to turn the same fury on Winchell and his newspapers, she pooh-poohed the idea as unimportant.

She closed—in triumph, I admit—with long lines still waiting two days later. She never saw Las Vegas again. Even twenty years later she could not be given away there. She could not appear on a Las Vegas stage if *she* paid *them*.

They have long memories, those operators. And I do not blame them.

Chapter 19

"Stephen, I've been desperately calling you and trying to find you . . . Joe and I are going absolutely crazy. I went in to call half hour, and can you believe, she has changed the entire rundown . . . what it means is that we have to change curtains, and drops, and there is not a light cue that is any good . . . everything will be wrong . . . I tried to reason with her . . . and Miss Baker will just not listen . . . she just sits there and smiles at me . . . well, I tell you, it will be a disaster . . . and here it is, less than fifteen minutes to curtain time . . . well, if it weren't for you, I would walk out . . ."

(1961)

* * *

". . . where is that wonderful production manager and lighting director that we had in the Huntington Hartford Theatre? . . . Let's get them both again. I don't think I was ever better presented or taken care of backstage . . ."

(1973)

* * *

I first met Bill Taub in Hollywood through a mutual friend. He had engaged me to do some work with Hope Hampton, who had decided to go into the night-club business. Bill asked me to fly to New York to meet with Hope, which I did. It was an entirely pleasurable experience.

I had heard stories of her fabulous jewel collection and of the two houses side by side, one of them hers, the other her husband's, Jules Brulatour, who could only enter her residence when she wished to see him, and when she pushed the button that opened the doors between the houses. I recalled stories that she fired shots at him with a revolver; and it sounded bizarre. I looked forward to the meeting.

She was immensely rich; if I am correct, she still receives a royalty on all Kodak film that is used anywhere in the world.

Hope was a little eccentric, I thought, but then I was accustomed to eccentric ladies. Her dressing room was always at least ninety degrees, but she had had the heater removed from her limousine because she thought it was bad for her throat. It happened to be wintertime, and between the dressing room and the car I nearly died.

But it had all been a pleasant experience; I was paid well, and there were no problems. Hope decided to abandon her night-club career after a Miami engagement. She wanted to do a picture in Hollywood; it is too bad it was never done.

Hope's story was the white version of the Josephine Baker story: dime-store ribbon clerk to fabulously wealthy. The only difference is that Hope hung on to every dime. She did not try to change the world as Josephine did.

* * *

In Hollywood, everything seems to start and stop at the Beverly Hills Hotel, and it was in Hope Hampton's suite that Bill Taub told me he was considering bringing Josephine Baker over for an American tour. He had had some experiences with her in the past, and I told him about mine. We both decided that the tour was a good idea.

So begins another event that made news around the world. I have never been able to unravel exactly what did happen legally, or who was responsible for what. I have let it stay as it is.

As I mentioned, my one prior experience with Bill Taub had been entirely pleasurable. He had paid me well, and there had been no problems. After Hope Hampton's Florida engagement, he insisted that I stay on for a time at his expense and have a holiday. And on every succeeding visit to Hollywood, he never failed to telephone me and ask me to lunch or dinner, or to some small party.

With the beginning of what I believe was the second Taub-Baker go-round, we seemingly, almost for no reason, were at each other's throats.

It started with the musical scores and arrangements. They were sent to me to pass on to the conductor, who, I believe, was Irving Klase, a wonderful and understanding man who had known and worked with Josephine for many years. Parts were missing, whole numbers were missing, pages out of certain parts were gone. "These scores are in a real mess, Stephen," Irving said, "and unless we get them in proper order, you'll never have even a rehearsal at the theatre, let alone a performance."

I telephoned Bill at his apartment in New York and told him the story of the arrangements. Josephine happened to be there, and he put her on the phone.

"Why, if they are lost, Stephen," she told me, "then either you or Mr. Klase has lost them, as I personally checked every part before it was sent on to you. And if there is any money that is going to have to be spent, well, you will have to spend it. And that is only fair."

Bill got on the phone. He was very sympathetic. "Go ahead, Stephen, and do what has to be done, and I'll take care of it when I get out there." And he did. There were no problems.

But already, in New York, Josephine was beginning to give him problems.

I was aware at the time that Josephine was nearly broke. In order for her to come to America at all, I knew that Bill would have to advance substantial amounts of money to her. She needed a new wardrobe. She had the most pressing obligations to meet before she could come over, and then there were the transportation expenses—particularly for her vast amount of personal and theatrical baggage, which had to come by air—so there is no doubt that Bill did advance her a considerable sum of money. Much later Josephine denied that he had done so. I let it go at that.

But more important, Bill Taub did something that no one else could have done. One must examine the man personally a little. William L. Taub liked nothing better than a good fight. When he heard the word "no," he immediately set about turning it into a "yes." I am sure that when the fight started with the United States government, he would have fought it out tooth and nail, whether or not he was going to present Josephine, and whether or not he had any substantial investment. Just after her tour engagement had been announced in Los Angeles, it seemed that every time I talked to Bill on the phone, he was calling from Washington, D.C.

Josephine and Bill, I guess, even to the end were mortal enemies. The one thing he did for her, which no one else up to that time had been able to do, or even wanted to do, was that he opened the doors to the United States for her—no small feat, considering the hammering the press was giving her. There is no doubt that the doors to the United States were closed to Josephine, particularly since Walter Winchell had started his verbal assassination.

One day Bill phoned me from New York. He sounded exhausted.

"Well, it's finally finished," he said. "I have just brought back with me all the necessary entry permits for Josephine. I'm cabling everything now to France. But I cannot tell you what it has taken out of me. I hope she appreciates what I have done for her."

Josephine did not. She might have at the moment, but she forgot easily. The magnitude of the work Bill Taub did to get her into the country must have been overwhelming, considering that later it would require the intervention of the President of the United States and the attorney general to secure her entry. And Bill's job was done during a more difficult time—during a more difficult period in her life.

The Taub-Baker affair originated with the matter of the advances. Later I was to hear only her side, and not Bill's. What I believe happened is that, before she came to America, and after she had been advertised and publicized for her Los Angeles appearance, she put a demand on him for even more money.

Bill telephoned me late one evening. "I'm going over the brink with this woman, Stephen. Can you believe, after all I've advanced, she is now demanding even more? Contrary to our written contracts, she is now demanding all her salary in front before she will come. It's blackmail."

I had to agree, for I had read the contract, and nowhere did it stipulate that she was to be paid in advance. I thought of the creditors, and the payrolls, and the food, and the other expenses that would be piling up during her absence, and I understood that part too.

Then I made a serious error. In trying to help, I lost the friendship of Bill Taub. The error I made was my suggesting that the theatre advance the necessary sums. I explained to the management that they would have to, since the money that they had advanced thus far would go down the drain if she did not appear. They were trapped.

The theatre managers agreed to advance the sum.

Now Josephine employed the famous "Judy Garland plan," as it is known in Hollywood. Whenever Judy was dissatisfied with something, she began pitting one associate on a set against another—the divide-and-conquer routine. Then, when everyone on the set was up in arms against everyone else, she would waltz in, exceedingly happy, amid the chaos that she had created, and set about to right the wrongs.

And so Josephine arrived, exceedingly happy. She moved into a suite with a kitchen at the Château Marmont in Hollywood, and started cooking and started thinking. She decided to abrogate her contract with William L. Taub. *It was a disastrous mistake.*

But to break it she needed reasons. And for Josephine, during that period, that was the easy part.

If there could be a defense of what she did, and I believe there is to some extent, she must be judged by the prior actions of her theatrical colleagues. She did indeed abrogate her contract—but then, so has every other star in the business. The stories of abrogated contracts are old business in

Hollywood and New York and would fill volumes. It was "the thing to do." And usually these stars, women particularly, learn this fine art very quickly, and they practice it with razor-sharp tactics. Marilyn Monroe became a master of it, as did Judy Garland. They always waited until exactly the right moment.

In Monroe's case, the "right moment" would be near the end of a picture, with an expensive set with five hundred to a thousand people working on it. She would let the studio heads sweat for a few hours. The first call would say she would be late; the second call (usually after lunch) would say that she was ill, but "I'll be there about four o'clock" (the beginning of Hollywood unions' "golden hours"). Then she would not answer her phone at all. Eventually the studio capitulated to her demands.

It was the same with Judy Garland and all the others. With Josephine, it was slightly different. First, she was not that well known in the United States. She might be able to flex her muscles in France, but not here. Secondly—and her biggest mistake she was abrogating a contract with the man who was solely responsible for her being in the country in the first place.

I suggested ironing out the problems. There was no ironing out.

Opening day was a madhouse of rehearsals and changes. Joe Privatier, the lighting director without whom Marlene Dietrich never worked, was setting in the final lighting. At the end of every Dietrich engagement, she handed him a blank check which she had signed. He could fill it in for any amount.

Allan Cooke was Josephine's production manager, and he went to great lengths to see that everything came off perfectly. He told me during rehearsals, "Stephen, Joe and I have just had a dress parade of her costumes for lighting. I've had them all around the stage for Joe, and I must say I've never seen anything like them. There isn't a thing at Fox or Metro that could compare. You'll be thrilled tonight when you see them."

I walked onto the stage and checked around a little. Josephine came from her dressing room as I was discussing something with Stanley Seiden, our general manager. She walked over and spoke with us for a moment.

"Excuse me. I just want to tell you, Mr. Seiden, how happy I am with everything. I know it is going to go beautifully."

Stan Seiden, always the gentleman, made some flattering remarks, and after that she started to leave. Then she turned and very quickly said:

"Oh, Stephen, will you see, when you and Mr. Seiden have a moment, if you could go to the box office and draw me a little money?"

"How much do you need, Josephine? I'm sure we can take care of it."

"I think about five thousand would do while I'm here."

It did not seem an unusual request, and there was money in the box office that would eventually belong to her after her engagement.

I noticed that Stanley did a double-take but said nothing. Josephine returned to her dressing room.

Then he told me what had gone through his mind. "I knew that not even Josephine Baker, as outrageous as she is, could spend thirty thousand in less than fifteen minutes." Then he informed me that Bill Taub had just drawn $30,000 on the box office, ostensibly for Josephine.

It was one-upmanship. After all, Taub still held the theatre contract, and he had a perfect right to withdraw any funds, either for himself or for Josephine. The amount he withdrew that day probably did not even cover his expenses, let alone the amounts he had advanced to her.

I reported to Josephine at once. She went pale. I commented on it.

"Don't be silly, Stephen. I'm a colored woman; how can I go pale?"

Then she looked into the mirror. "Why, my God, I *am* pale. It has been such a shock to me. This has never happened to me before, that the blood has drained from my face, and I actually have become pale."

She shrieked with laughter, momentarily forgetting the immediate problem. It was the last laugh for a long time.

When we tried to telephone Bill Taub at his hotel, he did not answer.

To make matters worse, when I spoke to Seiden about business, he said, "Not too good, not too good. But don't get me wrong, Steve, she's a wonderful lady, and she's got a fabulous show, and in thirty years in the theatre I've never seen such a wardrobe; but they just ain't lining up outside. Not yet, anyway."

They never really did, and it was not a successful engagement. It was the 1960s, the period of the beginning of rock 'n' roll, and things were different in the theatre from what they had once been. That she lived fifteen years longer was lucky for her, for when she reappeared in the early 1970s, America was riding a great wave of nostalgia, and Josephine was in her real element. I wish she could have lived a hundred years more. But this was still the sixties, and it was still rock 'n' roll time.

The managers of the theatre agreed to assume the obligations for the engagement, and the show went on. She was beautifully received by the press, and by the people who came to hear her. It is unfortunate that they were so few.

While we were in Hollywood I received a call from the manager of the Palace Hotel in San Francisco, who offered a suite to Josephine if the rest of the party would stop there. He was French and an old fan, and after we checked in he treated her royally and made special concessions to everyone. He must have regretted his gesture, for during the next four weeks he went through hell with the rest of us.

Taub, feeling that perhaps Josephine was now coming into some money, began a series of moves in federal court to attach her possessions, her wardrobe, her orchestrations, and the rest of her theatrical appurtenances.

The second laugh came on stage at the Alcazar. While we were rehearsing, the U.S. marshals walked in with subpoenas for everyone from the dresser to the conductor. They would be months defending themselves, and Josephine would pay for it all. Apparently it was Bill Taub's intention to embark on a plan of harassment of the entire company to get Josephine to acquiesce to his demands for a refund of the money he had advanced. But, first of all, she did not have it; and even if she had, she would not have parted with one cent.

When the marshal approached Josephine on stage, she happened to be rehearsing her theme song, "*J'ai deux amours*." This time I don't think she really meant it as she had forty years before.

She refused the subpoena, and the marshal threw it at her feet. As the marshal left, Josephine shouted, "Tell Taub he can attach Ann Sheridan with his court order." This was an inside joke, and only she and I and her maid and a few others knew what she meant. The line destroyed us, and Josephine herself. We fell apart with laughter, and the rehearsal had to stop.

The origin of this joke is worth recounting. Tommy Wonder, a remarkable young dancer with a great sense of humor, was in this company. He had been under contract for many years at MGM. He had appeared in countless pictures there and knew everyone. He also had a remarkable act that everyone, particularly Josephine, loved. He danced with a beautifully dressed life-size doll which had a wardrobe that was almost equal to Josephine's. The doll looked remarkably like Ann Sheridan; in fact, everyone called it Ann.

Tommy would attach the doll's feet to his, and then, holding her by the arms in a dim stage light, he would do a beautiful dance with the doll. Audiences never realized until the end that it was not a living partner. When the act was over, he would just drop the doll, and it would fall in a heap on the floor. The audience would go wild, and he always did an encore.

On opening night at the Huntington Hartford, when Tommy came to his dressing room, the doll was missing. He searched everywhere. Finally, in a dusty and unused dressing room, he discovered "Ann Sheridan." The doll had been raped: its dress was over its head, its panties ripped off, and even the telltale stains were there, as evidence to the ravishment of poor Ann.

Everyone in the backstage area howled with laughter. But the incredible part is that no matter how much he tried to hide the doll, even locking it away, somehow the rapist always found it and committed his vile deed. At the end of the engagement, the poor doll was a mess. Indeed, Tommy had already started having another one made up.

The "rapist" was never discovered. But by the time we got to San Francisco, our next city on the tour, "Ann Sheridan" was in a dreadful state, and that was when Josephine made the remark to the marshal. It is too bad the joke was lost on him.

When we returned to the hotel to have some supper, the phone rang in Josephine's suite and I answered it.

"Miss Baker, please."

I asked who was calling.

"Who are you?"

I said that I was Stephen Papich, her director.

"This is Agent"—I have long since forgotten the name—"Federal Bureau of Investigation. We wish to see you and Miss Baker."

I laughed. I thought it was a joke. I answered that we were busy and if they wanted to meet with us they would find us later in the Crystal Room, which was the famous dining room on the lobby floor of the Palace.

They found us, and it *was* the F.B.I. We were interrogated on and off for four weeks—in the theatre, out of the theatre. They obtained court orders to have our rooms searched, and when Josephine refused them admittance to hers, they broke down the door.

They demanded to know if we were plotting with a communistic group to overthrow the government. It was such an absurd suggestion that even the thought of it seemed insane. But it was still the F.B.I., and they were relentless. I have always felt that it was Walter Winchell who had urged the F.B.I. to conduct this investigation. Senator McCarthy's investigation had proved fruitless, so Winchell now took this tack. It was just another harassment on top of the one we were getting from Bill Taub and the federal court.

Now Josephine ran to telephone her friend, the attorney from the Las Vegas incident. She desperately needed legal aid. The friend agreed that she surely did—and demanded a retainer of $7,500. Josephine was crushed. Perhaps she had it coming to her, but I felt terrible and was genuinely concerned for her.

For the first few days, to prevent any attachments by the marshal, every night after the performance all of Josephine's wardrobe, the orchestrations, and even "Ann Sheridan" would be put into large canvas bags and spirited up into the flies. It was some sight to see the doll being hoisted up with a rope around her neck, to swing from the rafters.

The case was fast and sweet. Perhaps Josephine should have lost; Randolph Hale, the theatre owner, had the best attorneys. But the judge refused to issue any judgments to the plaintiff, William L. Taub, on the grounds that there was insufficient evidence that money had been advanced. He also issued a restraining order against Taub, preventing him from any harassment of Josephine Baker and her company anywhere in the United States.

It did not cover Canada, unfortunately.

Josephine was in seventh heaven. Taub was outraged. He persuaded some of the cast to leave, and even tried to get me to desert her. But I stayed on; she had already been deserted once by "my fair weather Las Vegas friends," as she called them.

* * *

Business was still not good. Then, a week before the closing of the San Francisco engagement, we received an offer for Josephine to appear in Canada. It was to be in a club known as the Faisan Bleu, in Montreal. I traveled out there to look the place over. It was perfect for her: it held more than five hundred people, and the money deal was a good one.

The engagement was a sensational success—and not only because of Josephine's drawing power and star appeal. She soon was to become a curiosity as well. When I returned to San Francisco to report on the situation, she was still being hounded by the F.B.I. Then they started on me again.

Only within recent months have the roles the F.B.I. and the C.I.A. played in the lives of many innocent victims in the United States, and the roles they played in the lives of citizens of other countries, been brought to light. Now these agencies approach situations with some trepidation. But such was not the case then.

Even years later, as our dossiers in those agencies continued to grow, it took the intervention of the President of the United States and the attorney general to stop the harassment of Josephine. President Kennedy, at the urging of his brother Robert, then attorney general, investigated the entire case. It was during a particularly trying period when she was being detained by immigration authorities who had been drawn into the case. In the course of this investigation, Josephine Baker was totally absolved of any participation in, or any attempt to enter into, any communistic or subversive organization in the United States or elsewhere. I too was absolved.

Not long afterward, Josephine was to march up Pennsylvania Avenue with Dr. Martin Luther King, Jr., in the great rally for civil rights that was being held in Washington. She thanked President Kennedy personally when he received her at the White House. It was then that she made a wonderful comment to the President and his staff. "I guess you can just say that Josephine Baker is lily white," she said. "I'm referring to the investigation, of course, not to my color, Mr. President." Kennedy loved it.

* * *

Bill Taub was not without his own connections, and he was not without ability of his own. More important, he was outraged, and rightly so, over her behavior. It is sad that she was to repeat almost exactly this same scene, though without the arrest, with Jack Jordan and Howard Sanders ten years later.

Again, what she took out on her producers and on her staff, and perhaps on her husband, she should have taken out long ago on those who had really done her injustice. She did not do it then. Now she did. And many times she struck out at the wrong people.

> . . . I will see that Josephine Baker never works another day in America. By God, can you believe it, maybe Winchell was right after all.
>
> (Bill Taub)

> . . . Josephine Baker, my staffers report, is suing her manager, Bill Taub, in federal court in San Francisco. There goes her last friend. . . .
>
> (Walter Winchell)

> TAUB HITS JOSEPHINE BAKER WITH SUIT FOR $157,000
>
> (*Variety*)

> It is difficult to believe the really fabulous Josephine Baker . . . she is ageless. Last night in the Huntington Hartford Theatre she showed Hollywood a thing or two. . . . She dazzled them, she knocked them out. . . . If anything, her advertised wardrobe of $200,000 cost more than that. She is ageless. . . . One wonders how long this incredible lady will continue . . .
>
> (Los Angeles *Times*)

> Bill Taub is the reason of the separation of my husband and I. Jo warned me not to go with him, but I did, and now you can see that I have come to this.
>
> (Josephine Baker)

> Miss Baker . . . you don't know me from Adam. I'm just a maid in Beverly Hills. But my mama and my daddy told me all about you, and I had to come here to see you. And you know, you're even more fabulous than they said you were. I expected some old lady, and here you are. Josephine, *you . . . are . . . something else!*"
>
> (A fan backstage)

> I never heard of Josephine Baker until I heard about her coming to do a show in Hollywood.
>
> (An announcer on NBC TV News)

> . . . In almost sixty years in the business, I was never on a show, or with a show, that had such problems. . . .
>
> (Jack Present, company manager, in San Francisco)

> Stephen, I've been desperately calling you and trying to find you . . . Joe and I are going absolutely crazy. I went in to call half hour, and can you believe, she has changed the entire rundown . . . what it means is that we

> have to change curtains, and drops, and there is not a light cue that is any good . . . everything will be wrong . . . I tried to reason with her . . . and Miss Baker will just not listen . . . she just sits there and smiles at me . . . well, I tell you, it will be a disaster . . . and here it is, less than fifteen minutes to curtain time . . . well, if it weren't for you, I would walk out . . .
>
> (Allan Cooke, production manager)

On and on it went. Josephine would throw the most outrageous curves to every person and department, yet her performances would manage to come out all right. If anything, in Hollywood that night it was better than the carefully rehearsed show. In the past, when Josephine "acted up," as she would say, the managers, impresarios and producers usually would just lick their wounds, take their losses, and walk away.

But Bill Taub was not the type to retire and lick his wounds. He moved, and he moved with speed. For a period of time, not only were he and Josephine mortal enemies, but he was a mortal enemy of mine as well. He moved against me at the same time he moved against Josephine, and he dealt us some telling blows. I must say I retaliated in kind. When I was arrested and thrown into prison, so was he.

In the end, the only people who "won"—and I hate that word—were the attorneys. Taub's legal bills must have been astronomical; I know mine were. And all the money Josephine had earned in the United States went to her attorneys.

Later, in Canada, Bill Taub was to make some very serious charges against Josephine Baker. And he almost made them stick. I have always wondered why he never pursued his case and his claim. Perhaps he wanted only to teach her a lesson once and for all, a lesson that she would remember and that the world would hear about. He did that, certainly.

The lesson had no effect on her.

Chapter 20

". . . I have given him [the author] this worry so you can get in touch with him if you wish, because there must be someone to take care of my business there in the U.S.A. Remember, he stuck with me while I had all the trouble there and really stuck his neck out to help me and showed his courage by doing so, and it's quite natural that I choose him as my representative, don't you think? Because I have the utmost confidence in Steve, so have I in you, but you have so much to do, therefore you cannot take other responsibility on your shoulders; in any case, when your plans are settled, you can contact him . . ."

* * *

The above is an excerpt from a letter Josephine wrote to her friend Dr. Carlton B. Goodlett, on May 12, 1961. Dr. Goodlett had been trying to help her in various ways with the famous "life story and film," and she was asking him to turn the matter over to me.

She referred to the "trial by fire," as she called it, in Canada. And it was some trial by fire.

"I knew Bill Taub was going to try to get even—and for what!" said Josephine. "But I never expected he would do that. Sometimes now I remember how they held those numbers up in front of me—mugged me, they call it—and I started to get the shakes. Like a common criminal.

"All my life, whenever I entered a theatre, people were taking pictures of me. Pictures for the production, of course, but then pictures in the street and all that. And I always loved it, and I always asked them to bring them backstage to me, or to mail me a copy, for I loved to look at them. Even those bad snapshots. But I never asked to see that one. And you know . . . they made me take off my glasses, too.

"My God, how did I ever live through that? Sometimes I think it was worse than losing the Milandes. I sometimes think that when my heart got that first shock that was so bad, it never really recovered, even now.

"After that, everyone here [in France] and abroad knew I was finished, and later events proved that I almost was. Well, you have seen me on stage. Just before I go on stage, I take one huge breath of air, and out I go. And that's what I did after that. I just took one huge breath of air, and on I went with my life."

* * *

When we arrived in Canada, we did not know that Taub had preceded us there. He moved quickly. He engaged one of the most prominent attorneys in Montreal, Queen's Counsel Cohn. In his complaint Bill stated that Josephine had stolen funds and wardrobe from him, that he had invested considerable money in her and her current performances, and that she was now traveling into Canada and crossing the border with stolen property.

Cohn in turn convinced a judge in the superior court of Montreal that he had a valid case, and at nine o'clock that same night secret indictments were drawn up, and warrants of arrest were issued for Josephine Baker and Stephen Papich.

Cohn must have regretted this move for years to come. With all that happened, I felt then, and still feel, that he was an honorable man, and so did Josephine. He allowed himself to be led down the wrong path.

At 9:30 that evening, less than thirty minutes after the warrants of bodily seizure were issued, the Montreal police were pounding on my door. They were pounding on Josephine's at the same time.

She was in her stage makeup, geting ready for her performance that evening. Why they sent five officers to her door and only two to mine, I do not know. As I said previously, it took all five to handcuff her. I submitted without a struggle; I knew there was no choice.

We were taken to the lobby, surrounded by the police, and were herded into the waiting police cars.

We were booked, separated from our personal possessions, photographed, numbered, and thrown into a cell. It was the only concession they made to her: they allowed her "the company of her friend" while in prison.

It was only when the heavy barred door clanged shut on us as we sat together on the narrow little bed that the real seriousness of our position hit both of us at the same time.

Perhaps it was beginning to hit Cohn and the federal judge, too. After all, Josephine was a person of international fame. They conferred shortly thereafter, and Cohn suggested that maybe he had acted hastily and perhaps the warrants had been premature. Perhaps it should have been a matter for the civil court instead. But by then it was too late.

It was morning in France, and as Parisians wandered out of their homes to pursue their daily chores they saw the headlines.

JOSEPHINE BAKER ARRESTED!
Held as a common criminal in
Montreal with her manager.

That was one headline. Every other newspaper in the world carried a similar one.

The French were outraged. The Ambassador to Canada in Quebec was routed from his bed, and he sped by special car to Montreal.

* * *

Josephine and I were held in a common cell in the federal prison for three and one-half hours. When I asked her what we should do, she replied simply, "Talk."

While the wheels of Canadian justice rolled ever so slowly, preparing our eventual release on bail, she talked. It was then that I heard the story of her great love. Perhaps the little bracelet which they had not taken from her when she was booked had reminded her. Somehow it had become caught in the cuff of her blouse and they had missed it. It was a pathetic little thing that could not have been worth $150. It had a tiny diamond. She looked at it for a long time. Then she told me how her arms had been covered in jewels many years ago.

"Me, Josephine—and look what they have done to me."

Gradually the story came out from deep inside her. Little by little, as it always did when she either loved what she was about to say or was distressed by it. It was then that I heard the story of the crown prince, and the romance, and the snows of Sweden.

She told me of the jewels, and the sable, and the little band playing her favorite song as the train with its private car pulled out of that wintry station under the leaden sky.

And she told me of her favorite piece of jewelry.

"Where is my horse with his shining little eye? Where is my king who would help me now? Where are they all now? Where are my friends when I need them? Oh, my God, somebody help me . . . please help Josephine . . ."

For an instant she terrified me by beating herself against the bars. She was trying to escape—to escape from some danger that she could not understand. Just as I ran to grab her, the police came to release us on bonds that had been posted by the operator of the Faisan Bleu.

It was the following day, when we were arraigned in criminal court, that the judge and Counsel Cohn realized the gravity of what they had done.

They called up one corridor and down the other for William L. Taub, as is the custom in those courts. Taub was not there to press his case. He had gone. He had done his damage.

That the arrest and imprisonment of Josephine Baker on such flimsy charges was a disgrace to be reckoned with is indicated by the actions of the judge who had signed the warrants. He came personally to the hotel to apologize to Josephine. She took it gracefully. She invited him to the show, and he and his wife accepted.

At that time Josephine did a piece of material called "*Donnez moi le main*"—"Give me your hand"—in which she went into the audience and told fortunes. During her performance that evening, she moved toward the judge, and in her inimitable style she took his hand and, while telling his "fortune," spoke of his honesty and his fairness in the pursuit of justice.

Then she made a remarkable statement which I have never forgotten: "Now I know how the people in America feel when they are brought to justice for their alleged crimes. I only hope, sir, that they are dealt with as fairly as you have dealt with me here."

No one in America ever saw the statement; it was printed in Canada and France and elsewhere, but no one read it at "home."

* * *

When Josephine and I returned to Paris, we carried with us almost $50,000 that she had earned at the Faisan Bleu. By then she needed $200,000 more at the Milandes.

With all that she had gone through in America and Canada, she now began to feel the real pressure. It bore down on her relentlessly. She did not spend one cent of the $50,000 on herself, pouring it instead into her venture into humanity, her "*capitale du monde de la fraternité*"—"my little capital of the world of brotherhood."

She should have saved her money.

Chapter 21

"I cannot collapse now. I must go on, for if I collapse, the rest will go with me. Then everything I have done will have been done in vain."

* * *

Josephine and I returned to the Milandes after the arrest in Canada.

I believe it was the arrest that most disturbed Jo Bouillon. He was a changed man. He was never around, and would disappear for days; and when she screamed for him and at him, he ignored her. Between them, a crystal wall, a crystal curtain, had descended: they could see each other, but there was no communication. One day he left.

It seemed that everything was going wrong. Even on our flight from Montreal, our plane was stranded in Newfoundland for five days.

But in France they waited for her. Her chauffeur did not leave Orly Airport for five days and nights; he slept in the car. He met plane after plane, as did the press.

To please Josephine, her friends at Chez Madame Arthur, the famous club of the French impersonators, arranged to meet her. For those five days, the running back and forth to the club and to their homes to restore makeup, to change underthings and to give a gown a final press must have been a nightmare.

Josephine met *herself* when she came off the plane. She also met Mae West, Katherine Dunham, Bette Davis, and Mistinguett.

Josephine screamed with delight: the impersonators had gotten themselves up in complete drag of those famous ladies. It caused some commotion in the airport, even at four in the morning.

Then, exhausted as we all were, nothing would do but to return to Chez Madame Arthur and watch them perform the show they had prepared for her. They had prepared a hilarious skit in which Josephine, portrayed superbly by one of the impersonators, is arrested in Canada. Two outrageous policewomen rushed through the audience to arrest her as a felon. She shoved them aside. "You cannot arrest me yet—I haven't sung '*J'ai deux amours.*' " The police ladies politely backed off.

Even at that hour of the morning it was one hilarious joke after another, and the performers were absurd. "Madame Arthur" himself, a marvelous character performer, was dressed as Yvette Guilbert, and looked just like the Lautrec poster. He kept charging through the little playlet, screaming, "I am the greatest star of the Folies Bergère."

I had never seen Josephine so happy. She was glad to be home, and I was delighted at the little respite.

As we were leaving the club, a little incident happened that signaled new events. It was an omen of what was to come.

As the car was pulling out and away from the curb in front of the club, one of the waiters came rushing out, waving a check. It was for $80 plus the service.

She was devastated. In her entire association with that club they had never presented her with a check. She and her friends had "spent" thousands there since the club was started.

I grabbed the bill and handed him a $100 note.

"*Merci . . . au revoir,* Josephine. *Bon chance . . .*"

As the car sped away, Josephine fell back into her seat and stared straight ahead. I hated them at that moment. I hated "Madame Arthur," and "Bette Davis," and the rest.

Josephine never mentioned the incident. She asked the driver to take us through the Place de la Madeleine. As we entered, she asked him to stop the car for a moment while she gazed over the empty square. The sun was coming up behind the church. I could only imagine what thoughts were going through her head.

She got out of the car and put a scarf over her head, for it was in the damp of morning. I got out and stood beside her, leaning against the car. She pointed across the plaza to the church.

"You know, Stephen, years and years ago I came here after my opening night. Things were so crazy that I just had to leave those crowds. So much had happened to me, and I couldn't understand it. I didn't speak their language then, and it was hot and crowded and smoky, and I just sort of walked out very quietly.

"Then I found myself here in the Madeleine. I walked over there, up the steps of the church, and I sat down and I thought it all out. And it came to me, and I understood it.

"If I were to walk over there now and sit down in the exact same spot and start thinking, I know it would not come to me. I would not be able to think myself out of this problem. Then they were only problems with the theatre, and with my associates in the theatre. Now it is much different. I should never have left the theatre to go to the Milandes. Maybe it is punishing me—what do you think? It is punishing me for leaving it, and I think it will be a long time before it ever forgives me. I hope one day that it does, for it had really been good to me, and I deserted it.

"Then, a few nights later, at the same kiosk over there, I was here again, thinking some more, and I was all alone. Imagine being all alone in the Madeleine then. Now you would get a knife in your back. But that night when I was leaving, I saw these two old Frenchmen in their smocks putting up something. As they unrolled it and slapped the glue on it, I saw that it was a poster of me in my banana costume—of me, imagine! A poster of Josephine. And they daubed it good all over with the glue, and then one of them slapped the poster on the little ass with his brush and laughed. I just looked at them and laughed too. It was such a strange, unusual experience. And I thought, Well, Josephine, I guess you are something when they put your picture up all over Paris.

"And as I walked away, here came an old concierge in her wooden clogs, with a bunch of loaves under her arms. We were the only ones passing, and she must have been the first in the bakery. When I passed her, I smelled that great bread, and I got so hungry. And then I just said to her, 'Bonjour, Madame,' and I gave her my big smile. And it must have sounded so funny to her with my strange American accent, and she looked at me kind of funny, and I repeated it. 'Bonjour, Madame.' Then she smiled at me and said, 'Bonjour, Mademoiselle, bonjour,' and she walked off in the other direction.

"And I remember that that was about the first time I started trying to speak French."

She stood there a little longer, and we got back into the car. We passed through the ancient gates of the city of Paris and wound our way through the French countryside. We followed the River Dordogne to the Château des Milandes.

Josephine was coming home to face the real music.

* * *

I stayed the entire summer. I did everything I could. I went with her from club to club, and from theatre to theatre. There was nothing that was *right* for her: it had come to that. What it really meant, though, was that they did not want Josephine. Indeed, the times were changing. Thank God they were to change again in her lifetime.

I studied the situation carefully with her accountants. It was impossible; voluntary bankruptcy would have been the only solution. She might have at least saved the furniture, and not be under the pressure of court orders. The property itself could have been divided and sold piecemeal, and she could have recouped some small part of the fortune she had invested. But she would not hear of it.

Then, as the summer came to an end, I had to return to America. She begged me to stay, but I could not. She said that she needed someone with her who "understood." There was nothing I could do. I offered to stay if she would accept the advice of her accountants and solicitors, but she still refused the advice. And her reasons were understandable: she did it simply to save her capital of the world of brotherhood. She had to save it. It was her one wish to help not just the blacks but all humanity.

As these things sometimes happen, her wish was granted. But it was not granted at the Château des Milandes. When it did happen, she did not immediately realize the magnificence or the importance of the event. It was the next day when it hit her. Then, when she telephoned me, she sounded happier than she ever had before, even with all the problems still hanging over her head back in France.

* * *

But this event occurred sometime later. Now, as I prepared to take leave of the Milandes, she insisted on seeing me off at Le Havre. I boarded a P&O liner that was sailing for Los Angeles, through the Panama Canal. She came aboard to have lunch with me for the short time the ship was at the dock.

She talked of running away again. We laughed; she had no money to run away. She could stow away, she said. She was like a little girl again. "Maybe they'd let me sing for my supper. It is an English ship, and you know they love me in the Palladium.

"When I ran away from St. Louis," she continued, "I only had a quarter."

"How much have you got now, Josephine?" I asked.

She opened her little change purse. "I've got two francs. Twenty cents. My God, I haven't even got a quarter!" A slight film came over her eyes.

When the captain of the ship heard that Josephine Baker was aboard, he came into the salon and introduced himself. He begged her to come to his cabin for an aperitif, and when she asked for Cinzano on ice, and it was not in his stock, he told his steward to go pell-mell down below to bring up a bottle.

He then did something that I knew thrilled Josephine, and brought many a tear to the eyes of the passengers. As the all-ashore gong and the horn of that beautiful steamship were sounded, he personally escorted Josephine to the gangway.

I kissed her good-bye, and she kissed the captain on one cheek and then on the other. The captain then did something that only an English gentleman would have thought of. He knew of course, as did the entire world, of her humiliation in Canada. But that day in Le Havre, as she moved toward the gangway, the ship's band played "*J'ai deux amours*." He stepped back and saluted, and the other officers saluted also. And they held it until the song ended.

I took Josephine's arm and pointed high up to the mast. The captain had ordered the Union Jack to be dipped in her honor, and as we watched, it moved slowly down the mast, and then with the last few bars of music it returned smartly back to the top. A breeze came up, and the flag fluttered proudly for Josephine Baker. It was one of the great moments in my life. I have never forgotten that scene.

Josephine stood waiting by the car as the ship pulled out of the harbor and sped to the breakwater. I stood at the rail until we were out of the sight of land.

Evening

Chapter 22

"Stand up, Josephine, and tell it like it is!"

"But when I ran away, yes, when I ran away to another country, I didn't have to do that. I could go into any restaurant I wanted to and I could drink water anyplace I wanted to, and I didn't have to go to a colored toilet either, and I have to tell you it was nice, and I got used to it, and I liked it, and I wasn't afraid anymore that someone would shout at me and say 'Nigger, go to the end of the line.'"

* * *

The one thing that Josephine had wanted most in her life was accomplished in less than a day. Actually, it was accomplished in about twenty minutes. It happened in the early 1960s. And it happened in the United States, in Washington, D.C., in front of the Lincoln Memorial. It was as it should have been.

After some difficulty, Josephine was admitted to the United States through the efforts of President Kennedy and his brother Robert, the attorney general. She had been invited to march in the great rally for civil rights with Dr. Martin Luther King, Jr.

The experiences for these people in the march had been trying, and Josephine came for the last day. Word of her arrival spread among the marchers. They were delighted. For some reason it seemed to give them new strength and determination, a new urgency.

Josephine had no intention of speaking to the people, and was not prepared. But soon she was to accomplish in just a few moments what she had been trying desperately to prove and accomplish for thirty years. She had spent her fortune trying to prove that brotherhood and equality could work, and that the Bill of Rights for blacks in America was the same Bill of Rights that whites lived under.

While her own formula did not—and, I believe, could not—work at the Milandes, her big moment came in Washington, D.C., where she accomplished so simply what she had wanted to accomplish for so long: to instill in her people in America a sense of pride, equality, and hope. She wanted to give them some of the fire that had burned in her for years. She wanted to send them out as ambassadors for the cause of brotherhood. She was like an Olympic runner who had carried her torch a long time and now must pass it on.

Dr. King was introducing the guests on the platform. By police estimate, there were fifty thousand people attending the rally. It had been a dreary day, but now the sun was beginning to break through the clouds.

Then he came to Josephine, and as she rose, a great roar swelled up from the crowd. It seemed that the applause would never stop; finally she raised her hand and stepped forward. She wanted to greet them with just a few words, then return to her seat so that they could hear the message of Dr. King.

When they quieted down, someone shouted, "Stand up, Josephine, and tell it like it is!" It was a new expression at that time, and Josephine had never heard it before. But she knew what it meant.

When she called me the next day in Los Angeles and told me the story, it was goose-bump time.

Slowly she walked to the microphone. There was absolute silence. They were ready to listen—finally, after all those years.

She spoke very quietly. She did not scream or rave or rant. "I spoke for twenty minutes," she told me, "and I never knew what I said until it was over."

She began speaking. "Friends and family . . . you know I have lived a long time and I have come a long way. And you must know now that what I did, I did originally for myself. Then later, as these things began happening to me, I wondered if they were happening to you, and then I knew they must be. And I knew that you had no way to defend yourselves, as I had.

"And as I continued to do the things I did, and to say the things I said, they began to beat me. Not beat me, mind you, with a club—but you know, I have seen that done too—but they beat me with their pens, with their writings. And friends, that is much worse.

"When I was a child and they burned me out of my home, I was frightened and I ran away. Eventually I ran far away. It was to a place called France. Many of you have been there, and many have not. But I must tell you, ladies and gentlemen, in that country I never feared. It was like a fairyland place.

"And I need not tell you that wonderful things happened to me there.

Now, I know that all you children don't know who Josephine Baker is, but you ask Grandma and Grandpa and they will tell you. You know what they will say. 'Why, she was a devil.' And you know something . . . why, they are right. I was too. I was a devil in other countries, and I was a little devil in America too.

"But I must tell you, when I was young in Paris, strange things happened to me. And these things had never happened to me before. When I left St. Louis a long time ago, the conductor directed me to the last car. And you all know what that means.

"But when I ran away, yes, when I ran away to another country, I didn't have to do that. I could go into any restaurant I wanted to, and I could drink water anyplace I wanted to, and I didn't have to go to a colored toilet either, and I have to tell you it was nice, and I got used to it, and I liked it, and I wasn't afraid anymore that someone would shout at me and say, 'Nigger, go to the end of the line.' But you know, I rarely ever use that word. You also know that it has been shouted at me many times.

"So over there, far away, I was happy, and because I was happy I had some success, and you know that too.

"Then, after a long time, I came to America to be in a great show for Mr. Ziegfeld, and you know Josephine was happy. You know that. Because I wanted to tell everyone in my country about myself. I wanted to let everyone know that I made good, and you know too that that is only natural.

"But on that great big beautiful ship, I had a bad experience. A very important star was to sit with me for dinner, and at the last moment I discovered she didn't want to eat with a colored woman. I can tell you it was some blow.

"And I won't bother to mention her name, because it is not important, and anyway, now she is dead.

"And when I got to New York way back then, I had other blows—when they would not let me check into the good hotels because I was colored, or eat in certain restaurants. And then I went to Atlanta, and it was a horror to me. And I said to myself, My God, I am Josephine, and if they do this to me, what do they do to the other people in America?

"You know, friends, that I do not lie to you when I tell you I have walked into the palaces of kings and queens and into the houses of presidents. And much more. But I could not walk into a hotel in America and get a cup of coffee, and that made me mad. And when I get mad, you know that I open my big mouth. And then look out, 'cause when Josephine opens her mouth, they hear it all over the world.

"So I did open my mouth, and you know I did scream, and when I demanded what I was supposed to have and what I was entitled to, they still would not give it to me.

"So then they thought they could smear me, and the best way to do that was to call me a communist. And you know, too, what that meant. Those were dreaded words in those days, and I want to tell you also that I was hounded by the government agencies in America, and there was never one ounce of proof that I was a communist. But they were mad. They were mad because I told the truth. And the truth was that all I wanted was a cup of coffee. But I wanted that cup of coffee where *I* wanted to drink it, and I had the money to pay for it, so why shouldn't I have it where I wanted it?

"Friends and brothers and sisters, that is how it went. And when I screamed loud enough, they started to open that door just a little bit, and we all started to be able to squeeze through it. Not just the colored people, but the others as well, the other minorities too, the Orientals, and the Mexicans, and the Indians, both those here in the United States and those from India.

"Now, I am not going to stand in front of all of you today and take credit for what is happening now. I cannot do that. But I want to take credit for telling you how to do the same thing, and when you scream, friends, I know you will be heard. And you will be heard now.

"But you young people must do one thing, and I know you have heard this story a thousand times from your mothers and fathers, like I did from my mama. I didn't take her advice. But I accomplished the same in another fashion. You must get an education. You must go to school, and you must learn to protect yourself. And you must learn to protect yourself with the pen, and not the gun. Then you can answer them, and I can tell you—and I don't want to sound corny—but friends, the pen really is mightier than the sword."

Josephine hesitated a long time, just looking. There was not a sound in the crowd. Someone came up and handed her a piece of paper. She read it, placed it on the podium, and continued in a low voice.

"I am not a young woman now, friends. My life is behind me. There is not too much fire burning inside me. And before it goes out, I want you to use what is left to light that fire in you. So that you can carry on, and so that you can do those things that I have done. Then, when my fires have burned out, and I go where we all go someday, I can be happy.

"You know, I have always taken the rocky path. I never took the easy one, but as I grew older, and as I knew I had the power and the strength, I took that rocky path, and I tried to smooth it out a little. I wanted to make it easier for you. I want you to have a chance at what I had. But I do not want you to have to run away to get it. And mothers and fathers, if it is too late for you, think of your children. Make it safe here so they do not have to run away, for I want for you and your children what I had."

She paused a long time, then very quietly said, "Ladies and gentlemen, my friends and family, I have just been handed a little note, as you probably saw. It is an invitation to visit the President of the United States in his home, the White House.

"I am greatly honored. But I must tell you that a colored woman—or, as you say it here in America, a black woman—is not going there. It is a woman. It is Josephine Baker.

"It is a great honor for me. Someday I want you children out there to have that great honor too. And we know that that time is not someday. We know that that time is *now*.

"I thank you, and may God bless you. And may He continue to bless you long after I am gone."

* * *

For a long time the huge throng of fifty thousand people sat still. Then there were screams and shouts and dancing and jumping. It was one of the greatest ovations she had ever received. She was proud, and justifiably so.

Josephine Baker accomplished in that one little unrehearsed speech what she had been trying to do for years. She had instilled in those people a feeling of pride, of brotherhood, and of equality. Each one walked away from the Lincoln Memorial that way with a new sense of pride in himself, and that was what she wanted. She needed no Milandes, and she did not need to create emissaries, as she had tried to groom her children to be. She did it herself, and that is how it should have been.

When she left, she marched straight to her meeting with President Kennedy. He was waiting on the steps of the White House for her arrival.

Chapter 23

DECEMBER 19, 1964

STEPHEN PAPICH
HOLLYWOOD, CALIFORNIA.

DEAR DEAR STEPHEN. I WANT YOU TO SEE ZSA ZSA GABOR AND TELL HER THAT YOU ARE A VERY DEAR FRIEND OF MINE AND THAT SHE IS THE KINDEST AND THE BIGGEST STAR. OF THE SCREEN, THE CABARETS, CONCERTS, BECAUSE ZSA ZSA CAN DO IT AS BRIGITTE BARDOT DID HERE. SHE HAS THE CLASS AND CONNECTIONS NECESSARY AND THAT WILL BE TREMENDOUS FOR HER IN THE WHOLE WORLD. I WILL COUNT ON YOU TO DO THE UTMOST FOR YOUR HELP IN COLLABORATING. YOU ARE THE ONE PERSON THAT I HAVE CONFIDENCE IN. I WISH HER TO COLLABORATE WITH YOU IN HER NATIONAL APPEAL TO SAVE THE MILANDES MY LITTLE VILLAGE AND FOR THE BUILDING OF MY BROTHERHOOD SCHOOL THAT WILL BE UNIQUE IN ALL THE WORLD. THIS APPEAL SHOULD START AS SOON AS POSSIBLE. I SUGGEST THE END OF JANUARY. OR THE FIRST DAYS OF FEBRUARY. I CAN COME FOR CONFERENCES AND CONCERTS WITH ALL THE ORGANIZATION IT WILL BE PERFECT. NATURALLY THOSE THAT WILL WORK IN THIS APPEAL WILL BE PAID BY THE ORGANIZATION. MONEY WILL COME FROM THE DONATIONS OR CONCERTS. THE REST OF THE MONEY GIVEN ENTIRELY TO THE VILLAGE OF THE MILANDES. LOVE, COURAGE, MERRY CHRISTMAS, AND HAPPY NEW YEAR TO ALL OF YOU AND YOUR CATS INCLUDED. WRITE.

JOSEPHINE

* * *

The desperate times were starting. I read the cable over and over. It was eight pages long, and written as Josephine talked. She had tried to cram a thousand thoughts into those few words.

Brigitte Bardot had gone on network television in France to appeal for funds to save the Milandes. The French had responded immediately, and substantial sums poured in. And not a moment too soon: the electricity had been disconnected for nonpayment, and the vendors in the village had again stopped deliveries. But it was still not enough.

The squeeze was beginning—but only just beginning. The Bardot money only relieved the current obligations. It did not touch the mortgages, and it did not touch those debts and liens that had been piling up for years.

I knew what Josephine thought. She thought that the same excitement for her village could be mustered in America. Unlike in France, however, Josephine was almost unknown in the United States. She had been an expatriate for a long time. Americans cared little. And they cared even less for her village of brotherhood.

I had written to and seen everyone for her. I had extracted promises—but no checks. The timing for her venture was wrong.

I had advised Josephine on countless occasions to walk away from her village—to walk away from the obligations—in order to protect her health. I had advised her to go to work, and this time to save her money and not pour it into a venture that I knew was bound to fail. Now, after having read her cable several times, I decided to do nothing.

Then I received the second cable.

DECEMBER 22, 1964

STEPHEN PAPICH
HOLLYWOOD, CALIFORNIA

RECEIVED CHRISTMAS CARD THIS MORNING. SENT LONG CABLE YESTERDAY. LONG LETTER TODAY FOR YOU CONCERNING PROJECT. IN JANUARY. YOU AND ZSA ZSA ARE THE ONLY ONES CAPABLE OF FULFILLING IT. IT NEEDS SO MUCH FINANCING TO KEEP THE MILANDES. WE CAN START CONCERTS FOR MYSELF FIRST AND AT THE SAME TIME ORGANIZE AN APPEAL TO SAVE THE MILANDES AND BUILD THE SCHOOL OF BROTHERHOOD AS IS OUR PLAN. ANOTHER LETTER FOLLOWING. LOVE. MERRY CHRISTMAS TO ALL OF YOU.

JOE AND TRIBE

I had done so much work to help the Josephine Baker dream. I had spent so much time, so much money.

Perhaps it was my fatalistic attitude; perhaps I should have thought positively, as she did. I decided to make one more pitch. As a special Christmas gesture to Josephine, I decided to go see Zsa Zsa.

* * *

I knew Zsa Zsa Gabor quite well. I had presented her in Mexico and had been her escort when President Johnson invited her to the White House. I also knew that Zsa Zsa was conservative when it came to money, and when it came to causes.

She was very cordial. I sat on her bed while I told her the entire story. She was forever fixing her hair and asking how she looked. The answer was obvious and the truth: she looked fabulous.

After eating some Hungarian sausage with her, I left, feeling that I had done my best. I had given it a good pitch.

It seemed it was always about two A.M. when the phone rang. It was never at a convenient hour. I remembered it was the day before New Year's. When I heard the buzzing on the line, I knew it was France.

I waited for the long "Haaloooo." Then it came out as fast as she could talk. "My God, Stephen, you have done it. Can you believe it! Zsa Zsa sent a draft to my bank. She is the only one in America who has helped me.

They all talk of brotherhood, but she really practices it, and isn't it wonderful? You and I know about the others."

I asked Josephine to please put the money into her private account. There had been no strings attached. I knew the hard times were coming. I wanted her to start a little nest egg.

It was too late. "I sent it all to the bandits who hold my mortgages, and they have agreed to give me more time."

I was thunderstruck. I knew it was a drop in the ocean, but had she kept it for herself it could have gone a long way toward easing some of the pain she was to go through. Unfortunately, it only gave her encouragement. The agony was to continue for almost three more years.

* * *

I continued to do what I could by mail and telephone for Josephine.

Then, again at two in the morning, in the summer of 1967, the phone rang. I knew she was ill the moment I heard her voice. I knew the inevitable was near. Could I come to see her?

On the eighteenth of January, 1965, I received a detailed letter that she had typed herself. It went on and on. I read it and reread it, over and over again, and it made little sense.

Now she was discussing the terrible situation with anyone who would listen, and, assuming she had discussed it with me, she poured it all out in one letter.

I had not heard that a Mrs. Blowe in Chicago had been trying to do something for her. I had already informed Josephine that we could get no help from the NAACP, but it wasn't taking.

The letter rambled on and on. That is when I realized it was really a desperate time, and that I must go to her again.

This is what she wrote:

Mrs. Josephine Baker
Les Milandes
Castelnaud-Fayrac
(Dordogne)

Les Milandes, January 1, 1965.

Mr. Stephen Papich
6377 Bryn Mawr Drive
Hollywood, California
U. S. A.

Dear Steve,

I was so glad to hear your voice over the phone yesterday. You are harder to reach than all the leaders of the world. Nevertheless, as the saying goes, better late than never.

But let's start from the beginning.

I hope my last letters received you safely, for now you'll certainly begin to understand the situation better, and see how desperately I am fighting and what odds I am in front of.

As you certainly will understand, sincere Mrs. Blowe had me wait three months, then she wrote and said we will have to wait three months more, and finally she wrote and said that we'll have to wait until May or June, which makes six months more. During that time, which covers the first six months of waiting, I made promises to my creditors, bankers, etc. . . . but little by little, they all began to lose courage, because as you know, when you do business with business people, and continue putting off your payments, they finish by not believing any more in your promises. That has been my case, and is the reason why I can't ask for any more credit nor waiting time. I have a deadline for the 11th of February, that's why I was so eager to come over and do these concerts right away. If I get $125,000, i.e., if I come back with this sum, after having come there on the 7th Feb., and leaving on the 11th, that will stop the first howling wolves, and the rest can be waited upon until we do our concerts, provided the concerts do not start at an inconvenient time for the creditors. For instance, we here in old tired Europe, don't think of organizing concerts so far in advance, because the publicity alone will suffer in as much as the progress is so quick that people forget if it is done too long in advance. We here engage our artists or whatever it might be that we want to produce in advance, but in the same time we don't start our publicity before the last moments, let's say: from 10 to 15 days before the opening so as the people will have in mind what they expect to see or buy. In that case the expense of publicity is not lost. But we double the publicity pressure so as it can be effective on the public opinion. We call that "stabilize publicity." If we do things (which are well done, well thought of, and have 100 percent results) here in these old countries, why in the world cannot it be done in a young country that is bubbling over with life, energy, and knows publicity from A to Z? That's why I so agree, with my coming over there so as to put all these ideas together with all of yours that are excellent.

We are leaving the 18th of January, as I said I can come on the 7th of February.

I forgot that I have a ticket from last year and my accountant reminded me of it this morning when I talked about our financial situation that you have to know about and with which you talked to me over the phone, but I hadn't expected this demand, so I told you a figure from my memory which in consulting my accountant I found out to be inexact.

As I told you before, if somebody can pay my return ticket from Los Angeles via London and Paris, which is the shortest way, and the way that I'll be coming, plus the difference, if there is any, from the ticket I have to Los Angeles, because my ticket is Paris/New York. But I'll see this through the Pan American company here in Paris.

Here are the figures my accountant just gave me: 160,000,000 old francs, approximately corresponding to about

$332,000	
$125,000	now, that is, when I come on the 7th, and leaving on the 11th, thus leaving us
$207,000	that we can pay once the concerts are started—and other things will be in function too, like donations, etc. . . .

As soon as Zsa Zsa Gabor returns to Calif., please go to see her, because, as I said before, she knows all the people who are interesting for us, and she will help us, I am sure.

Have you got in contact with Mrs. Blowe yet? If not, please do, as she is a good woman and extremely active. But to my mind, a little slow, in as much as we need action, but quick action, because of time running away with the situation. I would like you to make all these appointments so that when I come over we can all put our heads together for final decisions.

Thank you for your hospitality. It will be better for me to stay with you; in that way we will save time and work better.

No, I have never made any promises to the New York branch of the NAACP, nor has Mr. Krellberg who engaged me on my last tour, although this gentleman was approached by the NAACP's representatives, they never got together because the NAACP people of New York never wanted to pay enough money. So that will assure you concerning all the rumors that might be going around. Personally I am very happy about your changing from the NAACP to the Urban League, although I am friends with both of them. I repeat, only because the NAACP wants all the money, and in our condition this can't be like that. We too must get a lot of money.

When I came over in May, I came as a benefit for the NAACP combined with CORE and the Urban League, but it was understood that I should get no money for that, which I didn't.

According to your figures, 32 or 33 concerts will get us the $332,000 needed net of traveling expenses, hotels, dressing maid, food, transportation, etc., plus the pianist's fees (my pianist), that the organization must pay at the rate of $350 a week for the concerts, plus his transportation, hotel, room and board.

I hope I have explained everything clearly.

I am sending a copy of this letter to Mr. Browning to prevent you from going through all explanations and details.

Thank you again in advance for your so kind hospitality you offer me when I come.

I have left aside the school, etc., because I know that the other countries who are very small and have financial troubles of their own will unite in giving what they can towards that. But the most dangerous and the most urgent need is now, and that includes the sums that I just mentioned to you and that we can only get in the U.S.A. I think that it is good that you know that the world appeal I made in June brought in 70,000,000 francs; all of this money was paid out. The balance is the above sum. We were stopped by the beginning of vacation time and you know when things stop it is always hard to start again in the same rhythm or enthusiasm.

While we are there, we can start talking to people like Zsa Zsa Gabor or Nat King Cole's organization (films) or other film industries that you think would be interested in making a series of three episodes of my life story that must be a part of the rest plus all the different ideas you might have that may help bring in money. . . . I am not talking about TV, because you will tell me when I arrive what you think about it. For if it ruins our business, then it will be better not to think about it and put it aside for another time. Because TV can make or break an artist. Everything depends on how she or he is photographed, and that depends on the cameraman. We'll not risk anything.

Get all the people together for my coming.

Try to see the B'nai B'rith religious organization that is very well known and organized in Calif. I know that they will help.

I talked to my doctor after having finished our conversation over the phone, and he says that we can put off the operation [removal of abdominal strictures occurring as a result of the Goering poisoning] until the tour is finished. That is, we will do it in the spring after a little rest so as not to take any chances.

So we must work hard and quickly. That too can be done, Steve. Can't it?

I'll be waiting for the return ticket, etc. So don't let us lose any more time; I know you'll agree to that.

You were right about the phone call . . . $100, but at least I got you at last, and we got a little nearer to our goal.

Please don't let me wait for answers too long. Because as I am naturally worried about all these terrible situations and problems, that makes me worry all the more.

Love to all of you, not forgetting the Kitties.

Josephine

She signed it "Your Joe, with her human and animal family."

Within a few days I caught an Air France plane.

When I arrived, she was there waiting for me. I discovered then that things were even worse. Her immediate needs were for $500,000. Since my last visit I could see that things had been going steadily downhill. Jo Bouillon had left her. The château and its environs were a beehive of creditors. It was a ballet of ducking bill collectors, not answering doors, hiding in her bedroom, trying to disguise herself so that she could avoid the subpoenas when she went outside. . . .

We sat for a long time in her bedroom. Her accountant was there also. She was in bed, and for the first time I had to admit that she looked dreadful.

The accountant was still flogging the proverbial dead horse. We begged her to leave now, to leave quietly with the few francs she had left, before the onset of the scandal we knew would surely come.

Josephine lay in bed, staring straight ahead, thinking a thousand thoughts. Then she broke her reverie. Again she had not heard one word we had spoken.

She asked us to bring her some chocolate, and to take some ourselves. She even insisted that the accountant smoke and make himself comfortable. "You know what I have just been thinking?" And then it started.

Again she took us back, long, long ago—long before my time with her. She took us riding through the French countryside with her Italian lover, Pepe, at the wheel of her Bugatti Royale. The name of the car rolled off her lips beautifully. We rolled along with her through the sunny time of the early 1930s. It was the time when she had first seen the Château des Milandes.

We already knew this story. It was the same one we had heard many times before. But it seemed to make her momentarily happy to tell it again, and we waited patiently for her to finish.

* * *

When I returned to America, I decided that I would make one last-ditch effort. And I did.

It would be pointless now to name those people I met with. Some were famous, some were not. Most did not return my calls, even after I had made several. I met with executives of black car firms, insurance companies, and other important black organizations—and white ones as well. I met with the leaders of the NAACP and even of the B'nai B'rith. I called on everyone she asked me to. Everyone, of course, was excited about brotherhood. They all said that they believed in Josephine and pledged to support her. But no one, with the exception of Zsa Zsa, ever helped her.

It would have been different if these promises of aid had not been made. It is one's privilege to do what he wants with his own resources; but making promises one had no intention of keeping was, I felt, something else again.

I wrote Josephine a detailed letter, and she answered immediately: "You have done all you could, and all that I asked of you. As Mama would say, now we leave it in God's hands."

I regret to say that God handled it most unsympathetically.

Nighttime

Chapter 24

". . . The cat's food dish brought five francs. But a framed letter from General De Gaulle sold for one franc—one franc, mind you! So I guess that is what they thought of me . . . and in the letter he had thanked me for my services to France . . . and mind you, too, it was a solid silver frame . . . yes, one franc for all that I had done . . . but, my God, do people forget fast . . . I cannot tell you . . ."

* * *

Josephine called me late one night in July of 1968. Gradually the details came out.

Early in the morning she had been served with a vacate order. It said that the furniture would be auctioned on the following day, and those funds applied to her debts of about $500,000. In the event that the furniture did not bring that sum, the farm of the Milandes, and all its parcels in the village of Castelnaud-Fayrac, by the order of the court would be sold to the highest bidder, immediately following the sale of the furniture.

It had been a dreadful experience for her. Several creditors armed with court orders had burst into the house that afternoon and begun grabbing anything they could carry off to satisfy their judgments. Somehow, she and the servants had barricaded the doors, and that night, in her nightgown and wrapped in a blanket, she sat on the doorstep. No one dared cross. She spent the entire night there without sleep, waiting for sunup. On July 16, there was no sun. Only the rain. It came down in torrents.

Now came the local constables. They persuaded her that she must go inside, and she ran to her bedroom. Before she could close the door, other constables started removing her bed and furnishings.

Two hundred people stood in the driving rain at the auction of her personal possessions. Into the downpour went the Aubusson carpets, the Bergère chairs of Louis XIV, the Pleyel pianos from the music room, the Sèvres porcelain.

There was a madness among the bidders, but not the madness of outrageous bids. When the porcelains came out, what should have brought thousands brought hundreds. A Sèvres rose urn that a month later sold in Paris for $9,000 went to a dealer for $500. And so it went. The vitrines, the *bombé* chests, the Tremeau mirrors. Items that could be thrust into a pocket were grabbed off tables by some of those employed to assist with the auction, never to see the auction block. Mementos of a lifetime were lost forever, dropped into the pocket or bag of some helper.

When the fine furniture was gone, there came the beds of the children, the furniture in the servants' rooms, and then the kitchen. The last item that was sold was the cat's food dish. It brought five francs—four and a half francs more than it was worth. A framed letter from General De Gaulle thanking her for her services to France went for one franc—twenty cents.

The finest antique furniture, worth $250,000, went for less than ten cents on the dollar. The buyers scurried to cover their priceless bargains from the driving rain. They used coats and blankets and sheets.

All the while, Josephine watched from her bedroom window, through the rain.

In less than two minutes, the château, all its surrounding land, all its outbuildings, its farms, hotels, restaurants, and servants' quarters were sold. With the property went the little church and the cemetery where her mother was buried. Its appraised value was $4,000,000. It was sold to cover her debts—about a half million.

Josephine refused to leave her bedroom. The door was broken in, and she was pulled and shoved down the ancient stone stairs, through the now empty rooms. She did not utter a sound. The only sounds heard were the dragging and pushing of the constables.

As she was pushed into the kitchen, she managed to break away long enough to pick up her little cat. Then she was shoved through the kitchen door, out into the still-driving rain. They slammed the door behind her.

She stood leaning against it for a moment. Then, slowly, she slid down as her legs gave way beneath her, and there she sat. She pulled her coat up around the little cat to protect it from the rain.

The photographers' bulbs flashed. Next day the picture ran on front pages around the world.

Standing to one side, the servants cried for her. The bidders at the auction ran down the hill with their bargains. They tried to avoid her gaze.

Slowly she mustered that last bit of strength I always knew she held in reserve. Very quietly, she rose. For a long time she looked at the piles of wet furniture, the wet carpets, and the Playel piano covered against the rain with a thin blanket.

"Don't cry for me, friends. When I was a little girl, they burned my home. During the war, the Germans destroyed another one. Now this one has been stolen. I have not been a good businesswoman, but I am still a star. *Je me battrai.* Now I fight!"

Then she walked slowly through the dirt and the mud. The rain kept falling. She passed the bidders, who were running off with their purchases. She never looked back. She never returned.

Slowly she eased her tired body into a friend's car. Still holding the kitten, she stared straight ahead. As they passed the great château that had brought her to ruin, she did not turn to look.

Josephine had two more bad years, then her wheel turned again.

Now the trial by fire for Josephine Baker was over. She had survived all those terrible trials one by one. First the trial by water, then the trial by air, and the rest. It is incredible that she withstood the last. Her trial by fire was almost mortal.

As her car moved out of the park which had once been her property, and where she had spent some of the best and some of the most disastrous moments of her life, she slumped forward in her seat. The little kitten uttered a sound of terror.

It was the first of her three heart attacks.

Chapter 25

"But that day I knew that racism had come all the way to the south of France to find me—Old Man Trouble was really giving it to me now. And then, when it was over, I cried for myself and my family, but I wept for France too. For now I know there is no hope for anyone in that country either. And that is why you have heard me say several times that I might even come back to America to live."

* * *

It was really not until 1973 in Cuernavaca that we had time, without the ringing of telephones and the knocking on the doors to interrupt us. It was my second night with her in Cuernavaca, at the beautiful home of Robert Brady. She talked for a long while about the eviction, and her feelings.

"Stephen, I just do not know what to do. *What is happening in the world?* I thought that, after the war, things would change for the better. But you know they have not.

"Did you ever think you would hear me say that maybe now I should stay in America? Maybe I should even move to America? The wheel has turned for me, Stephen, but it has turned for the world too. And do you know how the situation has changed in France?

"When I told you the other details, I never wanted to admit to myself or anyone what was really happening. *But it took me some time to believe it myself*. I will never understand why they didn't kill me then. Can you believe that all the stories you hear, about the colored being beaten up and hurt badly in America, actually happened to me too? But can you believe it if I tell you *it happened in France, of all places?*

"I have spoken of the life I have lived. And if it was good, that's the way it was. And if it was bad, I told it that way too. And I cannot tell you how it destroys me to tell about that day.

"You see, what actually happened was that they got some young thugs, about eight or ten of them. I learned they paid them only a few hundred francs to go in and rough me up a little.

"Imagine that if you can. When I told you the story long ago, it was mild compared to what actually happened. Can you believe that there are—what I even hate to say—that there are real nigger-haters in France too? Can you believe it? You know, I am old. I know it. *I feel it.* And it is hard for me to tell it, but that is what happened.

"They were paid to work me over, but they were not to work me over as good as they did. They were young French punks. I know you don't speak or understand enough French to understand the language of the gutter, but when you hear what they shouted at me you will never believe."

Now she leaned over and spoke in a whisper, so that no one else should hear.

"They said words, and I can hardly repeat them to you, like 'motherfucker,' and 'nigger,' and 'a black bitch who fucks white men for money,' and they actually had me in the mud, and I could not believe it, but they were doing it to me. *To me, mind you!* And it was in France, and it was the scum of the French earth who were doing it to me, and when I heard all that in the most vile French, I was destroyed, and I felt there was just not much hope left for me. I thought I was dead then, until some of the servants ran up and these kids, these thugs, ran into the house and stole everything they could lay their hands on.

"They stole from me legally later. They didn't have to bother to steal from me like criminals.

"But that day I knew that racism had come all the way to the south of France to find me—Old Man Trouble was really giving it to me now. And then, when it was over, I cried for myself and my family, but I wept for France too. For now I know there is no hope for anyone in that country either. And that is why you have heard me say several times that I might even come back to America to live."

Chapter 26

1973

"You know, I was just thinking about myself, I'm like that famous bird in the old mythology, what do you call it? The Phoenix [the legendary bird of ancient Egypt that is consumed in fire by its own act, and rises in youthful freshness from its own ashes]. Yes, that's it—that's me! I was so happy this morning when I got up and looked out over toward the ocean here in California, I called up the secretary and wrote another fairy tale. Here, read it, while I order some chocolate for us . . ."

* * *

She had suffered the first of three heart attacks. She had another one in Copenhagen two years later. The final one came in 1975.

Josephine recovered slowly. But, as the gods, who survived all their trials, including the last by fire, are rewarded, so now was Josephine.

Her friend and benefactor Princess Grace arranged for her to have a villa in the hills above Monte Carlo, in the village of Roquebrune. It was to be her last home—although, again, not really a home. For her home was the theatre. That was the one she loved most, and that was where she died.

Josephine now began to appear in a series of small clubs. I am sure she performed there reluctantly. She sorted out the best of her wardrobe. It was a pathetic effort, the reports I received from her and others confirmed. But she pressed on. The time was not just right. Not yet.

Josephine had never really believed that she would make the fantastic return that she did.

"My God, how is it possible?" she would say over and over after she was led off the stage each night. But it was. It was, I am sure, one of the greatest returns for a star that has ever been.

Undoubtedly, many stars could have done it—if they had lived long enough. In this respect, Josephine qualified. She lived just long enough.

It seemed that overnight she was picked up in the cheap little clubs on the continent and dropped quietly and easily on the stage of Carnegie Hall in New York City. It is exciting, and it was to Josephine, that her "return" —that is what she called it, for it was true—should happen for her in America. Until her appearance on that stage in June of 1973, she had never, by her own admission, been what she called a "really huge success in America." That performance changed it all.

The two gentlemen who were responsible for this achievement were Jack Jordan and Howard Sanders. That it was all to end up in the courts again was typical of Josephine. I knew it would from the beginning. Unfortunately, this time the cases were marked "plaintiff deceased."

I liked both Jack and Howard. We had a few skirmishes, but I always gave them credit for one thing: they, and they alone, took the enormous gamble of bringing Josephine back to America. Jack and Howard thought now was the time. It certainly was. That June day in 1973 happened to be her birthday.

Josephine had asked me to come to Cuernavaca to meet with her before this comeback, as she called it. I told her I didn't think of it as a comeback, because she had never really been out of the picture.

My plane was late getting into Mexico City. Robert Brady's chauffeur was waiting, and we spent another hour and a half winding our way over the mountains to Cuernavaca.

Josephine was visiting Bob at his magnificent centuries-old monastery. She was waiting for me as we arrived. She looked thirty, and was radiant in a splendid white Mexican dress from the state of Veracruz. I threw my arms around her. She asked me if I liked her dress, which I did, of course. As I studied her in that dress, she just seemed to belong, as she did anywhere.

She told me all about her coming engagement at Carnegie Hall, and expressed the hope that others could be arranged to follow that one. I told her that very likely they could.

Then she astounded me. She said that Sanders and Jordan had agreed to pay her $10,000 a day. She then decided, on the spur of the moment, that it should read $10,000 a "performance," and she added $20,000 more for the matinees. It totaled $80,000 a week.

They *had* agreed to pay her $10,000 a day, but it was to include the matinees. I knew their little venture was doomed from the start. It was not in the cards, particularly when they were paying all the other expenses.

I decided to take a firm stand with her. I explained that they would lose about $30,000 a week even if they *sold out* each engagement. I went over the figures very carefully. She was learning. Incredibly, she agreed to accept $35,000 a week. I told her it was that or failure, because even the wealthiest promoters could not live with the other contract.

I conveyed this to Sanders and Jordan and they were overjoyed. Their joy was brief. The old Josephine was coming out, and she began to demand a nickel here and a nickel there. They sent for their attorneys, and she sent for hers. It went back and forth. And it was in the same suite in the Beverly Hills Hotel in Hollywood where the famous Taub affair had taken place. It is true: everything in Hollywood showbiz starts and stops at the Beverly Hills Hotel.

Whether they made or lost money with Josephine I do not know. One thing is certain: they gave her a marvelous production.

When Josephine Baker appeared for the last time in Carnegie Hall in New York, it was the old Josephine. It was the feathers and the sequins and the gold dust and the diamond dust. It was furs and egrets and towering headdresses and jewelry. It was something!

She wore dungarees, and rode motorcycles, and cracked jokes, and conducted the orchestra. She did everything but sing "Bake That Chicken Pie," and I was surprised that she did not. The audiences went crazy for her.

"You know, Stephen," she said to me, "they are making more noise for me now than when I first appeared in Paris at the Folies, or at the Casino de Paris. I thought they made noise then, but this is really something. Why, I cannot even hear the orchestra!"

It was true: even the band was drowned out.

She repeated this performance in Los Angeles, San Francisco, and Detroit. Then she returned to France for an engagement at the Bobino Music Hall. After that, she was to return to America for a cross-country tour. It had been almost fully booked. Unbelievably, the theatre owners were guaranteeing her $50,000 a week. This was against a percentage that would easily bring that up to $80,000 or even $90,000. So much for a "one-woman show." She could, they felt, command a $25 ticket.

The last night in Detroit, Brian Avnet, the company manager, and I walked into the house to watch her. On this tour, Josephine was using material by several contemporary composers, and as we arrived she was performing her show-ending "My Sweet Lord" number. I am sure that all who read this are familiar with that beautiful piece of music. As she entered, great silver curtains descended and surrounded her. She appeared in an egret-and-coq-feather headdress that was at least three feet tall, with shades of lavender, green, black and gray. She wore the greatest gown I'd ever seen her in, a simple black silk velvet with a huge train. She was covered with jewels—arms, neck, and waist.

Slowly she turned, and as the music started, she began singing. As the number continued, she removed her headdress, then slowly began removing the jewelry—first those pieces around her waist, then her necklaces, and finally the bracelets. She just dropped them to the stage.

When she had removed all the jewels, from the audience came a choir of a hundred singers in gray and silver robes, and each was carrying two candles. They slowly filed onto the stage and sang with her.

"I really want to see you.
Yes, I really want to see you . . ."

Looking back, I feel now that Josephine knew her time was coming soon.

Then the stage lights faded, and only a small lavender spotlight remained on her face. The stage was illuminated only by the candles held by the singers. Reflected in the silver curtains, they seemed like a million flickering lights.

At the end of the song, Josephine just fell to her knees and raised her face upward. The lights faded and the curtain came down.

The audience went wild. It was the old Josephine Baker formula—the Baker mystique. And it was still working.

In New York, Los Angeles, San Francisco, and Detroit, Josephine was the "new" sensation. She was a sensation to those who remembered her; to those who had heard about her but had never seen her; and to those who had never heard of her but came out of curiosity.

* * *

We continued working on her new tour for 1975 after she returned to France for the Bobino Music Hall engagement.

Perhaps the Bobino producers too had become infected by the Josephine Baker magic, for they gave her a production that could hardly have been rivaled even by her former great appearances at the Folies and the Casino de Paris.

The critics raved. On opening night, when the fifteen-minute ovation ceased, she just stood on stage, holding up her hands. For a time she just waited, looking at the audience, looking out over the theatre. She looked into the wings and at the stagehands, and other artists could be seen peeping out from behind the curtains. Every eye was fastened on her. There was not a sound from anywhere.

She put her hands on her hips and spread her legs apart. It was the *old* Josephine. The *real* one.

Perhaps going through her mind, like some great high-speed motion picture, was her entire life, with its ups and downs, its triumphs and its failures. Perhaps little Ethel the chimpanzee flashed out to her with the tiny jewels, and perhaps a crown prince, and a private railroad car, and perhaps bananas, and maybe her mother, and those washboards, and Bessie Smith, and Mr. Browning, and Bert and Benny . . . and the children scooting along the oil-covered linoleum floor, and that great château that had been hers.

Perhaps Pepe, and that beautiful Bugatti, and perhaps she recalled singing at the top of her voice, speeding at a hundred miles an hour through the French countryside.

Perhaps she thought of Guilbert. "Take my stage, you beautiful black queen of the music halls of Paris . . ."

And then maybe that audience went suddenly silent for her, and she could not hear the applauding and screaming and shouting. Perhaps she saw also, in some strange flash, that hearse winding through the streets of Paris, and those silent tens of thousands waving their little white handkerchiefs and removing their hats.

Then she made her little four-word statement. And as the audience left the theatre that night, they wondered about it and discussed it among themselves.

But in her mind, very likely Josephine knew what it was about. She had ridden that great wheel through its entire revolution. She had resurrected triumph from her ashes, as if she were the Phoenix.

What she had said was, "Now I can die."

Two days later she died.

And they did carry her high and proudly on her shield of victory, and they mourned her the world over, and they carried her to visit the places she loved. They took her to the church of the Madeleine, and she rested there a little, and they took her down those great avenues and past those great music halls, and the men removed their hats, and the women waved their handkerchiefs. And they mourned her in silence, for that is their way.

And they placed her in a tomb, and from it you can see the waters of the sea and, beyond that, the country she really always loved—America.

But she is not in her tomb. You must go and visit those dark theatres the world over, and the summer breezes will carry to you her little laugh, and you will see those egrets, those feathers, and that diamond dust, and she will flash her smile on you.

And if she knows you, you might hear her thousand violins playing their haunting melodies . . . and maybe even while you are watching, a prince will come and take her in his arms, and they will wrap themselves in sable and dance. . . .

Index

Abtey, Jacques, 122, 124
Ahmanson Theatre, 106
Albertini, Pepe d', 95, 98, 141, 220
Alcazar Theatre, 192
Alhambra Theatre, 58
Anderson, John Murray, 101
Atkinson, Brooks, 107
Aux Iles Hawaii, 60

"Bake That Chicken Pie," 27, 28, 230
Baker, Carie (Mama), 11, 21–31, 63, 78, 149
Baker, Margaret, 11, 12, 22
"Baker-Fix" (Hair Formula), 69
Balanchine, George, 106
Balenciaga, George, 69, 95, 104, 106, 182
Balmain, Pierre, 182
Banner, Robert, 5
Barbette, 58
Bardot, Brigitte, 153, 156, 214
Belafonte, Harry, 58
Benny (of vaudeville's "Bert and Benny"), 21, 26–30, 32, 34–40
Bert (of "Bert and Benny"), 21, 26–28, 32, 36–37, 52, 61, 63
Beverly Hills Hotel, 90, 187, 230
Beverly Hilton Hotel, 4, 162
Billingsley, Sherman, 173–175
Blake, Eubie, 40–43, 45, 51, 63
B'nai B'rith, 219–220

Bobino Music Hall, 6–7, 48, 58, 230–231
Booker T. Washington Theatre, 20–21, 25, 28
Bouillon, Jo, 80, 121, 136–137, 149, 201
Boxcar Town, 12–13, 16–19, 78
Brady, Robert, 226
Brice, Fanny, 101, 105–107
Brioni, 70
"Brotherhood, Treatise on," *see* "Treatise on Brotherhood"
Brown, J. Mardo, 42
Browning, Haroldine, 4
Browning, Ivan, 4, 40, 42, 44–45, 51, 63
Burke, Billie, 100–104, 181

Cantinflas, 114
Cardin, 70
Carnegie Hall, 7, 97, 229
Carton, Louis, 68
Caruso, 98
Casino de Paris, 6, 58, 80, 95, 97, 102, 112, 230
Cerdan, Marcel, 80
Chanel, Gabrielle "Coco," 69–70
Chevalier, Maurice, 56, 59–60, 66, 79
Chez Josephine, 98, 113
Chez Madame Arthur, 201–202
Chocolate Dandies, 42–47, 56, 81
Chrysis, 58
Clair, René, 56
Cole, Nat King, 219
Colette, 58, 93
Colin, Paul, 56, 61
"Comme il banque," 167
Cook, Joan, 150
Cooke, Allan, 190, 196
Cooper, George W., 42
CORE, 218
Cotton Club, the, 39–40
Creole, La, 112, 127
Critica, La (Argentina), 178

Daven, 51–52
Davis, Charles, 42
Davis, Sammy, Jr., 5
De Gaulle, Charles, 7, 56, 62, 127, 223–224
De Gaulle, Madame, 156
"Dengoza," 98, 113
Derval, Paul, 44, 101
Deslys, Gaby, 58
Detroit *Free Press,* 123
"Diamond Thief, The," 176
Dietrich, Marlene, 190
Dinner at Eight, 100
Dior, Christian, 69, 106
Dodge Sisters, the, 58
Dolly Sisters, the, 58
"Donnez-moi le main," 200
Dunham, Katherine, 3, 176
Dylan, Bob, 74

Erté, 95, 103, 106, 115

Faisan Bleu, 194, 199–200
Fanny, Madame, 58
Farman Company, 110
Farouk I, 131–132
Federal Bureau of Investigation, the, 12, 176, 193–194
"Feelin' Like a Million," 167
Felix, Pearl and Seymour, 100
Fernandel, 59
Fitzgerald, Scott and Zelda, 56
Flory, 58
Folies Bergère, 7, 51, 53, 55, 58, 68, 71–72, 75, 78–80, 101–103, 136
Foujita, 79

Gabin, Jean, 98, 112
Gabor, Zsa Zsa, 214–215, 218–220
Garland, Judy, 189–190
Gaynor, Mitzi, 176
Gee, Lotte, 42, 63
"Georgia Camp Meetin'," 14
Gert, Valeska, 58
Gizencka, Crystina, 123–124, 127
Goering, Hermann, 115, 117, 125–126, 128–129
Golder, Jenny, 58
Gomez, Tommy, 3
Goodlett, Carlton B., 197
Grable, Betty, 176
Granville, Christine, *see* Gizencka, Crystina
Great Ziegfeld, The, 100
Greenwood, Charlotte, 34, 46
Guilbert, Yvette, 56, 58–59, 62–63
Gustav VI, 56–57, 75–77, 81–90

"Haiti," 65, 99
Hale, Randolph, 193
Hampton, Hope, 186–187
Hann, W. A., 42
Hayes, Arthur Garfield, 118
Heller, Seymour, 180
Hemingway, Ernest, 56, 66, 79
Hitler, Adolf, 94, 115, 128
Hola, 114
Hope, Bob, 101, 105–106
Huntington Hartford Theatre, 176, 186, 192

"If You Ain't Never Been Loved by a Brownskin, You Ain't Never Been Loved At All," 43, 81
Illinois Theatre, 42
"I'm Just Wild About Harry," 40, 43, 52
Imitation of Life, 162
In Bamville, 42–45, 56, 103
INTERPOL, 12

"J'ai deux amours," 94–96, 192, 202, 204
Johnson, Lyndon B., 215
Jordan, Jack, 195, 229

Kaye, Danny, 119
Kennedy, John F., 119, 142, 157, 194, 209, 212–213
Kennedy, Robert F., 119, 158, 194, 209
King, Martin Luther, Jr., 194, 209–210
Klase, Irving, 187–188
Klee, Paul, 117
Krupp family, 66

La Creole, see Creole, La
La Critica, see Critica, La
Ladd, Tommy, 79
La Sirène des Tropiques, see Sirène des Tropiques, La
Leon, Jean, 120–121
Liberace, 180
Los Angeles Music Center, 4–5, 106
Lou Tornoli Club, the, 178
Louis XIV, 139–145

McCarthy, Joseph ,175–176, 193
Maquis, the, 120–127, 129–131
Mare, Rolf de, 56
Martin, Richard, 11–12
Maxim's, 67, 68, 72
Meir, Golda, 33

Melba, Nellie, 71–73, 98
Merry Widow, The, 100, 111, 138
Milandes, Château de, 14, 116, 135–149, 153–159, 162, 220
Miller, F. E., 40
Minnelli, Vincente, 106
Mistinguett, 56, 59–62, 66, 130
Mitchell, Julian, 41–43
Monaco, Princess Grace of, 228
Monroe, Marilyn, 65, 112, 190
Moulin-Rouge, the, 58
Mountbatten, Louise, 77, 79
Murray, Mae, 100–101, 111
Music Center (Los Angeles), *see* Los Angeles Music Center
"My Sweet Lord," 230–231

National Association for the Advancement of Colored People, the, 216–218, 220
Nederlander, James, 5
New Harmony, 149
New York Times, The, 150, 156
Nicolska, la, 58
North, Sheree, 112

Offenbach, Jacques, 112
Ohrbach's, 69
Old Desert Inn, the, 180–182
Olympia Music Hall, 58
Otere, la Belle, 58

Palladium, London, 99
Paris Monde, 69
Paris que remue, 94
Paris Sisters, the, 58
Payton, Lew, 41–42
Perón, Eva, 178
Pétain, Henri, 56
Piaf, Edith, 56, 59–60, 79, 145
Picasso, Pablo, 66, 79, 117
Poiret, 115, 129
Polaire, 59
Present, Jack, 195
Prosser, Monte, 173

Rainbow Children, the, 135, 137, 149, 162
Randolph, Amanda, 42
"Razzazza Mazzazza," 14
Red Cross Nurses Corps, the, 120
Regine, 58
Revue Negre, the, 47–48, 50–51, 63
Rocky Twins, the, 58
Ryan and Burke, 58

Sanders, Howard, 195, 229
Scotto, Vincent, 94
Seiden, Stanley, 190–191
"Sheik of Araby," 66–68
Sheridan, Ann, 192
Shuffle Along, 41–44, 56
"Silver Heels," 14, 16
Sinatra, Frank, 106
Sirène des Tropiques, La, 112
Sissle, Noble, 41–45, 63
Sixteen Baker Boys, the, 109
Skolsky, Sidney, 112
Smith, Bessie, 20–21, 25, 28–35, 38, 63
Snow, Valada, 42
Soeurs Broquin, les, 58
Sorel, Cecile, 59, 112
Spinelly, 58
Stork Club, the, 172, 174–178, 186
Stravinsky, Igor, 56

Tam Tam, 112
Taub, William L., 138, 186–198, 200
Tauber, Richard, 108–109

Théâtre de Champs Elysées, 7, 51–52
"Times They Are a-Changin', The," 74
Tito, Josip Broz, 119
"Topsy Anna," 45
Treatise on Brotherhood, 148, 154–160
Trotobus, Michel, 123–127
Tucker, Sophie, 58
"Two Loves Have I" (*"J'ai deux amours"*), 94–96, 192, 202, 204

Urban League, the, 218

Van Cleef & Arpels, 67–68, 90
Variety, 46, 195
Varna, Henri, 6, 50–56, 61–62, 71, 74–81, 94–96, 109–110, 112, 45

Waldorf Astoria, 104–107, 173
Waters, Ethel, 47, 67
Winchell, Walter, 48, 118, 133, 138, 174–177, 185, 188, 193, 195
Wonder, Tommy, 192
Wood, Robert, 4–5, 136, 162
Worth, 69, 95
Wright, Frank Lloyd, 114

Zanuck, Darryl F., 112
Ziegfeld, Florenz, 94, 101–104, 211
Ziegfeld Follies, the, 101–106
Zou Zou, 98, 111